Filippo Graglia

A TOUBABOU ON THE HORIZON

25000 km of emotions by bike

Copyright © 2021 Filippo Graglia

First published in Italy
2020

All rights reserved
ISBN 9798509345043

Cover Designer: Debora Faragalli

To mum, who travelled and suffered with me

To a child who is fond of maps and engravings
The universe is the size of his immense hunger.
Ah! how vast is the world in the light of a lamp!
In memory's eyes how small the world is!
CHARLES BAUDELAIRE, LE VOYAGE

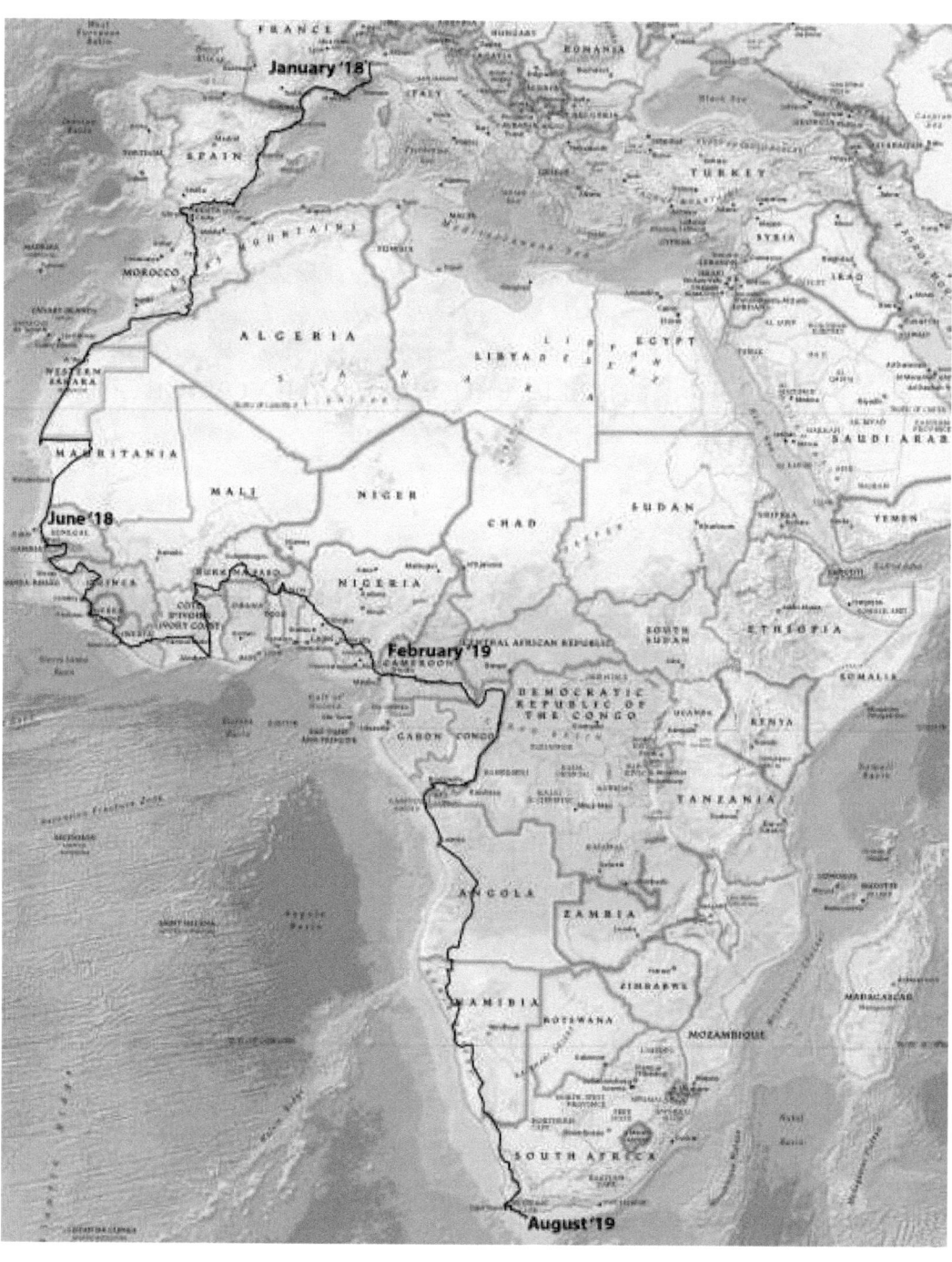

A ROUNDABOUT

I open my eyes. Many faces are looking at me, but it's difficult to recognise them while my sight is still blurry—the fuzzy autofocus of a broken camera lens.

I close them and try to feel every part of my body, starting from the tips of my fingers. They move, *I feel no pain, good.* I send my neurons to stimulate my arms: everything responds properly. And the legs? Let's try. The right one, analysis in progress: okay. Left, Warning. I try the movement again, and a stabbing pain spreads from my left foot up to my ankle. Shit.

My heart is beating to the rhythm of a devilish dance, and blood rushes to my brain. In a dangerous situation, the adrenal glands have pumped adrenaline into the bloodstream, which is now coursing through my body, ready to react to any stimulus. To be honest, I'm not in great enough shape to respond to it. Primordial instincts still guide our actions, with those defence and self-preservation mechanisms that our ancestors passed on to us.

All this is happening inside me. Whoever is observing me sees only a motionless body. I am still lying on the ground with my helmet firmly on my head and my eyes closed.

Various people are whispering around me, and some voices are calling me. I recognise Andrea, a colleague of mine.

"Hi Andrea" comes out spontaneously, and I try to smile as I open my eyes.

"Oh, so you're still with us," he replies, visibly relieved. "How are you feeling?"

"I can feel, so I'd say pretty good."

"Does it hurt anywhere?"

"My foot, Andrea. It feels heavy and painful; something might be broken. I'm afraid the Greenland trip is off this year." My words are coming out fast and confused, and my voice is still trembling—another effect of the adrenaline.

"Come on! Hang in there; the ambulance is coming."

The faces around me come and go, some I recognise, some I don't. I close my eyes and try to recall the events of a few moments before.

Like every morning, I was riding my scooter to work. I have an aggressive driving style, I admit, but to get around Turin on two wheels, you must be assertive. Two hundred metres from the gate of the company that has raised and nurtured me for five years, is the last roundabout, one of the many that create traffic jams at five in the evening. At 8:13 a.m. I approach the roundabout at a good speed; no one is nearby. My right of way, my roundabout. At 8:13 that morning, a car approaches the right-hand entrance to the same roundabout; nobody is nearby. His right of way, his roundabout.

Behind me, I hear the car slam on the brakes, but too close. Then the collision: a crushing of plastic, a sudden blow and I'm knocked to the ground. I instinctively twist my torso and put my left arm on the asphalt, trying to roll over and soften the impact. The scooter crashes down with me and violently crushes my foot, which gets caught between the bitumen and the vehicle's frame. In the meantime, the car has stopped, and the number plate is stationary less than half a metre from my head.

Only in retrospect do I remember that after pushing the scooter away, I stood up and shouted furiously: "You bastard! I'm going to Greenland tomorrow!" The next moments are hazy, but it is easy to imagine that someone helped me to move from the roundabout onto the sidewalk, where I am now lying and thinking about recent events.

Greenland. I have spent a lot of time over the last six months organising this expedition. Three friends, two planes, a helicopter, a snowmobile, and a dog sledge to set up base camp on a glacier on a small island. For the next two weeks, we could explore every nook and cranny on skis and sealskins, wandering across immense expanses in the hope of (not) meeting the local inhabitants—the polar bears.

But this book is not about Greenland, it's not about hostile, icy tundra nor its furry inhabitants, and it's not about howling sea-view descents[1] on skis hidden under thirty centimetres of fresh snow.

But someone had decided differently. There were other plans for me and until 8.13 that morning, I still didn't know.

In Christian doctrine, it could be your guardian angel. Plato baptised him Daimon. He is Jiminy Cricket in "Pinocchio". However, the name does not matter now. The key to the story is that *inner voice*, that so many of us sometimes hear. We hear it, but do we really pay attention?

This friend within us is the bearer of our destiny. He is our guide and motivator, faithfully and resolutely whispering to us each and every day. We need silence on the outside, but above all on the inside, to pay attention to him. In tough situations, however, he protects us by raising his voice, and by *instinct*, I tend to follow his instructions.

I imagine that my friend is quietly tucked away in my stomach. He must have thought it was the best place, considering the amount of food I swallow every day. When I was a kid, I imagined him as a microscopic little furry monster who spent his days stuffing his face. And every once in a while, he'd get up and give me a jolly good pinch to make himself heard. Something is about to happen, something important. A little pinch, to get me dreaming again. *That way, you have to go, Filippo, that way.*

---

[1] The author of the book is known among his friends for his euphoric shouting, which is not appropriate for a chaste mountain environment during ski-mountaineering descents.

That evening, back home after a day in the hospital, and in the following days especially, I had a definite itch in my stomach.

TIME

No one told you when to run,
You missed the starting gun.

PINK FLOYD, TIME

Three months have passed since that day. The fracture has healed, and the injured foot is working again. Three months stuck at home have given me a lot of time to think. About what? To sum up in one line: I was lucky because something much more serious could have happened to me.

Only one thought wandered through my mind in those days of home monotony. *Just do it!*

In 2012 I discovered travelling by bike. Three short experiences in the following years showed me the potential of this means of transport. A transfer to the starting point, two weeks of cycling, the return. And repeat.

In two weeks on the bike, your butt doesn't even have time to get used to the saddle, and then you're back in a comfortable chair in the office. But your mind, on the other hand, stays on the road for a few more days. It takes you a while to get back to normal.

I remember vividly that at the end of each trip, I would say to myself: *I wish I could try out a more complete experience; I would like to travel without a fixed destination, or a return ticket.* I would be free from the pressure of time; I would make time my ally, to be shared without being measured. Time would become an asset.

Especially for those who already know me, it is easy to imagine me sitting on a chair during those months, the computer resting on my lap, painting long brush strokes on the map. Asia with the Silk Road, South America and the *Carretera Austral*... these excellent routes are known to cycle travellers from all over the world. I can find all kinds of information on the net, from travel diaries to a compendium of practical information. Photographs of landscapes are breathtaking, and I can't even imagine the excitement I would feel if I were immersed in them.

As an engineer, I have a perverse love for Excel files. For each trip, I have a spreadsheet in which I catalogue all the information: borders, itineraries, stop-off points, and so on. If I can only travel for two weeks, it's better to avoid the unknown and prepare for every eventuality. And yet, I think to myself, this trip doesn't have to be like that. There would be a lack of exploration and discovery. There would be no taste for the unknown.

I reopen Google Earth, the reliable digital tool of dreams, and the answer takes shape. Africa. East or West coast?

My instinct says West: Atlantic coast. Great, there's only one blog on the net. The itinerary's off the beaten path. I'll go down there.

At that moment, as a tree shakes off the snow that has fallen in the night, I shrug off my lethargy; energy begins to sparkle again in my body, after an instant rush that sends chills down my spine. I love the moment when the idea of a trip takes shape in my mind. I'm full of adrenaline as the pieces of the puzzle fall into place in quick succession. *There* my journey begins. This moment is always more intense than the physical departure when I board the plane or jump on the bike.

I instinctively bring my hand up to my neck and caress the necklace I have been wearing for almost ten years. I smile. And I hold back a tear. The shape of Africa carved on a piece of tin bought at a market in Zanzibar has always been there with me—silent.

I spend the whole day watching the door of my manager's office, looking for an opportune moment to talk to him. Many chances come and go during the day. Now that it's coming to an end, I have not yet had enough nerve to stand up and knock on that door. I'm not waiting for the right moment; I'm trying to get enough courage. A pleasant job in a reliable company, with good conditions and excellent colleagues. It will be hard to explain why I want to leave.

It was a moment waiting to happen. I have come to this decision quite naturally: the facts and time just going on have led me to this moment. I took the decision serenely; I did not have to think about it too much. Yet, today I hesitate. What invisible forces are holding me back?

I summon up courage: after this final step, the road will be clear, and all I have to do is jump into the saddle. Now is the time. My legs are trembling, my heart begins to beat wildly. I approach the door and knock. Or maybe I didn't, I just grazed the door, and my boss didn't hear. I breathe in deeply, three times.

Knock, knock.

JANUARY 2

We shall not cease from exploration.
And the end of all our exploring
Will be to arrive where we started.
And know the place for the first time.

T.S. ELIOT, FOUR QUARTETS

On the frosty morning of January the second, the sky is a murky blue. The mood at home is not the best. After a silent breakfast, I go to get my bike on the terrace; it has been leaning against the wall for days with its load of luggage, waiting only for me. I stop for a moment to contemplate it, my life companion for the next few months. Back then, I could not yet imagine that that frozen piece of steel had the power to warm my heart.

I grab the handlebars and push the bicycle slowly across the garden and down into the yard. My beloved dogs are jumping around me, asking for attention. Bombo has the inseparable battered ball in his mouth, but I'm not in the mood to play with him.

I have little desire to talk. Maybe I wouldn't know what to say. It was a hard blow for the family to receive the news of my departure, and to accept the big sacrifice that I asked of them.

Mum, Dad and Grandma are waiting. Their expressions are worried and melancholic. I pretend to check for the umpteenth time if anything is missing on the bike so that I don't have to bear their gaze. Finally, I propose a photo all together. The result is a sad shot, appropriate to the moment.

"Mum, I'm going."

The moment I jump on the saddle, tears try to escape from my eyelids. I can hardly hold them back; it's only for a few months, I think. With one foot on the pedal, I set off, raise an arm for a last emotional goodbye, and off I go!

The first two months quickly go by on the calendar. I rapidly settle into my new rhythms, dictated by day and night. If it's Wednesday or Thursday, I no longer know, and I don't even care.

I leave the Ligurian coast behind me in a few days, as well as the French one. So much rain, so much wind in that cold January. At the end of the month, I cross the Pyrenees, and a warm sun welcomes me to Spain. Through Catalonia, Valencia, and Murcia, down over the Sierra Nevada, where the snow allowed. I fall in love with Granada and with its charm, but not only with the city. I am enchanted by the warmth and feeling of the flamenco that echoes through the streets. But mainly, I am enchanted by her blue eyes and how our minds have begun to vibrate in unison.

When I leave the city, the sun disappears behind ashen clouds for weeks on end, and the rain pours incessantly. On a cold and humid night in the low mountains, a big dog visits my tent and lies down on the flysheet, uprooting a peg. I try hard to push him away before the tent collapses, and that's when I feel him shivering. I understand and let him in to keep both of us warmer.

Another night a passing stream visits my tent and enters, this time without authorization, soaking everything and taking with it much of the equipment scattered inside.

I arrive in Cadiz with all my clothes soaked, as well as my sleeping bag and the rest of my equipment; there has been no way to keep them dry. The mobile phone spends the next forty-eight hours buried in a jar of rice. They might seem like miserable days, but, God, I had so much fun. The night when that big dripping dog licked my hand to pick up the last crumbs of the biscuits I brought him; the night when I ran out of the tent in my underwear to chase my few possessions as they were carried away by the water, the breakneck descents in the mud of Andalusia...

MOROCCO

*I was nothing but a mortal
lost among the sand and the stars,
aware of the only sweetness of breathing.*

ANTOINE DE SAINT-EXUPÉRY,
WIND, SAND AND STARS

March 2018

Climbing up the steep alleys, where the multitude of street stalls and the joyous crowds press in and obstruct the path forward, I struggle upwards, pushing my bike by my side. A relaxed atmosphere welcomes me. Evenings in the medina of Tangier are colourful, noisy, and fragrant. Teenagers joke and laugh with each other, and I am drawn by the unmistakable smell of grilled meat. There's the cook, calling me and pointing a fork at the tempting legs of goat sizzling on the coals. Despite the hour, many of the small shops are still open. The intense yellowish glow of the hanging lightbulbs illuminates all kinds of goods: fruit, preserves and fancy fabrics. Inside one of the many cafes, a crowd is watching a game on the big screen and explodes into raucous cheering as a goal is scored.

The upper part of the medina is less busy at this time of night. Some of the ladies sit on their doorsteps, enjoying the coolness of the evening air as they chatter after finishing all their chores. I imagine their husbands sitting in the cafe and sipping tea. Up here, the alleys feel more closed in by the intimate half-light, only a few lights here and there just enough to find your way. Through labyrinths and up flights of steps, I reach the hostel, booked from the ferry a few hours earlier, for my first African night.

That morning, I had been at the port of Tarifa, on the other side of the Mediterranean, in Europe, yet only a few kilometres away. Bad weather and strong winds whipped up white horses in the sea for most of the day. It was only in the late afternoon that the company decided it was safe to travel. Jolted here and there in my seasickness, I finally set foot (and wheels) ashore at the port of Tangier after night had already fallen. The port welcomed me onto African soil; noisy and confusing. As I came out of the gates, I was immersed in the city traffic, a jumble of horns and headlights in every direction. On the opposite side of the wide avenue is the medina, perched on the hill and behind its walls. Far behind me, I catch a glimpse of a few pinpricks of light, the Spanish coast.

On the ferry, I met a Swiss guy, and together we leave the hostel and go into the lively maze of streets of the old city. We sit on the terrace of a cafe from which a small group of men is leaving. The game on TV must have just finished. I order tea. Obviously. Had I met Francis the night before in Tarifa, we would have drunk a toast to the journey with two large beers. Here, in a Muslim country, the drink of company and friendship is tea.

The waiter arrives with two small transparent glasses filled with mint leaves and the teapot, in which a sugar iceberg is floating. I think back to the trick of the ship in a bottle. How did a lump of sugar so big get into that teapot?

I couldn't have imagined a more enthralling entrance into Africa than this. I share with Francis the emotions I felt as I walked up the streets of the medina a few minutes earlier. I was immediately at ease, among the warmth and friendliness of these strangers, who welcomed me and greeted me: "*Bienvenue*!" The impact of this new world was as intense as it was delicious.

It is almost ten o'clock in the evening; the shop lights are going out, and the streets are emptying. At the cafe, three young men remain, humming to the rhythm of guitar strings, while at a table inside, a man in a colourful headdress is intent on rolling a cigarette. The bartender is wiping the counter while watching a movie scene on TV. I fill my glass one last time, smelling the freshness of the mint, and we return to the hostel at the end of the labyrinth.

The first few days in Morocco were a surprise: the first of many. As soon as I leave the fascinating Tangier, I climb the Rif mountains, which lie at the foot of the Atlas mountain range.

My pace is sluggish due to the constant uphill stretches. But I am still in that phase of the journey that I am sure some of you will understand. Never give up, so getting off and pushing, despite the unquestionable saving of energy, would be dishonourable. I plod along at turtle-like speed, passing through mountain hamlets usually consisting just of a mosque and a few houses. A man is working in the field right next to the road. I greet him, he pauses and cheers me on with a big smile and a Berber shout. The children are greatly amused and entertained by the sight of me passing by. They chase over towards me, exchanging Berber comments and laughing their heads off. When they reach me, there is no need to run; they can walk faster than me anyway. One of them understands my fatigue, grabs the rear rack, and starts pushing me. Two others join in. I stop pedalling, turn around and laugh, and they with me. Even some ladies are watching the scene from a doorway. I feel like I'm flying on the pedals. Ah no, it's the kids who still haven't let go of the bike.

I stop to catch my breath. It's just gone one o'clock. I run my gaze over the gentle slopes in front of me that gradually climb into the peaks on the horizon. Fast-moving clouds paint changing hues on a palette of cultivated terraces. A few scattered houses interrupt this green carpet on which the wind blows lightly and continuously. A rooster crows in the distance. A farmer exhorts his donkey with shouts that I can't understand. A few moments later, a speaker amplifies the double tap of a finger on the microphone into the air. It works. "*Allaaaaaaaaaah Akbar.*" The last syllable, sharp, echoes. "*Allaaaaaaaaaah Akbar.*" God is great. Come now to pray. Come now to salvation. The call to prayer interrupts all activities. Those working in the fields roll out their prayer mat[1], those who remain in the village go to the mosque. I put a foot on the pedal and set off again.

These are days of interminable ups and downs. Under an ashen sky, I wander through landscapes which appear always to repeat themselves. Entering the umpteenth village, a sign to Ramla indicates the end of the climb. I stop to ask for directions. A kid, I would say 6 years old, approaches me.

"Do you want some hashish?" With the same innocent tone as his friends selling biscuits at the market, the young seller shows me a brown cube on the palm of his hand.

"*No merci, mon ami,*" I refuse the biscuit this time.

The rain begins: the first time since leaving Spain. I thought, I hoped for some respite after those three soggy weeks. Instead, here I am, looking for a shelter, waiting for the downpour to stop.

I find refreshment and warmth in the cafe of a petrol station, where I order tea and an omelette to appease my hunger. While waiting, I contemplate the water falling relentlessly outside the windows.

Shortly afterwards, a young man comes in, about my age. He is the mechanic from the garage next door; I had greeted him earlier when I arrived at the service area. He asks if he can sit with me at the table for tea. "*Bien sûr.*"

He's shy and holds back, although he seems to have a lot of questions. It's up to me to tell him some details of my journey, and little by little, he opens up. Mohammed started work selling hashish as

---

[1] In Arabic, it is called *Sajjāda*. Carpet sometimes used for prayer. The prayer must happen in an appropriate place, clean. When it is not possible, this carpet is rolled out turning it towards Mecca.

a child and never had the chance to continue his studies. He's now in his thirties and doesn't feel like hitting the books again, so he works on engines in his uncle's workshop. Unfortunately, he barely has enough to live on and is worried that he may never be able to leave the village.

In a moment of silence, we both look out at the rain. There is no sign of it stopping soon. "Would there be a place here where I could bed down for the night? I'm leaving early tomorrow." I throw the idea out to Mohammed.

He phones a few people, but I can tell from his frown that his search is not going well. Moroccan hospitality must be respected, so he invites me to sleep in his flat. It's small, but it'll be enough for two, he tells me. In reality the flat is a corner in a warehouse, with hundreds of spare parts scattered around on the greasy black floor. With a curtain, he has separated the cubbyhole where he sleeps and eats. On the wall are the flags of his faith: Morocco and Real Madrid. *Not much, but better than a night under the rain.*

"Mohammed, Mohammed," someone shouts from the workshop below. It's the owner, his uncle. They have informed him of my presence, and he has rushed over to invite me to sleep in his house, "nice, big and air-conditioned". This is a filthy dump, judges the uncle. A glance at Mohammed is enough to understand that he regrets the missed opportunity to share an evening and his hospitality with a foreigner. I decide in an instant.

"Thank you, sir. But I have already rolled out my mattress and sleeping bag." Although I haven't.

"Too bad. Next time then. Come on, let's go to the cafe and have a chat so you can tell me about yourself while Mohammed prepares dinner."

We don't go to the cafe; instead, he takes me to his brother's shop, a dreary little room whose walls are hidden behind stacked boxes. The air is filled with smoke, and I instantly recognise the smell of marijuana. Ayman, his brother, is sitting on a pile of plastic containers with a joint between his fingers, the biggest I've ever seen, without exaggeration. The man must be at least ten years older than him, and they don't look at all alike.

"Would you like some?" he asks after the customary greetings.

Best not offend local hospitality. "Yes, of course."

"Do you know what we deal with here?" *Sure, I know. It's the biggest hashish production area in the world.* I keep my answer vague. "I guess so, but you tell me."

"Hashish. Everything depends on that around here. Our family owns several hectares around here."

"Seven," points out the younger brother, Ibrahim.

"It's a few more than that... never mind, it's not important. What I wanted to say to you, and I'm telling you this because you seem a reliable person, is that we're looking for partners."

"Ah, interesting." *Let's see where the conversation goes.*

"Every year, we look for new backers and new partners. We are slowly expanding our production. We always need new machinery and someone to help us import seeds." He throws the butt end on the ground and rolls another joint at once. "We don't have them here. Usually, there is someone who imports seeds from Spain. A lot of people there are interested in the business."

"I've heard talk about it. Once the goods are ready, do you send them back there?" Despite the topic, the atmosphere is relaxed, and I'm curious to push the discussion a little further. "And how could I work with you?"

He smiles. "Wait, wait, don't be hasty. Tomorrow, if you feel like, go with Ibrahim to see the fields, so you can get an idea." He doesn't leave me time for an answer and continues: "There are no plants yet. We haven't sown any seeds yet this year. With all this rain, the soil is soaked, and the seeds would rot."

"Alright then, tomorrow morning."

With a gesture of his hand, Ayman closes the subject, while with the other he brings the joint up to his mouth.

Mohammed has prepared a succulent tajine: potatoes, olives, peppers, and chicken. "Fresh fresh." Two other people have joined us, engrossed in a discussion about Real Madrid's convincing win of that day. Cristiano Ronaldo, who bagged four, is the main topic. They are all Real Madrid fans, and as there's no way to take the debate any further, they soon involve me in their discussion by asking about my trip. We get on well together and exchange anecdotes throughout the evening and into the night.

The next morning, I find neither Ibrahim nor his brother. I leave the petrol station with an unsatisfied curiosity: I would have liked to know the end of the story. I set off imagining myself sitting on a tractor ploughing these fields, and I think back to the life of the Berber peasants of these areas, one of the poorest in Morocco. Neglected by the government, they have found (economic) relief in the cultivation of marijuana. *For the first night spent with locals in Morocco, it was fascinating!*

In the Rif mountains, surrounded by cannabis fields, lies the town of Chefchaouen. The medina, painted entirely in various shades of blue, is a sight to behold and attracts tourists from all over the world. However, it lacks the warmth, the boisterous and thriving street life I had come to love in other cities. It is a breeding ground for tourists, where visitors can roam around freely and take hundreds of photos. After wandering aimlessly for a few hours, I finally found the market and the human life in it, in a square in the upper part of the city, outside the medina.

On the way to the house where I am staying, I guess from the hubbub of a crowd of schoolchildren who have happily poured onto the streets, that classes have just finished. A small group of kids approach and shyly follow me at a distance. After discovering that I wasn't going to eat them, they walk along with me and become what they are again: friendly, noisy, and curious! The oldest girl speaks a little French, as do a few of the others. So, it falls to her to translate for the other kids. They pepper me with questions, and we joke about our terrible French. I reflect on these children's desire for knowledge and how important it is that I never lose mine.

Arriving at the beginning of the little street where I live, I put the little child I was carrying on my shoulders down on the ground, say goodbye to them, and off I go. A few moments later, the older girl calls out after me, and stepping forward, she places a little yellow flower in my hand. "Because you have been kind to us," she says, with a smile on her lips and in her eyes.

Like me, the little group had appreciated the gesture and one by one, they all pick a flower off the ground to bring to me. Last comes the little girl I had on my shoulders, who hands me a small stone to seal the moment.

They walk away, and tears run down my face. Such purity, so genuine. Here is another essential lesson brought by these professors of life. Don't be afraid to express what you think, don't hold back your emotions if you want to break through and touch people's hearts.

I spent ten days in Fes, a city rich in history, culture, and humanity. I wandered around and got lost countless times in the medina, said to be the largest in the world. A maze of alleys often similar to each other. In the first few days, the impression of being in a labyrinth is intense: *haven't I been here before?* The ancient Moroccan city is, in fact, a maze built for defensive purposes. It has been beautifully erected, and incredible treasures are hidden among its meanderings. The only way to find them is with a guide, or if fate wills it.

Walls, nondescript and dilapidated, conceal behind them elegant riads, typical Moorish dwellings built around an internal courtyard or garden. Often an elegant fountain dominates the space overlooked by the balconies of the rooms of the house, rich in mosaics and wood inlays. In the hustle and bustle of the medina, these are islands of peace, where the outside world's noises are far away, muffled.

Often, equally hidden among the houses are the mosques, especially the smaller ones, whose presence is revealed only by their minarets. Or by following the stream of the worshippers who go there at prayer time. Fes is also home to several important madrasas and the oldest university in the world. And so it was, wandering through this maze of narrow streets, I happened to discover some of these wonders.

Goods are moved by donkey or on carts pushed by energetic youngsters. It often happens that pedestrians get caught up in a bottleneck with the traffic of goods being delivered. In this tangle of people, everyone sure of their destination moves quickly. Tourists and myself, on the other hand, wander slowly, contemplatively.

For me, an unmissable stop in the morning is at the shop where a short, skinny cook serves *bessara*, a traditional soup of broad beans and garlic. Customers sit in the backroom, crowded, intimate and familiar. Here, I met some merchants who invited me to visit their shops in the medina. I don't think I ever managed to find one, relying only on their directions.

The cook never abandons a strategic position which allows him to draw from the steaming pot and serve the customers' table at the same time. He doesn't speak French, and verbally our relationship never got beyond "how are you" and "good soup". Yet as the days go by, we make friends, or at least we enjoy each other's company.

Having stocked up on energy, it is now time to enter the heart of the medina. On display at the butcher's counter, the severed head of a dromedary has been an important milestone in this labyrinth since day one. Next to it, two young boys prepare lamb roasts and beef with vegetables. The meat is often fresh, locally sourced. A shopkeeper sells eggs and chickens; a few metres away, a butcher kills and cleans the animal, which is then served in the little restaurant next door.

Hidden in the maze of the medina are enchanting little squares, like oases in the desert: some of them I reached once but then never again. Caged by the claustrophobia of the alleyways, to arrive here is a breath of fresh air. Looking up, I can see the sky again, clear.

The henna *souk* is my favourite corner in Fes. An enchanting, intimate little square with two central trees taking up the space in front of a small mosque. The stalls sell mainly cosmetics, some of which are henna-based. I made a friend here, Michela, who has been married to Mohammed for several years. They run a shop together, right next to a fountain and the mosque. I spent whole afternoons chatting with them and with customers passing by their shop. A purchase here is never made in just a few minutes, often leading to long conversations over a glass of tea. Time stands still, in such perfect harmony with this magical place. Only the comings and goings from the mosque indicate its flow until the sun sets.

A boy often comes by to visit Michela; I think he is charmed by her sweetness. He sits on the steps at the entrance of the mosque, and Mohammed hands him a tea and a handful of dates or almond pastries to go with it. I don't know his name, he is autistic and doesn't speak much, but he loves music. I play at guessing his musical tastes, switching between different genres on my mobile phone. The Red Hot Chili Peppers? He shakes his head, negative. Queen? He listens to them, starts moving his head to the beat. Yes, Queen are fine. And Mannarino? He listens and shakes his head violently. God forbid, no. Alright.

"This is Pink Floyd." He listens. "You like?" Not a word or a nod. I let the whole track play until it fades into the buzz of the *souk*. At that moment, he clenches his fist and offers it to me, and I touch his knuckles with mine.

Music, a universal language. I have learned to put it next to football and religion as topics that connect the entire globe. They have often helped me make valuable friendships or pass through customs unscathed.

We part with a warm embrace from which I feel this boy transmitting a powerful energy, and a shiver runs through me. Michela observes the scene and smiles: "He's a good boy, huh?"

On the way back, after passing the head of the camel that with its gaze points me the way out of the labyrinth, a stop is required at the stall selling *msemen*[2] filled with ricotta and honey, accompanied by a glass of yoghurt.

How I love this city.

It is early April when I leave the city of Fes to enter the Atlas mountain range for the first of two crossings. At the outset, a cold drizzle continued to fall, extending the feeling of winter. As I ascend in altitude, it turns into annoying wet snow. Here I am, perfectly dressed to cross Africa with its deserts and forests, freezing.

Conditions improve after a few days, and a shy sun reappears, creeping through the last clouds. I am in the heart of the mountain range near the village of Anefgou, one of the poorest areas in Morocco. The snow soon starts to melt on the branches and, blown off by the wind, it gives the impression that below it is still snowing.

At the top of the pass, I see the first earthen houses in the distance. I stop to contemplate this view with the perfect timing. The sky is finally clear, and the vivid light makes the colours sparklingly bright. A few white patches remain, scattered here and there on the sunny slopes, while the snow has painted the peaks, adding a further touch of colour to the panorama.

My gaze runs from the valley floor towards the peaks. The cultivated land near the roaring torrent gives way to a barren, uninhabited terrain. A wooded strip, almost all pines, frames the snowy peaks under the clear sky. The distant shouts of kids invite me to look down into the valley, where a football pitch has been skilfully wrested from the inhospitable slopes. How important it is to give the right amount of time to every action, or inaction. How lucky I am to be able to afford it.

---

[2] A thick crepe usually served for breakfast. It may be the equivalent of the American pancake.

In these mountains, the bike traveller can take his pick of numerous itineraries, all equally exciting. I have identified a track, very interesting by all appearances, which will take me to the Todra gorges in five days. I travel through remote villages, thundering streams laden with winter waters and high passes. No less hospitable than in the seaside and lowland villages, the people invite me into their homes countless times during the day. Whether to spend the night or chat, they offer me the inevitable tea. They teach me that in these parts, they warm the body by using wormwood leaves rather than refreshing mint.

I continue on, the icy wind from the west fades little by little, and increasingly, a new warm breeze now comes from the southeast, from the desert.

For thousands of years, the Todra river has carved its way into the reddish sandstone of this region. Today, a road runs alongside the watercourse; it is surrounded by overhanging cliffs that sometimes exceed three hundred metres in height. A breathtaking environment, which I had the opportunity to visit on a previous trip.

Todra is, in fact, a paradise for climbers, among them both a dear friend and me. Two years before, we were hosted in a small hotel at the exit of the gorge. Although it was not remarkable for its qualities, we were pampered by Hassan and his brother Harbi *Morgan Freeman*, and we spent some delightful days there.

I have a delightful memory of that stay, and I am now returning to them with a photo we took at the time as a sign of gratitude.

Morgan Freeman is sweeping up between the terrace tables when I arrive and leave my bike at the entrance. He doesn't recognise me: it's been a few years, and I'm not easily identifiable, dressed like that.

"Good morning, this is for you," I say, handing him the photograph. In the shot, Morgan Freeman and his brother are hugging my friend and me. A little confused, he examines the photo and studies my face. He takes another look at the picture and finally bursts into an exclamation of joy.

"Brother, come and see who has arrived." Hassan looks out from the kitchen, approaches, and repeats the same actions. A moment later, we are seated at a small table, sipping a glass of mint tea as we recount the highlights of recent times. Once again, they make me feel at home, the same pleasant vibes I had a couple of years ago. They haven't changed at all, and the place hasn't changed. In the evening, the noisy generator continues its work loyally into the night.

I leave behind the Todra gorges and this oasis of peace, heading southeast. The incredible variety of Moroccan landscapes reaches its peak here. A few days earlier, I was freezing in the snowy mountains, and now I am heading, wind in my favour, towards the arid desert on the border with Algeria.

Wandering through Morocco, you inevitably notice how Islam permeates every moment of the day for... everyone. Like it or not, I feel it all the time. Five times a day, in any inhabited area, the muezzin calls the faithful to prayer. When we share a meal, we use only our right hand to bring food to our mouth. When they offer me a hot dish, *Alhamdulillah*, thanks be to God. When the mechanic is about to saw off the axle of my pedal, *Bismillah*, in the name of God. When I arrive at a village in the Sahara after a hundred kilometres in the midday furnace and find all the shops closed because "it's Ramadan and they reopen tonight, then you can buy a coke." This is what I mean when I say that Islam permeates people's lives, it sets their rhythms and guides their actions.

I am moving away from Zagora, a tourist town on the Draa river[3] banks. The town still retains its original charm in many parts—at least I imagine it is the original—or if not, it appears more authentic. It is an oasis at the gateway to the desert.

---

[3] More correct would be to call it Oued, as it is a non-perennial watercourse that in the interior of Morocco is lost in desert areas.

To the west, thick palm groves hide the view of the river. I'm still not used to this heat, intensified by the afternoon wind. A warning light on the dashboard: sudden dizziness and shivers tell me that a stop is necessary. I take a track that sneaks through the palm grove, and I am amazed by the hidden world I find there. I skirt low earth walls that mark the boundaries of the properties, following the track that runs for several kilometres through the palm trees. The only encounter is with a farmer who is hoeing the land. He sees me and greets me with a hand after having passed it over his forehead to wipe away the sweat. Unfortunately, we don't understand each other because my French and his Arabic don't connect beyond the usual greetings. But he gives me a wave as I carry on.

A little further on, the shade of the palm trees is broken, and space opens up onto the square of a dusty village. The mosque on the opposite side dominates the scene. With the tired smile that characterises my afternoon arrivals, I stop by an old man sitting on a doorstep, intent on rolling up palm leaves already cut into thin strips. Once again, when the pleasantries are over, we no longer understand each other. Fortunately, a girl comes out of the house; I imagine she is his daughter. After exchanging a few words with her father, she tells me in good French that they will inform the village chief, and he will certainly find me a place for the night.

The old man's hands slide swiftly and painstakingly over the palm threads, learned from a lifetime's experience. I watch him for a long time as he weaves the thick fibres into a rope with a casual nonchalance. I approach him to study the details of the movements, and he, pleased with my interest, slows down his work and shows me the main steps.

Finally, I am joined by Mohammed, my host for the night. During the journey, I am learning the importance of recognising a person's intentions at first glance, or at least in the first five seconds. Mohammed has a serious but friendly face, a pleasant smile, and a firm handshake. Right from the first meeting, he gives me an excellent impression.

We walk towards his home while he shows me the village, enriching my visit with anecdotes and historical details. As in other similar villages on the banks of the Draa, everyone lives off the production of dates. There are at least five varieties around here, and he is keen to show me his plantation.

The time for the sunset prayer has arrived, and we move quickly to his house, where he leaves me in a room all to myself. "Let's go to the mosque together, tonight,[4]" he tells me before closing the door and leaving. *It wasn't a question, I guess.*

As I wash myself, I mull over what he has just told me. Only Muslims are allowed to enter mosques, so I find it strange that he invited me.

About half an hour later, he returns, calling me from the door, and invites me for dinner. Those who can afford it always dedicate a room to welcoming guests, sent by God. A rasping television welcomes us into the living room. The walls are bare, without decoration, as one would expect from a country house in the middle of palm groves. Carpets of various sizes overlap on the floor, covering the whole surface. Finally, to complete the setting, a few low sofas are arranged along each wall and three pouffes next to a low, wide table.

Two other people are sitting at the table: an elderly man with a charismatic look and another gentleman, who will introduce himself as the *Imām*[5] of the community. While his wife serves us a marvellous, hearty tajine, *Bismillah*, we help each other wash our hands. Starting with the oldest person at the table, our host pours water from a plastic

---

[4] Mohammed refers here to the night prayer, the last of the day. Five obligatory prayers, the *ṣalāt*, dictate the times of daily life in Islamic communities. Communities that are traditionally based on the position of the sun in the sky; the measurement of time, as well as geographical orientation and the development of trigonometry have contributed to the scientific determination of these times.

[5] Literally is translated as *guide*; he is the head of the Islamic community. In a more general sense, *imām* is for Sunnis also anyone who leads daily prayer.

teapot over his hands and into a small bowl to be collected. Finally, I offer to pour the water for Mohammed to help him with this ritual. Everyone expresses a gesture of approval. *I am learning something, at last.* I am the youngest at the table, and his son was not present in the room, so the task fell to me.

The topic of the evening is immediately evident. Just as I bring the first fragrant piece of chicken stew up to my mouth, the *Imām* asks me: "Philippe, what do you think about Islam?"

A delicate subject. I have spoken to several Muslims, and the impression I have gained is that for them Islam is the best religion. They do not understand why others persist in incomplete, or even worse, false beliefs.

So, I try a gentle approach. "I was struck by the similarities with Christianity. In short, love for God and neighbour. And I admit ignorance, but I was surprised to find Jesus also in the Koran. I think we really are brothers in this."

"It's an excellent thought," replies Mohammed. "Islam came to complete the shortcomings of Christianity. Its doctrine is complete, in every direction."

"We also have another aspect in common. The holy wars. Millions of humans beings have died in the name of God, and now in the Sahara in the name of Allah; Islamic terrorists are committing inconceivable massacres." I've abandoned delicacy too quickly.

Mohammed and the *Imām* look at each other, and the latter turns to me: "Be careful not to confuse things. This organisation you hear about, Islamists, they are not real Muslims, they act for money and power, and use Allah as an excuse to the people."

Mohammed interjects. "A true Muslim acts with love, in the name of God."

"But why have these groups thrived in the local populations? I mean, I've heard of many people who join their cause and no one opposing them."

Mohammed weighs up the question and continues: "Many countries where these events happen, and some regions, in particular, are weak. In the sense that the government has no way to reach them, there is no political interest, or they are poor in resources, and the populations feel abandoned. There is a lot of discontent over there; they have no schools, there is no security, and lack of food. And that's where these jihadist groups, or whole ethnic groups, intervene. They replace the state; they become the state. Do you understand? These people offer protection against bandits and provide weapons for fights against rival ethnic groups."

"They operate in border areas, far from the central government. There they can easily replace the state and build parastatal structures. After that, they can do whatever they want. Human trafficking, drugs. Nobody stops them," concludes the *Imām*. "Now I'm leaving; it's almost time for prayer. I'll see you there."

I am wearing long trousers, which are acceptable to Mohammed, but my red t-shirt ripped at the shoulder is not. He calls loudly to his son, who comes in from the next room with a shirt and a *qamis*, the foot-length white cotton suit worn by every man in Morocco. "They're for you. Try them on."

"Wow, but there's really no need."

"Wear them, for prayer it's better." Another command, not a suggestion.

I feel proud to walk beside him, wearing this outfit. Everyone is watching with curiosity and amusement the cyclist who rode through the village a few hours earlier. Someone exchanges a joke in dialect with Mohammed, who responds with a laugh; I look at him and nod, in a gesture as if to say: *I understand Arabic too*, and smile at him.

Before each prayer, a Muslim follows a cleansing ritual to enter the mosque purified. This explains why there are always washing facilities next to each mosque. Men on one side, women on the other. *Ça va sans dire*[6].

Mohammed is pleased as he explains every detail of the cleaning ritual to me, which has to be carried out in a precise sequence. Left hand washes the right, three times. Right hand washes left, three times. "Bring the water to the mouth with the right hand and gargle. Good, now inhale water into the nose. *Always* with the right." My mentor corrects every little mistake or omission. Now it's the turn of the face. "Roll up your sleeves; you have to clean your forearms well." Head, ears. Now the feet, and we're done. Interesting how Islam enters everyday life even with rules about hygiene, guiding every action of the believer.

Ablutions at an end, we enter the mosque. First of all, we remove our sandals, and with a nod, Mohammed indicates to me a corner to one side where I can sit and watch the prayers. The floor is covered with carpets, of an almost uniform red to adorn the room. The walls are bare, lacking the decorations and engravings usually found in the wealthiest mosques. The digital clock behind the *Imām* catches the eye immediately. It shows in large red figures the current time and the appointed time of the five canonical prayers for that day. The room remains spacious, albeit divided by regular arched columns, and about fifty men barely fill the room. In perfect synchrony between their words and movements, they prostrate themselves and rise up, guided by the words of the *Imām* I had met at dinner just a short while earlier. I am happy to have been invited to witness such moments, fundamental to the community. But I ask myself, *who knows why they have let me enter?*

On Friday morning, I accompany Mohammed to see the plantation and then afterwards to the mosque. On this day, the midday prayer represents the most important religious event of the week, a little like Sunday Mass for us Catholics. This time he takes me to a back room

---

[6] This goes without saying.

where there are already dozens of people dressed for the celebration, while a group of boys in a corner intone religious hymns. A rapid round of greetings and introductions, and I find myself face to face with the *Imām*.

"Good morning Philippe, today I would like you to become a Muslim." *Would you like some tea?* No, no, he asked me if I wanted to change my religion, not if I wanted a cup of tea, but he did so in the same tone, wandering between extremes of nonchalance and custom. I was speechless and, not knowing how to react, I looked around, trying to understand. In the meantime, the boys had stopped singing, and the adults are also waiting for me to say yes.

I turn my eyes to the *Imām*. "Look, I thank you very much for this opportunity. I am honoured by it. But I don't believe I'm in a position to make a decision right now. It's a question I have to think about."

Mohammed interjects: "No, it's not difficult, Philippe. It's sufficient to learn this phrase and after the common prayer recite it three times," and he continues "*La ilaha illa Allah, Muhammad rasul Allah.*"[7]

I feel very uncomfortable, under pressure, and I don't want to be here right now. If at first, I thought it was a joke, a few minutes have been enough to reveal the seriousness of the proposal. I play one last card. "Listen, it is not a question of choosing tea or coffee. It is a life-changing decision. I need to inform myself, and study what it means to be a Muslim."

The good Lord, or Allah, has decided it is time for prayer. The muezzin approaches the microphone, and the loudspeakers on the minaret the call to prayer out, amongst the palms. Upset by how the situation has evolved, the *Imām*, Mohammed and the others say goodbye and then go towards the prayer hall. I leave the room with

---

[7] "There is no true God, who has the right to be worshipped except Allah, and Muhammed is the messenger of Allah." Once a person has uttered the testimony of faith (*Shahada*) with conviction and understands its meaning, he adheres to the Islamic religion.

them, but I need some air, and I head towards the plantation and the house.

I leave Mohammed's house the next morning. We never talk again about what happened. Perhaps it never occurred. I leave with three abundant kilos of dates of the best quality and a nice shirt—from that day on, it will become my ordinance outfit, although often crumpled, for those moments when appropriate elegance is called for. Mohammed would have liked to add his religion to my luggage as well. Despite this disappointment, I think these were two constructive days for both of us. A foot on the pedal, a trumpet blast, and a smile to say goodbye. Off we go, the Sahara awaits.

I kept my promise, read articles and websites on Islam, started reading the Koran. I don't feel at ease with the dictates of this religion, which for me is restrictive, limiting in terms of opinions and free will.

But that's what a journey is for. You learn, you study, you grow. Now I know with certainty that a Muslim is not someone who commits massacres in the name of Allah. A Muslim is a brother who opens the doors of his home to me; a Muslim is someone who always has something to give to those who have nothing; a Muslim is the one who tries to resolve conflicts with love, not by fighting.

Come to think of it, what if I replace the word *Muslim* with *Christian*? Where is the difference? There is no difference. A Muslim is my brother.

When the alarm clock goes off, I'm already awake and agitated. I am close to the border with Algeria, in the bungalow of an elegant resort in the desert sands run by Luc, a Belgian cyclist who moved here several years ago. For the next three days, I will be on my own in the desert, and with this project in mind, I have slept little and badly. Yet the previous evening, Luc tried to reassure me several times. "You won't be alone. Berber shepherds are out there at the moment. If you have any problems, give me a call, and I'll come and pick you up with the *quatre-quatre*.[8]"

The track I will be cycling along is internationally famous for its charm. It is used by many rally competitions and tourists with a taste for adventure. Departure: M'Hamid Arrival: Foum Zguid. In between, the Draa *Hammada*[9]: sand, rocks and, I hope, some water wells. I found some GPS tracks on the net, but Luc informs me that conditions vary from year to year, and it's necessary to check with the locals. His hand follows his words by tracing curves and obstacles on a paper napkin.

He advises me against the track closest to the sand dunes, the great Erg of Chigaga. A strong wind in the previous weeks has blown a lot of sand onto the track, and it would be difficult to pass with a loaded bike. However, an old road runs at the foot of the mountains but is falling into disuse because it is in such terrible condition. For me, it will be perfect.

The sun and I start the morning together. For the first few kilometres, the track meanders between low dunes. I'll follow the track made in the sand by the 4x4s, but I could be in trouble even so. However, just like spring snow, early in the morning, the sand better bears the weight of the passerby: the humidity of the night makes it harder, and it should be easier to skim on the surface.

I soon realise that a three-inch tyre is not going far in a sea of sand unless I lower the pressure. I press my finger on the valve to release air. The hissing goes on for several seconds until I test the tyre's resistance to my touch, which I imagine to be under one bar of pressure. That should be enough; in fact, it's better not to go too far in reducing the pressure, or a protruding rock could tear the tyre casing apart. The price to pay: repairing a tubeless tyre in the middle of nowhere. Every cyclist's nightmare.

---

[8] The friendly nickname for 4x4 vehicles.
[9] One of three types of desert. Generally flat, barren and covered with gravel.

Before setting off on my journey, I thought through every detail of my bike, and there was no doubt about the tyres. Robust and wide enough, they proved to be an excellent decision. A bicycle of this type allows me to tackle *almost* any road without worrying about the kind of surface I will encounter. In short, it increases my perception of freedom enormously. Travelling by bike is freedom.

I make progress, but slowly. Often in the saddle or, when I struggle through mounds of windblown sand, on foot. It surprises me more and more how similar the behaviour of sand is to snow.

The trail winds through the dunes, which are never more than a couple of metres high. A few shrubs and thorny acacia trees add a touch of colour to the otherwise golden landscape. In an enchanting silence, I am lucky to enjoy all this nature in complete solitude. Perhaps it is too much for one person alone. I feel dwarfed and have the sensation of disappearing into this immense environment.

It's ten o'clock when the odometer informs me that I have covered ten kilometres since the start of the track. The lack of effort while pedalling suggests that I have now finished sinking into the sand.

Little by little, the landscape has levelled out, and a vast expanse opens up in front of me. Only a mountain range continues to run to my right, far to the north. The track now splits into multiple paths: traces of the *quatre-quatres* that avoid the washboards searching for less bumpy surfaces. Yet they all continue in one direction, in search of the place where the sun daily goes to rest. Even I enjoy leaving fresh tracks in the ground, as I like to do early in the morning when I climb the snowy slopes of my mountains.

In the early afternoon, I arrive at an oasis. On the map that Luc has sketched out on a piece of paper, it has the high-sounding name of *Oasis Sacrée*. A shepherd, who until a few seconds before was dozing under a palm, tells me there is a well on the opposite side of the oasis, with plentiful water. There are no dromedaries around. God only knows how many hours ago he fell asleep. *His herd must be in Algeria by now.*

Luc hasn't indicated any other wells on the map, at least not in the next fifty kilometres. *It's hot, extremely hot, maybe I should go on in the morning.*

I am tempted to pitch the tent under those two palm trees near the well, protected from the sun and the wind. I weigh up the option while I throw some water on my neck to refresh myself. I go back to the bike to get the camping equipment. *Stop!* A white snake is slithering up the front fork and has now reached the handlebars. Its head is hidden; indeed, my guest is less than half a meter in length, yet it paralyses me with terror.

What to do? I have no knowledge of the species in this area. I scroll through the list of options; the only wise one seems to wait for the reptile to voluntarily leave the bike that it has taken hostage—it is now studying the brake mechanism. Having rejected the idea of pitching the tent near the well, I move away, searching for a new shelter for the night: a small abandoned shed a few hundred meters away seems the right place.

Meanwhile, a furious wind has started to blow. I go back to retrieve the bike while the sand, which gravity had kept in its proper place until a short while ago, is now swirling in the air. The snake has left the bike, and I am reassured by a quick check of the surroundings. I grab the handlebars and drag the bicycle into the shed. A nifty stroke of luck: in a few moments, a raging sandstorm hits the oasis. From the hut, I can safely admire and film it. The sand penetrates the shelter but, out of the wind, it just covers everything with a thin golden layer. Despite this, I sneeze; better to wear my scarf and cover my mouth and nose.

Outside, the rushing wind blows hard from the west, and the palm trees dance, possessed by an ancestral spirit. I sit like this, waiting, contemplating this alien landscape of vigour and wonder.

By the time the storm subsides, the sun has set. Venus is already shining in the sky; the other stars emerge shyly. It is time to rest.

The dromedaries passed by the shed several times during the night, waking me up with their grumbling. As I try to sleep, my thoughts go to the magic of the previous day and to the place where I am camped. The new day brings with it more challenges, and my tiredness does not help in any way. Early in the morning, I tackle the old track, which is more like a mass of wobbly stones. The same as riding on a pile of ostrich eggs. Now, continuous ups and downs and loose stones test my patience. I have no other choice, having discarded the sandy track a few kilometres further south; a sea of ostrich eggs separates me from the other itinerary. I'm more and more in debt to these fat tyres. Who knows how today would have been otherwise?

A couple of hours later, a white tent shows up at the end of the rollercoaster, a few dozen pedal strokes from the track. I imagine they're the nomadic shepherds Luc told me about. I approach, but it seems that they have already spotted me; a man is standing at the entrance of the tent and looks to be weighing up my presence there. With the excuse of asking if there is another route in better condition, I approach to chat with them. I'm really curious.

The whiskered man is the head of the family: he lives with his wife, two daughters and two grandchildren—I imagine this is only a part of the household, as six people would be unusual in the numerous Maghrebi families. Following the guide book of perfect Moroccan hospitality, the shepherd invites me into his tent for tea. Only after sitting in the shade do I realise how fierce the sun is today. A pleasant coolness accompanies my clumsy attempts at communication. After more than a month in Morocco, I can ask for "food, water, sleep" with my Arabic language skills. The conversation with my host then turns to the local food, water scarcity in the area, and the quality of sleep in such empty regions.

One of the two daughters enters at the right moment to break the silence that has been created. Raising my eyes, which were previously focused on the tea grounds, I am stunned. *Perhaps those numerous stones out there on the road were once travellers who, passing this way, fell under the spell of this extraordinary desert sorceress.* A marvellous face, elongated and thin, with thick eyebrows framing two dark eyes, is staring at me. I can't tell if those eyes are black or brown. But, at the same time, they are so bright, two stars in broad daylight. They shine with their own light and smile at me.

This celestial creature passes me by and sits down in front of us, followed by a little girl still swaying on her two plump legs. The same eyes, she must be her daughter. I risk asking for a photograph, but she shyly replies *"lla"* in response. No. At least for the next ten minutes, I won't keep reading tea leaves.

I approach the little girl to play with her. The mother smiles but doesn't interact, and after a few minutes, the old man decides it's time to resume work, so I say goodbye, and with a few pedal strokes, I go back to trampling the travellers turned to stone by this Berber Medusa.

According to Luc's map, I am heading towards a settlement, perhaps the only semi-permanent one in the region. But it will undoubtedly require a huge effort if I ever make it. The surface of the track is all broken up, if possible even more than before, while the high temperature is starting to exhaust me. I study the GPS to find an alternative. It seems that a track branches off a few hundred metres before my turn off to descend to the Iriki plain. On this other track, a cruising speed of more than five kilometres would at least give me a bit of a cooling breeze. Let's give it a try.

Lake Iriki, or rather what remains of it. After the construction of a large dam several hundred kilometres upstream, in Ouarzazate, the flow of the Draa river has diminished, and today it dries up between the towns of Zagora and Tagounite depending on the rainfall of the year. This lake, therefore, ceased to exist in its liquid form some fifty years before I came this way. So, this is where I am—an endless plateau with occasional bushes on hard ground. The terrain is made of hardened sand with a thin layer of salt from the drying out of the lake.

Cycling here is finally a pleasure: fifty or more kilometres of smooth, level ground awaits me. Tiredness goes on the back burner as I am enchanted by my surroundings. On the left, in the distance, is the sandy erg that I circumnavigated the previous day. Finally, on the right, continues the mountain range that has been with me for a few days.

Always head in the west direction towards the large flat-topped mountain that you see down there. Luc's advice resonates in my head. In fact, there it is, interrupting an otherwise flat horizon. *Easy*, I think.

The heat is unbearable, and I can't see anything on the horizon to shade me from the sun. Yet there is something magical, surreal around here, as if I were in a Dali painting. I try a couple of photographs, but I soon discover how difficult it is to capture the soul of this place in a few shots. Similarly, I find it hard to describe the landscape in words, or at least to convey the sensations that this environment offers. Countless whirlwinds of air and sand graze on the plain; a lake emerges in the distance, and an islet reflects on it. Wait!

The lake should be completely dry! In fact, there it is as a mirage, with a stunned cyclist admiring it. Instead, the big flat-topped mountain in the background continues to admire itself in the *lake that isn't there*, as it would have done a hundred years ago, in the *lake when it was still there*. I move forward, and the lake moves away. I chase it for at least half an hour, but the lake is still there, and it seems more and more unreachable. Only whirlwinds exist, and avoiding them was an amusing game during the crossing.

Equally surreal is the presence of three buildings arranged in a straight line a few kilometres apart, one hour's ride after diving into the lake. *Is the sun going to my head? Another mirage, maybe? Yet, I am covered up and well hydrated.*

A boy with a sleepy expression looks out into the scorching early afternoon sun. Clearly, my call has woken him up. "*Cocà, Fantà?*" he proposes as I approach. No, it is not a mirage. It is a hotel in the middle of nowhere. The poetry of the place fades, but it doesn't die.

I wake up in the mid-afternoon, and all at once, the heat is more bearable. Saying goodbye to the mirage of the innkeeper, I get back on the saddle. It doesn't take long for the military checkpoint, indicated by Luc on his hand-drawn map, to come into sight on the horizon. *Hopefully, they can put me up for the night.*

I set off in the direction of the building, which dominates the plain from a modest hillock. Another call from me and another sleepy face appears in the afternoon sun. He seems embarrassed at not having done his duty and not having seen me arrive earlier, so he tries to cover it up. "*Passeport, s'il vous plait.*"

No hospitality in the military compound. However, I get a valuable piece of information: there are no water wells in the next few kilometres until I reach my destination. So, I ask them if I can get water at the outpost. The young soldier willingly agrees to save a traveller on a bicycle from death by dry jaws.

Beyond the military outpost, the terrain begins to rise gently. I am now far from the plain, which is no longer in sight, and I pedal until I reach two shrunken bushes a short distance apart. It may not be the perfect shelter from the wind, but it is the only one in the vicinity. The ritual of setting up base camp follows, as the sun bends ever closer to investigate, intrigued.

The enchantment of a desert sunset. This is no ordinary sunset. It is the sunset I have earned through an intense day of toil and sweat. To get to this point, I have endured a gruelling day; I have faced obstacles and difficulties. That sunset is my sunset. Waiting for the water to boil for dinner, I sit on the ground, cross-legged, watching the deep blue night advance. With the sun low behind me, I contemplate the pyramid of the shadow of the tent stretching to the ground and, thinking back to the day, I can't help but smile. A few moments come back vividly in my mind: the stony road, the shepherd who offered me tea in his tent, the lake that is not there, *those eyes*... those eyes keep me company until I close mine for the night, and maybe even afterwards.

It's time to leave the sand. In the following days, I cross the Atlas Mountains again and return to the coast, more than a month after my last icy swim. Agadir and the surrounding beaches are a decent place where I can finally rest from the accumulated fatigue and enjoy surfing. A few days go by, the tiredness has been washed away by the salt, and I want to get going again. On my way to the south, the great Sahara is already calling me with its vibrant energy.

Guelmim is the gateway to the desert. At least that's what it's called. Don't imagine that an environment dominated by imposing sand dunes and devoid of any kind of life suddenly emerges just beyond this town.

Nevertheless, it remains a fascinating town. The arch built as you leave the city is reminiscent of a launchpad towards the deep south. As the city fades away, the landscape becomes gradually arid, the distances between the various outposts increase, and the wind becomes the master of the environment, no longer hindered by the Atlas range.

The Sahara excited me, but it frightened me even more. Intimidated by the idea of the great emptiness, I recall my high school maths tests. What's that got to do with it? You may ask. Very often, I was unprepared and consequently terrified at the idea of being questioned. I knew it would end badly with a poor mark on my report. Well, with mathematics, only a serious study helped me get through the test. I took on the desert with the same spirit.

I started my research with Google Maps to find all the outposts along the way. I took note of the distances. One hundred, one hundred and twenty kilometres. One day, I will have to pedal hard to reach a military base one hundred and eighty kilometres away.

The next step was to contact people who crossed the desert before me and ask them about the availability of water and any other difficulties. *The wind, check the wind*, a famous cyclist suggested. For this purpose, too, the internet is essential. I type *Western Sahara May winds*, and all sorts of useful information comes up. Most of the time, the winds blow from north to south, excellent!

That's why, as I passed the Guelmim arch, I was no longer afraid. Once I had organised myself as best I could for every possible difficulty, I felt prepared for the challenge.

A deep breath and off I go, to conquer the Sahara.

But Sahara cannot be conquered. The mere idea itself is crazy. There is no life here. Only proud men and the occasional tree have been able to adapt and survive. And they have not conquered it. Instead, they asked for permission to enter, adapted to its rules, and hoped for its mercy.

Especially in the first few days, the wind sets the pace. It has home advantage. With the ocean on one side and the desert on the other, it can blow where it chooses with nothing to stop it. And since the wind is playing on my side, many days literally fly by, pushed by its currents.

The vegetation thins out, and the last rocky reliefs plunge into the sand. The asphalt road runs monotonously and lazily through the barren landscape. Not so for the surroundings. Each day, I pass through different landscapes: a region of rocky desert; an uninterrupted expanse of hardened sand; dried-out river mouths washed by the daily tide, bringing life with it; an idyllic lagoon surrounded by white sand dunes where flocks of flamingos find shelter and food.

As I entered this emptiness, I began to feel at ease. The day goes by listening to an audiobook, or the music on the radio, or the wind. Sometimes a distant horn announces the approach of a sleepy truck and often accompanies a thumbs-up from a smiling driver. As the days went by, I began to recognise the buses that travel the route every day. One driver also seems to have recognised me, and if at the first crossing we exchanged a circumstantial greeting, at the second he slowed down to ask me if everything was going well, and finally, at the third meeting, he stopped, eager to know the reasons for the journey.

The road is an endless succession of itself, and I am always cycling in the same position. I had not thought I would find peace there. My legs were always spinning with the same rhythm: a hypnotic rhythm that enchants the mind. I contemplated the pure pleasure of the moment, with a clear mind and a fixed smile hidden behind my scarf, ignoring the heat and the numb seat.

In the desert, its inhabitants teach us that every part of the body must be adequately protected. Long, breathable clothes covering all your body, a cap pulled down to protect your eyes, and a scarf pulled up as far as your glasses. The latter proved to be an essential accessory for travelling: the air's extreme dryness dries out my body moisture within minutes, increasing the need to rehydrate.

For two days only, the wind turned. This was enough to put me on my knees, miserable and defeated. As always, the road is flat with nothing but sand and rocks roasted in the sun. An overbearing wind blows continuously and unhindered in the opposite direction to where I'm going. The fine sand creeps in everywhere, no matter what kind of protection I have; in the evening, I find it in my hair and in my underwear, crunching between my teeth and drying my throat. By mid-morning on the second day, I had covered much less ground than I had planned. If I was covering twenty-five kilometres every hour on a windy day, now I'm slowed down to ten measly kilometres per hour. The wind still hasn't given me a break.

So, I stop. At that moment, the only solution seems to be to scream. I pull the bandana off my face and scream in frustration. The wind can carry my furious sound waves to the sea, merge them in the sound of the waves, where my cries are dispersed. Who wins? I rest my arms on the handlebars and my forehead on my arms. A deep breath. Two, three. I have to be patient; that's how it is today. Today it's the wind and me. I can't fight it, and I can't beat it. So, I will have to be with it; we will have to be One.

I need a few minutes of rest, after which I start off again more serenely. I find myself humming a song, and I let the wind take it where it will. The desert is a great teacher for those who know how to listen.

A few kilometres from Tarfaya, a police patrol stopped me for a routine check; their escort to the town was less usual, *pour votre sécurité*. Over the next ten days, I would hear this phrase said dozens of times, repeated like a mantra by the police and military.

Another patrol is stationed at the entrance to the city and, without getting out of their cars, the officers do their duty with few words. When the first car has left, one of the two policemen approaches with a friendly manner and an official smile.

"Good morning, so you would be an Italian cyclist?"

"Good morning, officer. Yes, I am."

"And you are going to Mauritania, by bike?"

"Yes. Or at least I'm trying to." I accompany the joke with a smile and a shrug.

"Where are you going to sleep tonight?"

"Well, I think I'm going to stay here in town. I'll probably ask to pitch my tent somewhere."

"No, better not. *Pour votre sécurité*, you should sleep in a hotel."

"I'm sorry, officer, but I'm on a long journey and can't afford to pay for a hotel every day."

The two talk among each other, and after a quick phone call, the policeman continues: "Follow us on your bike to the hotel, and we will talk to the owner."

Yes, sir.

When we reach our destination, the policeman behind the wheel gets out, lights a cigarette, and goes to sit on the bonnet of the car. I put my bike against the wall and follow his colleague, who in the meantime has entered the hotel. He is talking with a guy at the reception desk, who looks up and peers over the officer's shoulder when I enter. That night cost me one euro and fifty cents.

Before leaving, the policeman asks me again: "Where are you going tomorrow?"

"On the road along the coast, towards…" I check the map, "Foum el Oued."

Without abandoning his polite yet firm tone, the policeman replies: "Better not, continue on the main road to Laâyoune."

I'm starting to get annoyed by this behaviour. "Why, sir?"

Pointless question. You can imagine the answer. *Pour votre sécurité*.

Early in the morning, after a breakfast included in the B&B rate, I leave the hotel when the sun has not yet risen. The world outside the hotel is still sleepy. A boy pushes a cart through the otherwise deserted street, while an individual across the road absent-mindedly smokes a cigarette. Maybe I've seen too many spy movies, but it seems to me that the man starts a phone call as soon as he sees me leave. I take the side streets in order not to pass in front of the police station and take the road along the coast.

A strong wind is blowing, and the road is almost entirely covered with sand, a thin layer, but enough to make me think that it is not being used. As I drive along the coast, I pass two wrecks, one of which is a passenger ferry. In 2008, when leaving the port of Tarfaya, due to strong winds and stormy sea conditions, the ship was thrown onto a reef and damaged beyond repair. Other wrecks have suffered a similar fate and now lie in this coastal museum.

I had just taken the last few photos of the wreck from the beach when a car pulls up on the side of the road, next to the bicycle. I retrace my steps and already sense the reason for this visit.

"*Monsieur*, you can't stay here, *pour votre sécurité*," the large but affable man reproaches me. He introduces himself as the commander of the Tarfaya police. I don't even try to argue the point, and they force me to go back with them. The officer at the wheel gets out of the car and helps me load the bike into the boot. On the way back, we converse calmly, like old friends. As soon as I try to find out more about why they stopped me, the commander doesn't reply and shuts up. They drop me off a few kilometres down the main road.

I start pedalling again, finally resigned to following their instructions, and only after a couple of minutes do I stop and turn around. In the distance, I can still see the outline of the car and the commander, his elbows resting on the car roof as he checks that I'm following orders. After that meeting, to make my life easier, I decided to behave like a blameless tourist.

Their house, their rules.

WESTERN SAHARA

Oh Saharawi, revolutionary people!
We are the revolutionaries!
And the free land of the Sahrawis is for the Sahrawis!

MARIEM HASSAN, HAIYU

May

Off I go, escorted by the policeman's gaze. Why so many police and all this need for control, you might ask?

The town I have just left, Tarfaya, is the last outpost in southern Morocco. This is partly untrue if one considers Western Sahara as a Moroccan region. Formally, this is the case; this territory is an integral part of the Kingdom of Morocco. But opinion is not unanimous, the argument not yet settled.

Until 1975, this vast desert region was a Spanish colony. Later, the Sahrawi population that inhabited these lands, supported in particular by the Polisario Front, founded the Sahrawi Arab Democratic Republic so they would get international recognition. Morocco, through a *peaceful* initiative, the so-called *Green March*, invaded the North with three hundred thousand civilians. In the meantime, the Spanish government formalised the division of the region between Mauritania and Morocco. War broke out. After several defeats, Mauritania withdrew from the conflict, leaving only Morocco to fight against the Front. Morocco escalated the fighting and conquered a large part of the territory through a mighty military operation and, above all, through the construction of a wall that they continued to lengthen over the years. Guarded by the army and surrounded by minefields, this wall blocked the Sahrawi advance. Since then (1991), they have been confined to a small part of Western Sahara, although today, most of the population is in exile in the refugee camps of Tindouf in Algeria.

Morocco's interest in Western Sahara is still very high. The main reasons are phosphate mines and the fishing industry. In addition to being heavily militarized, the government has invested substantially in road construction, expansion of ports and industrial parks. The government has also created new villages to entice part of the Moroccan population to migrate to these lands, attracted by tax breaks and fair wages. I have seen many settlements along the coast, both new and abandoned.

Western Sahara amazes me with the variety of its landscapes. Or rather, remembering how I imagined it, a flat and sandy expanse, I realise my mistake. On the coast, the arid desert ends abruptly with a fifty-metre cliff down to the beach, and finally to the sea.

In addition to the semi-deserted villages I mentioned earlier, several fishermen's huts are scattered along the road. These shelters are often just shacks, made of a few wooden planks and covered with rags to stop the sand from coming in. The scraps are, in turn, held in place by worn-out fishing nets to keep the wind out. These waters are plentiful, and fishing is the primary source of livelihood for the locals.

Some stretches of this endless coastline are fabulous. Overhanging the sea or sloping down a sandy hill, they invite the cyclist to slow down and stop several times. The atmosphere is permeated with saltiness, which blurs the long-distance vision, creating a mystical scene.

I am sitting on the edge of the cliff having a snack while absent-mindedly watching a fisherman untie his nets on the beach. I play at imagining us from a plane. We would be two tiny dots in this solemn scenario. We might just be two dots, but we are not insignificant at all since we contribute to, and are part of, this Oneness. At that moment, in tune with the grandeur of the Universe, an intense peace has spread through me. A phrase by Terzani came to mind, and I was moved:

"What a mistake it was to get away from nature! In its variety, in its beauty, in its cruelty, in its infinite, unparalleled greatness, there is the whole meaning of life.[1]"

I spot the path the fisherman has taken and follow it upstream with my eyes. As I do so, I notice a battered hut perched just below the top of the cliff, again with a few rags and some nets from which clothes are hung. Evidently, the cabin was built in that precarious position to shelter from the incessant Saharan winds. There, he is one of the few proud men who have learned to live with the desert and dedicate themselves to a life of hardship. In all of this, I see the image of Freedom in that fisherman.

I cover almost four hundred kilometres in two days. Forced marches to reach the military outpost of El Argoub.

The commanding general can't make up his mind, clearly taken aback by my appearance on his doorstep. *Pour ma sécurité* he would not want to leave me camping alone in the desert. *Pour leur sécurité* makes it risky to let me sleep in the military base or, even worse, in some family member's house. I am exhausted from the interminable day spent in the saddle, as always at the mercy of the strong winds. I patiently follow him with my eyes as he strolls back and forth on the porch, with his thumbs in his braces, fastened over a white vest. The soldier who accompanied me to his home is also waiting, silent. The general calls him closer and gives him an order before shutting the door behind him without further words.

Private Ibrahim explains the compromise solution to me. I will be able to pitch my tent outside the base, near the communications antenna. This way, I will be within sight and protected from the wind.

---

[1] Terzani, Tiziano. *Un'idea Di Destino*. Milano: Longanesi, 2014.

I jolt awake. The headlights of a car illuminate the tent from a few metres away. The door closes gently, and the gravel crunches under the ever-closer steps. The stranger walks around the tent and talks to another man, whom, I assume, is still sitting in the car. I'm stuck and don't know what to do. If they want to come in and rob me, it will take two seconds, and I would have no way to fight back. I try to take them by surprise, hurrying out of the tent and shouting so that someone from the nearby base can hear: "Who are you? What do you want?" The car's headlights light up a holstered pistol.

The intruder raises his hands in front of him, not towards the gun. He shows his hands as a guarantee of his good intentions while justifying himself: "*Monsieur*, don't worry. We are the police, and we are here *pour votre sécurité*." A policeman in plain clothes, appearing late at night! I am taken aback and mumble something to apologize for my reaction. Yet, I would have liked to tell him something else, especially as they scared me so much.

"We'll stay here in the car and keep watch."

"Sir, thank you. But I don't think it's necessary. I'm sure nothing will happen, so close to the military base."

Obviously, the objection brings no result. The policeman approaches the car as he replies, "We're here. If you need something, call us. Good night."

"Good night."

I return to the tent, zip up and slip into the sheet bag. The interior is still brightly lit.

"The lights!"

The car's headlights go out. Now, yes, it's a good night.

The next morning, I wake up early. The car is still there, and the two policemen are sleeping on the reclined seats. I remove the tent, prepare my bags, and have breakfast. When I have finished, I approach the car and knock on the window. The policeman wakes up suddenly and turns the knob to lower it.

"Thanks for keeping watch. Goodbye, Sirs."

I've lost count of how many patrols and checkpoints I've encountered on this road. Each time, the same questions on my trip, the document check, the usual queries about the luggage contents. And finally, I arrive at the border with Mauritania. No, that's not quite correct. In front of me lies a no man's land—a strip of land of a few kilometres wide belonging to the Polisario Front, but today uninhabited.

I've read some unpleasant things about this frontier, but I will soon discover that these are typical exaggerations by some travel blogger. The only truth is that a sign warns me to be careful because I'm crossing a minefield, although the latest information I have says that the area has now been cleared. Today this strip of land is under the control of the United Nations. My initial fears vanish as soon as I see the Blue Helmets. Along the five kilometres separating them from Mauritania, I meet some patrols monitoring the traffic. I stop near a guard car to look around. My heart is beating fast, even though everything is calm around me. I'm in one of the dirtiest places I've ever seen. It's also a giant graveyard for cars that have got stuck in this area for different reasons. They got bogged down, hit a mine, or were abandoned by smugglers.

It has to be said that, apart from the first paved kilometre, there is no real road. Using common sense, I follow the tracks of other vehicles, and in no time at all, I am on the other side, at the door of the customs officer.

MAURITANIA

Talghiwen assohatnen
Itadj asemman anneghabint
-
In difficult times, we share our suffering
As we share a glass of tea.
TINAIRWEN, ASSUF D'ALWA

May

With the curtains drawn and the window closed, I seek shelter from the fierce, glaring rays of the sun, from the sand carried in the incessant whirl of the wind and from the noise on the street below. I am curled up on the bed in a hotel room in Nouadhibou, studying the route on the map. In the half-light and the longed-for quiet, I run my finger along the line of a railway, which in the absence of obstacles runs straight east, hundreds of kilometres into the desert. A straight line, the border, runs parallel to the railway, there being no significant barrier to divide Western Sahara and Mauritania. Officially, it would be the border between Morocco and Mauritania. But to be precise, a narrow strip of the desert to the North of Mauritania is claimed by the Sahrawis. To make a long story short, it is not clear where Mauritania's northern border is.

I have to laugh, a bitter laugh though, imagining those gentlemen standing around a table in late 19th century Berlin[1], ruler in hand,

---

[1] Berlin Conference, 1884. The great European powers divide up Africa and formalise the colonies. Despite the fictionalised vision proposed here, the initial intention of the Conference was the exact opposite: to open Africa to free trade and civilisation. See Reybrouck, David van. Congo. Milan: Feltrinelli, 2014.

intent on dividing up Africa on the map. "Hey, Leopold the Second, what do I do? Do I draw the line here?" "Yes, that's fine, Von Bismarck" or "leave me some more territory, you've got that interesting region over there."

According to their whims, bigwigs, who never actually visited Africa, shared out the continent to avoid conflicts and safeguard their own commercial interests. And the Africans? A little here, a little there. Now you are Nigerians; you are Cameroonians. A nationalism only in name but not in fact.

Before the arrival of the Europeans, there were thousands of tribes on African soil, each with their own dialects, their own customs and habits, and they uniformly populated this continent. On closer inspection, the only distinctions between the various groups were dictated by the environment. Desert, savannah, or forest. Nothing more. One of the most significant failures of the colonial period was precisely this: to separate an ethnic group into two or more nations, and, conversely, to unite under a single flag tribes who had been rivals for centuries.

At the market, several voices confirmed to me that in the early afternoon, the train should leave the station in the northern suburbs of Nouadhibou. This train and its unique journey are a legend. The SNIM (*Société Nationale Industrielle et Minière*) railway connects the company's headquarters on the Nouadhibou peninsula with the Zouerate mine, considered the richest source of iron oxide in the world. It is said to have been discovered by pure chance by Saint-Exupéry (that's him, the writer of *The Little Prince*), who flew over the area and noticed the magnetic compass going crazy.

My intention was to jump aboard this freight train and travel to the remote outpost of Choum, then cross into the heart of the Mauritanian desert in the Adrar region.

Saint-Exupéry wrote of Nouadhibou: "There is a fort, a shed and a wooden hut for our crews. All around, the desert is unlimited. This makes Port Etienne[2] almost invincible in spite of its modest military power.[3]" In eighty years, a city had sprung up where before there was only a fort. As in most African cities, a small city centre contrasts with a vast suburb made up of shacks and sand that continues for several kilometres north along the main road.

I arrive at the station well in advance. The place would still be deserted if it were not for the watchman. As soon as he notices me, he shows up at the door from the little room where he was sheltering from the fierce wind and invites me in.

He closes the door behind me and makes me sit on some sacks lying on the ground. I sit with a puff of dust and sand, which makes me sneeze. It must be a storeroom: besides the stacked sacks, there is only a teapot on the flame in the centre of the room. Everywhere you go in Mauritania, there is always a teapot on the go. I sip the sweet tea while we chat about this and that. Finally, he asks me how much I am willing to pay to load the bike in the wagon.

"Well, I'll load it, don't worry."

"You can't do it by yourself. You have to lift it four metres off the ground. I'll help you."

"Listen, I'll call you if I need you, okay?" The watchman doesn't seem satisfied with the negotiation but changes the subject anyway.

A train heaves into view. But in the opposite direction to the one I have to travel in. With its load of iron ore and goods, it has just arrived from the hinterland. In front of me, the wagons of the longest train in the world are flowing, endless and identical, slowing down more and more, until a puff announces the complete stop.

---

[2] Former name of Nouadhibou.
[3] Saint-Exupéry, Antoine de. *Terre Des Hommes*. Gallimard, 1939.

A sudden bustle breaks out among those I thought were passengers like me. Quick as geckos, they climb onto the train to collect all the goods stored on top of the mountain of iron dust before it sets off again. At first, they take care of the goods, but with the minutes ticking by, they start to carelessly throw them on the ground. The activities are not yet complete when the driver starts the mighty engine a kilometre further south, and the train lazily resumes its motion.

It's a race against time to retrieve all the goods before it's too late to jump off the wagon! The last package is unloaded when the huge convoy has not yet reached full speed. The *looter* jumps off the moving train, just like in the best robberies in all good westerns. While all this is happening, a few metres from the railway, a family is preparing dinner. It's a meat stew, I would say from the smell. In a few minutes, the sun will set on the horizon, and they will be able to break their fast for Ramadan.

I know about the famous *African pace of life*, yet I am astonished when, at nine o'clock in the evening, they announce that the train will arrive *perhaps* in a couple of hours. Since midday, I have been at the station; two more hours to wait will not be a problem.

By now, I have exchanged a few words with everyone, and everyone knows me. Several people have offered to help me load the bike on board, which is indeed a challenging undertaking on my own. Who are they?

There is Mohammed, who is from Senegal. He has heard that they are looking for miners in Zouerate. Several guys are going there *on business*, but they don't tell me what. A soldier waits by himself in a corner of the station. He has been granted leave and will visit his family. In short, everyone has a good reason, and then there's the travelling cyclist who only discovered the existence of the train a few months earlier and wants to have an extreme experience. I have read many travel stories. And often, even before finishing the book, I find myself dreaming I'm there. I take over from the author: I play at shaping that world; I imagine the sensations; I weigh up the difficulties. The journey on the iron train was in one of those tales.

A distant whistle in the dark and the approach of a beam of light announce the arrival of the train. I check my mobile phone, which reads 23:30. A mechanical fault has delayed the departure, but it has been fixed. My drowsiness from the long wait suddenly gives way to the excitement and anxiety of the moment. I only have a few minutes to load all the luggage and the bike. As soon as the train is stopped, two friends, Rashad and Ibrahim, nip up the ladder and reach down to take my luggage.

A minute later, I am on board and can catch my breath. About ten individuals are in the carriage with me, including Rashad and Ibrahim. This three by ten metre box will be our home for the night. Meanwhile, the loading operations continue a few wagons away. Shepherds are loading a flock of goats, which are hoisted a few metres off the ground before landing in the wagon with a bleat. The only light source is a veiled moon, just before the halfway point in its monthly journey.

A bang, followed by a juddering jolt, announces that the engine has started at the head of the train. Our carriage begins to follow behind, and we slowly make our way through the darkness of the desert. I would like to stand and observe the buildings and the few lights that are moving away from us, but the rush of the air and the sand push me back, so I return to crouching, leaning against the wall.

My friends are huddled under a heavy blanket to protect themselves from the wind and the cold in the night of these arid expanses. Ibrahim lifts a flap of the rug and beckons me to join them. They are preparing tea. Indispensable, even on a moving goods train. With them is another boy, whose name is lost in the din of the rush. Rashad is mixing the tea according to the long and delicate Berber ritual. Between one jolt and another, the drink is poured into the glasses with extreme accuracy, raising the teapot higher and higher. "It takes a lot of froth to make the glass beautiful'.

Enchanted, I admire this operation; not a drop is spilt. With his right hand, the dexterous boy passes me the glass. We toast and drink with much laughter. I don't understand anything my tea buddies are saying, but the atmosphere is magical, and the tranquillity of the moment is contagious.

It's cold now. All the passengers are huddled under blankets, pulled up over their heads, looking like corpses in a sack. Yet, they are warm and protected from the sand. I, on the other hand, have chattering teeth and a throat full of sand.

Fal is the SNIM technician I had shared a few laughs with during the afternoon at the station, and now he is calling me. Because of the chaos and the darkness, I hadn't seen him get on our carriage. He offers me a share of his blanket, and I gladly accept to hunker down there with him. I wrap the blanket around me, fixing it under my bum. The idea of just lying in the open is absurd. The cloud of sand raised by the two hundred or more wagons makes it impossible to breathe, and being immersed in it is not pleasant. Not at all.

The blanket is tiny, so Fal moves closer to me, and I can feel his breath on my face. He tells me a little about his life, and I share some moments of my journey. I am together with a Mauritanian boy huddled under a blanket on a goods train in the middle of the desert. Poetry.

A cold shiver wakes me up. I move the blanket away from my face enough to uncover my eyes and see the intense blue of the night fading away with the first light of dawn. I get up and stagger to the edge of the carriage. We are now heading east, and the crosswind blows the sand away, allowing me to see clearly ahead: an endless line of wagons projected in the orange light of dawn. Herds of dromedaries are grazing here and there on the expanse of sand, among the few bushes that survive the enveloping heat. The first rays of the sun light up the sand, which glows like gold. Waves of sand and the few surviving bushes create tricks of light and shade on the ground. To the north, the immense monolith of Ben Amira[4] interrupts the monotonous horizon.

My travelling companions lie motionless on the bed of the wagon. Huddled under their blankets, they look exactly like the bags of goods travelling with them. They have probably seen this view so often that it is no longer interesting. Instead, this moment will be etched on my memories for a long time. Heedless of the cold and the sand, I admire every detail, every perceptible variation in the colours of the sand, a few tents in the distance. If I am out of breath, it is not because of the sand. Finally, I curl up on the floor of the carriage and let myself be rocked by its jolting movements.

Ibrahim has woken up. He gets up, washes himself with the little water available, and unrolls his prayer mat. Facing south, but I don't correct him. Here too, on a moving train, a boy in his black cotton tunic does not forget to thank his God. Maybe I should follow his indirect suggestion and also do it more often.

The train slows down its already unhurried pace and, in a couple of minutes, stops. On a sandy track next to the railway, some jeeps are chasing the train. It could be the same *robbers* seen the previous day in Nouadhibou; those who will get on the train to collect the goods destined for the village, and me. After eleven hours, I arrived at my destination, in Choum, while almost all the other passengers will continue for another six hours to Zouerate, where the train will head back with a new load of iron and people.

Choum is an uninspiring outpost, consisting of a few shacks made of earth or cement, but with shops where you can still find

---

[4] It is considered to be the second-largest monolith in the world, after the rock of Uluru in Australia.

everything. The paved road, one of the three in the country, ends here. I suppose that the sensations of meeting human beings in such a remote setting are similar to what a pioneer might have felt on reaching a village in the American Far West.

I leave the town, and my wheels whizz along on the immaculate asphalt. The road seems to have been completed the day before. Time goes by indefinitely until the sweltering heat forces me to stop. It is even more suffocating than the previous weeks. But what could I expect, moving a thousand kilometres inland? So, I crouch down in the shade of a bush to drink some water and rest. I look around. Nothing catches my attention.

After some minutes, a shepherd emerges from the scorching nothingness and sits next to me, asking for some water. This is a trick of Mauritanian shepherds: they can materialise suddenly and without making a sound. Perhaps during the day, they stay under the sand, like snakes and scorpions. We can't understand each other, so we do not get much further than greetings and my destination. A few moments later, the shepherd thanks me and vanishes in a whirlwind of sand.

The temperature must be well over forty degrees, and a violent desert wind dries out the throat and nostrils. Fortunately, there are enough water wells on the way not to die of thirst.

On the plateau, a short distance from Atar, the capital of this region, lies the village of Chinguetti. It's an ancient, monochrome town. Chinguetti is built of stones and bricks created from the same earth on which it stands, with flat roofs made of palm wood. The old town was built on the edge of the desert, but now the sands are advancing inexorably. With UNESCO funds, most of the dwellings have been cleared of sand, but it is only a matter of time before the desert claims its own. No doubt, Chinguetti is a fascinating place with a precious treasure.

Let us take a step back about a thousand years to the 11th century. Like other towns in the oasis, Chinguetti was an outpost of vital importance on the Saharan caravan routes. During this period, professors and scholars travelled along these routes to disseminate knowledge of all disciplines known at the time: religion, astronomy, mathematics, and medicine.

Imagine these *teachers* arriving in the city on the back of their dromedaries, laden with precious texts and manuscripts. I find it a very poetic image, indicating a great love of culture. For centuries, scholars from all over West Africa travelled to Chinguetti to study the knowledge of the time. Most of the manuscripts that still exist are kept in this village's houses. There is a high risk that they will be lost due to the harsh environment and the inexorable passage of time.

The region around Atar is unexpectedly varied. To the east, the Adrar plateau plunges from an imposing cliff onto the plain below. Ancient watercourses have carved deep gorges. In one of these, there is a track climbing up to the oasis of Toungad, where Riccardo lives. But I will tell you about him in a moment.

The plateau is an enormous hilly expanse of volcanic origin. The ground is strewn with a myriad of volcanic stones that make the area look unattractive. As I bump along the stony track, I notice the oasis in the distance. What an immense relief for the eyes of the travellers who finally see their oasis in the desert!

A dry river bed cuts through the thick vegetation of palm trees and shrubs. Next to the palm grove, a few huts accompany the track, which continues for a few hundred metres. After crossing a dune, it ends in what could be described as the courtyard of Riccardo's house, who is there, on the threshold, waiting for me.

His is a fascinating story. Born in Rome, he worked for many years as a photographer, specialising first in fashion photography in

Los Angeles, and then in travel journalism. During a conversation, he tells me about a caravan expedition with the Tuareg of Niger. I am dying to see his shots, but he doesn't have them with him now that he lives here. Riccardo arrived in Mauritania with the idea of running a restaurant and accompanying tourists in this environment that he likes so much. Not long afterwards, he met Fatimatou, who became his wife, and together they moved into their current home in the oasis.

As Riccardo slowly walks towards me, he is overtaken by his two pesky little angels, Minatou and Nibroua, who come to greet me. I meet Fatimatou at the back of the building, making tea. I will spend two days with them; during this time, Riccardo will inspire me with his love for the desert.

As I walk around the house, with its stone walls and thatched roof, I come across an enclosure for the dromedaries, a dry well, an active well and some small huts. One houses the toilet while another, built of logs and palm thatch, is the pantry. There are several water tanks on the floor and a goatskin hanging from the ceiling. This ancient practice of the Sahara peoples is used by both camel and truck drivers. Several times, I have seen these goatskins dangling between the trailer wheels behind trucks.

In the late afternoon, the family rests on mats on the shady side of the house. It is Ramadan, and the sun has almost set. This marks the end of the day's fasting. Fatimatou has prepared a tray with plenty of dates and some almond biscuits while her brother is making tea. The other jugs contain dromedary milk and *bissap*[5] juice.

I am struck by the calmness with which they approach the buffet after the whole day spent without drinking or eating—another sign of respect for Allah and this fundamental religious precept. Throwing oneself into the food would perhaps give the impression

---

[5] One of the names by which the hibiscus tea is known in West Africa. It is normally served cold.

that the fast is an imposition and one is only waiting for the moment to break it. On the contrary, everyone maintains a composed and dignified attitude – they respect the fast of their own will.

In front of us, a pyramid of sunburnt rocks surrounded by dunes emerges from the sand. Sitting here with them, I savour the magic of the sunset in the desert, a fresh breeze arrives to cool the earth, the world turns golden, and the curtain closes.

The enchantment does not end here. I feel the wind blowing from the valley. The backdrop is inlaid with stars, and the Milky Way suddenly bursts forth onto the stage. The two daughters play happily and sometimes enjoy climbing on me. Fatimatou pours tea while I look respectfully at Riccardo. In his daily routine and with his family, he found the serenity made up of little things of everyday life. We are but tiny in this environment and have to act in harmony with it. His heart is full of love.

"A place that amplifies every little feeling and sensation. The isolation and loneliness of cities empty the soul. Our silence fills it. Relax, disconnect, listen to the wind, the silence, your own heartbeat."

This is Riccardo. Very nice to meet you, Riccardo.

There are hardly any distractions on this road. A slight variation in the landscape is the most exciting and noteworthy event to distract me from the blaze of the sun. Along the five hundred kilometres that separate Atar from the capital, there are few settlements, sometimes within an hour's drive of each other. A whole day in the saddle. I come across some *service stations*, as I would call them if I were on an Italian motorway. They are little more than huts, sometimes thatched, sometimes brick-built, where travellers can stop to escape the oppressive heat and drink tea or pray.

The design is often similar. Once you take off your shoes, you enter a large room. The floor is covered with carpets, with cloth drapes on the walls to block the omnipresent sand that creeps in between the straw. Next to the walls, there are thin mattresses where one can have a drink or rest. It is not uncommon for travellers from these arid lands to stop here for the night.

The midday sun heats up the already scorching asphalt, ghosts of heat and sand camouflage the horizon. A service station shows up in the distance. I go in, and a couple of friends invite me to join them.

If you are invited for tea, put aside your haste, every gesture follows a strict procedure. In fact, the ceremony can last up to an hour.

The eldest, a now-retired police officer, raises the teapot in the air and traces a golden thread that ends in the glass. Until he is satisfied with the amount of foam, he pours it back into the teapot and repeats the operation, slow and measured. It is a ritual and as such should be honoured. With a turquoise veil wrapped around his head, his travelling companion observes the procedure absentmindedly.

The officer serves me the glass on the tray before filling the one for himself and his partner. He boils some more water and repeats the whole ritual. After the second tea, I make a move to stand up and thank them: "*Shukran*.[6]"

How rude! "Wait, wait, there is still the third tea."

The first glass is as bitter as life,
The second is as strong like love,
The third one...

"What was the third one like?" he asks for his friend's help.

The third is as sweet as death.

---

[6] Thank you, in Arabic.

Over the next few days, the local people show their real character.

The Mauritanians are noble, proud, and rarely back down from their positions. Like most desert peoples. It has been the same for centuries, and their reputation is well known. They didn't let me pay for a single meal, not even a glass of tea.

I remember with pleasure while cycling on a particularly windy morning (but is it still worth mentioning the presence of the wind, since on the coast it blows incessantly all year round?) that a car draws up beside me. We go along at the same pace. The passenger, who, from his well-groomed appearance and clothes, seems an important person, says hello and asks if I need anything. I glance at my water bottles, all filled to the brim, before declining the offer.

"Oh, no, no. Let me give you something."

The driver stops the car, and I slow down beside him. He gets out of the vehicle and hands me a bottle of water and some bread.

"I don't have many things with me in the car." He thinks for a moment and then adds: "when you get to Akjoujt, go to I.'s restaurant. There will be a lunch paid for you." The cordial but confident tone does not leave space for any reply. So, I thank my benefactor and watch him leave as I get on the saddle again to face the wind.

In Akjoujt, I ask for I.'s restaurant and go in. Finally, some shade. Some customers are resting on the mats closest to the big fan. It's Ramadan, and coping with it in the summer months here in the desert is exhausting. Unable to eat, but above all to drink, most of the population lies resting in the shade, waiting for the sun to set. Only those with serious reasons, or those who travel, can abstain.

Sitting on the low sofa, I am enjoying a delicious meat couscous when two men approach, evidently interested in my appearance.

Chatting, I explain I prefer to cycle early in the morning because of the temperature. Therefore, I start before dawn and stop shortly after midday because, in the afternoon, the heat is oppressive. When I express my wish to stay in the village for the night, the two men argue about who should put me up. A not dissimilar scene had occurred the previous evening in another small outpost.

Hospitality is sacred, according to the Bible as well as the Koran. Especially in these regions, as in all inhospitable lands, where nature is unforgiving. There is no other solution for the people but to come together and share everything in order to survive in these conditions. Hospitality and sharing. Moreover, during Ramadan, believers can *gain credits* with God, and so they become more involved in charity and good works.

At night you sleep under the stars; it is the freshest place to rest. One night, I am lying down on a mat in front of a small shop, close to the road. A breeze has started blowing and pushes grains of sand into my face, thus waking me up. It's a full moon, but my attention is drawn to a silhouette coming towards me. It's only a few metres away from me, between the mat and the road. My heart beats faster while the stranger walks a few more metres and then stops. With the moonlight behind it, I cannot make it out. Then I recognise the profile of a dromedary. Intrigued by my movements, the animal is staring at me, adamant. How worrying! Am I dreaming? I close and reopen my eyes; he is still there. I take a photo that I keep as one of my favourites of this trip to prove that no, I was not dreaming. I let him do what he wants and lie down on the mat again. I fall back to sleep immediately after.

An uncertain amount of time passes. When I hear a murmuring confusion near me, I open my eyelids enough to understand the origin of the buzz: two men are squatting on the large mat. They are talking to each other as they prepare to go to bed. Everything seems to be in order. Therefore, I close my eyes, but at that moment, I recognise one of the two voices, the heavier one, nearest to me. "Bo!" I exclaim with great surprise. The figure shudders, turns and recognises me. His surprise turns into a big laugh and an equally big hug. Bo runs a shop three hundred kilometres east of here. He hosted me at his house two nights before. And now I find him deep in the night sleeping next to me on the roadside, where he has accidentally stopped to rest from his long journey to the capital.

What an extravagant and eventful night.

As I approach the coast, the landscape changes. Or rather, the sky. The deep, crystal blue fades to ghostly white. The sun in the sky is a round, pale blotch. The gusty winds stir up sand in the air, which is then trapped in the mist carried by sea. The buildings, sand, and everything reflect a blinding light, and under that deadly white sky, I arrive at the capital.

The immense, dusty, and bare spaces surrounding many African towns are filled with slums. These run for kilometres along the roads into the towns. The inhabitants put large stones on the corrugated metal roofs so that they don't fly off in the winds. It is a squalid neighbourhood. Unfortunately, during the journey I will get used to this misery on the edge of every large city.

But this is the first time. I don't even dare to look up from the strip of asphalt. All I see are the ever-present ladies, sitting on the side of the road in the sand and dust, intent on selling a few goods piled up beside them. They are stacked to attract the eye of the customer. But in this context, the pile just enhances the scarcity of the goods even more. On the opposite side of the street, a donkey lazily pulls a cart, overflowing with jerrycans of water to be delivered to the inhabitants of the suburbs.

Slaves live in this neighbourhood of glaring poverty. I am shocked when Emmanuel reveals this to me.

Known as Kastel to his friends, Emmanuel is a Cameroonian who abandoned his parents twenty years ago in Ebulowa, a small town in the south. He travelled for a long time, taking odd jobs to pay his expenses until he settled in Mauritania. I still can't understand why he made this apparently crazy decision. Today, he works in a hostel owned by a wealthy person in the capital.

Kastel tells me that slavery is no longer legal in Mauritania[7], but it is still tolerated and, even, widespread in society. As in many other cases on the continent, this is due to one ethnic group being traditionally subservient to another, higher caste.

The protagonists in Mauritania are, on the one hand, the *Haratin*, who are black Moors of Arabic-speaking and descended from dark-skinned slaves, and, on the other, people of Arab/Berber origin, above all the *Hassani*. The latter are a minority, yet they hold all positions of political and economic power.

For generations, the *Haratin* have belonged to the poorest caste, maltreated throughout Mauritania, and serving their *masters*. Slavery is a hereditary evil. If you are born the son of a slave; you are born a slave. As if it were a disease. Unfortunately, they don't see it that way. The slaves have to obey simply because their masters are of a higher caste than they are. This is what mothers teach their children. From slave to slave. To finally enter paradise.

Thanks to this information, I walk around the city with more understanding. The Moors of Arab origin are few in number, but they are noticeable everywhere with their elegant sky-blue *boubou*[8]. These slaves, on the other hand, are rarely seen. They work behind the scenes in society, in jobs considered to be the most miserable and burdensome. I have only met them in a few houses, where they carry out domestic work or accompany the animals to pasture. They collect rubbish or beg.

Some locals, as well as other travellers, suggested I visit the port of Nouakchott. Late one afternoon, I take a taxi to the dock. There are six of us in the car, plus the driver, so as to not waste space and

---

[7] In 1981, slavery was declared illegal. In 2015, a new anti-slavery law was enacted.

[8] Typical men's robe from Mauritania. It is a long cloth with a hole to allow the passage of the head, and with two large open sleeves on each side. It varies in tone from blue to white and is often decorated with gold and white embroidery.

air. Many taxis and other traffic are going towards the port, as it is one of the main economic centres of the country. Whether it's fish for family dinners to buy on market stalls or fish to be exported on an industrial scale, much of the catch passes through here.

Opening the car door, I am overcome by the pungent smell of the fish, mingled with saltiness in the air. Going from the car park towards the beach, I encounter a sea of humanity. Cheers and shouts from everywhere; ladies are calling out the fish of the day; customers of all kinds shouting their prices. People are moving in all directions, but I have the feeling that I am the only one wandering around without a specific destination. A young boy takes my hand, he wants to sell me some plastic containers.

On the beach, the situation is even more chaotic to the inexperienced traveller's eyes. Countless wooden boats, streamlined and painted in all shapes and colours, are moored a short distance from the shoreline. The porters walk around with the water up to their knees and load crates of fish onto their shoulders, handed to them by the fishermen on board. They then return to the beach to the guy who hired them. It may be a private individual waiting with his cart. It may be the guy who runs the whole business. Or maybe, it may be some other porters who then unload all the goods into their pickup truck and take the fish to town.

Large quantities of fish fall on the ground in this chaos, but nothing goes to waste. Here come the kids, slaloming between the various actors and throwing themselves on the fallen fish before it is covered by sand or trampled. Some of them are probably orphans or from destitute families, so they get food for dinner in this way. Others, on the other hand—you notice them because they walk with self-confidence through the crowd—immediately sell outside the harbour what they pick it up from the beach.

It's a time-honoured mechanism. Everyone has their role to play. During the rush hour, when the boats return, no one sits idly by. Only when all the fish have been unloaded, can the crew sit on the boat with their legs dangling and wait for the bustle to die down before pulling their fishing boat ashore.

I wander in fascination along the beach and the jetty, not wanting to miss a single moment of this seemingly chaotic babel. As the sun goes down, the beach empties out. Fishermen in groups head for their homes, laughing and joking, while an old woman lingers on the shoreline, scouring the ground, trying to find some left-behind fish.

It is time to leave the capital and the Sahara and enter the Sahel[9] and Senegal. I am still pedalling through the squalid southern suburbs of the city when I hear a crash, and the bike collapses under my weight. A quick check is enough to identify the fault: the thru-axle on the rear wheel has just broken.

This is followed by swear words that I cannot write here. *What now?* I try to keep calm and call Massimo, my trusted mechanic in Italy. In addition to having enviable mechanical skills, he has now become a reference point for calming anger and finding inner serenity in such situations.

"Fil, do you want it sent by courier?"

"Oh no, Massimo. No courier ships to Mauritania, I checked."

Five thousand kilometres away, there is silence. Shortly after, an idea.

"Have one made. It's a simple component."

Thank you, Massimo.

I take a taxi back to the hostel and go with Kastel to the craftsmen's quarter. We wander the streets looking for a turner, but it seems that no one works on Friday afternoon. We find one, particularly listless, who asks me the equivalent of fifty euros for the work. Kastel is furious with him. "You shouldn't treat tourists like that. Just because he's white, you're asking for astronomical amounts

---

[9] The Sahel, from the Arabic *Sahil, edge of the desert*. It is a transition region between the desert and the savannah.

of money." Then, turning towards me: "Let's go and look somewhere else."

The indolent man shrugs his shoulders and resumes chatting with his friends.

Finally, a young taxi driver sitting on his two-wheeled steed direct us to one of the best turners in the city, called Ahmed. He is a burly man of few words. "Seven thousand Ouguiya", and he goes to the machine to take the necessary measurements. Fifteen euros. I question Kastel with my eyes, and he nods his head. I am lucky to have found a professional, and an honest one, above all.

While Ahmed works, I sit on a pile of tyres. I remember a scene from a few months earlier, at a mechanic's in Fes, Morocco. I had destroyed the rear derailleur, and after a two-week wait, a replacement was delivered from Germany. The derailleur support plate on the frame was bent. I went to a mechanic to try and straighten it out.

I watched the whole process with apprehension.

"Please don't tighten the axle too much," I told him as he vigorously tightened the part.

In the next flashback, I remember removing the thru-axle and the wheel for a thorough cleaning during the first afternoon at the hostel here in Nouakchott.

I put two and two together, *et voilà*. The obliging mechanic had over-tightened the pin and, once removed for cleaning, the cracks that had developed on the threads spread, leaving me stranded after a few kilometres.

Over the next few months, numerous breakages would occur. Shit happens. What's done is done, and getting angry doesn't help. Even a bike breakdown can make you wiser sometimes.

Twenty-four hours later, with a feeling of déjà vu, I leave the hostel and head south.

In the whole trip, I have crossed a few really bleak landscapes. The region south of Nouakchott was one of these. A strip of asphalt in an insignificant environment. The sun reduced to a sphere of faint light by the sandy air carried by the desert winds. Occasional villages apparently inhabited by just a few people, buried under all sorts of rubbish. Abandoned to themselves and the winds.

A fork in the road leads me towards a minor frontier crossing called Djama. As I approach the Senegal River, vegetation reappears. Green surrounds me after months of sand and sky. The difficulty of the environment and the endurance needed to cross the desert had begun to test me, sucking up precious mental energy. Now, this sudden change in the landscape gave me new stimulus and energy.

The river banks are surrounded by marshland and cultivated fields, perhaps the only ones in the whole of arid Mauritania. Further downstream, the banks are invisible behind a barrier of tall reeds and shrubs. I pass through an enchanting area, the Diawling National Park, where abundant wildlife thrives on the river's waters. Lots of warthogs lollop away as I approach. Hundreds of flamingos, pelicans and other shorebirds watch me suspiciously as I go by, before returning to their own occupations.

Travelling along this green strip of land, the *Langue de Barbarie*, I arrive at the Djama dam in a couple of hours. Beyond it is Senegal, ready to welcome me with its colours, clothes and fruits, and its music of animated chatter and joyful laughter. The desert is over, the crossing is complete.

It is not a farewell, but a see you again. This inhospitable expanse and its proud inhabitants have won me over. At first, it shows itself as an empty container whose boundaries are sand and stars. But the desert does not give itself away so easily. You have to enter it, not only with your body but also with your spirit, and in doing so, its essence penetrates you.

The wind carries with it distant stories; the silence is a light for our soul, as if, pervaded with curiosity, we were descending into a primitive cave with a torch in our hand to explore its most hidden recesses. I am sure it will not be long before this dormant spirit of the desert awakens and begins to call out to me.

Au revoir, Sahara.

SENEGAL

Every time an old man dies in Africa,
it is as if a library has burnt down.

AMADOU HAMPÂTÉ BÂ,
SPEECH TO THE UNESCO ASSEMBLY, 1960[1]

June

There is rubbish everywhere. On the street, on the sidewalks, on the seashore and along the banks of the river that runs through the city. I am wandering through the streets of the centre, I have always loved walking, simply observing life as it goes by in its daily routines and trying to unmask its soul.

This place has a confused spirit: the picturesque centre of Saint Louis with its colonial houses in different pastel shades, which put it on the UNESCO Heritage lists, is just a façade that welcomes the traveller. Walking around the city should take me back in time to the colonial period, which the historic centre bears testament to. But, in the streets of this tourist wreck, I cannot walk for more than ten minutes alone, without somebody approaching me to offer a guided tour or to sell me a bracelet. I continue to wander in the desolate alleys, although this triggers great sadness, because of the overwhelming filth and state of neglect. The deterioration of the buildings is evident in every corner. Only a few have been refurbished and turned into tourist hotels.

---

[1] The quote, as reported here, is an (anonymous) reinterpretation of the original speech of Hampâté Bâ, whose meaning of the words is retained.

At street corners, or sitting on the steps of some abandoned buildings, hundreds of children ask for money. They approach me barefoot, in ragged clothes, and beg me to drop a coin in the rusty jar they carry around with them. What dismays me is the number of these kids: can they all be orphans? Or maybe they have simply been abandoned by families who couldn't afford to support them?

The road from the city to the south runs between the coast and a lagoon. On both sides, are an endless line of shacks where fishermen and numerous women sell fish. Those who cannot afford a stall have their wheelbarrow chock-full. Those who do not even have a wheelbarrow display the fish on worn pieces of cardboard on the ground. The nauseating smell of garbage mixed with that of fish will leave me with an unenviable memory of this city.

I rush off at full speed in search of clean air. The degradation of Saint Louis has left me frustrated and irritated. It could easily be the pearl of Senegalese tourism; instead, it is abandoned to itself and to its own filth.

Distracted by these thoughts, I don't notice that I have left the last houses long behind me. The track now proceeds straight and flat between millet fields, and, at last, the wind blows the pure smell of the sea onto the mainland.

Moving away from the coast, I find the typical vegetation of the Sahel, albeit more verdant than the previous days. The acacias are thinning out more and more, and different vegetation takes over the landscape. Finally, I see it, the first baobab. This is, for me, the highest expression of *Africanness*, together with the elephant.

The one in front of me is relatively small, without leaves, yet it stands out from the surrounding vegetation. It looks like an elderly giant who, motionless, enjoys the warmth of the sun. And, as with an old man, his presence requires respect. So, I leave the road, push through brushwood, and approach the tree to contemplate it. At that moment, not a puff of wind moves the dry air. The rainy season is still far away.

While planning the trip, I was unsure whether to change the departure date to avoid either the Sahara's summer heat or the rains in the equatorial forest. I feared the heat more, not imagining the surprises that the rains would have in store for me.

I stop daydreaming and return to reality next to the baobab. I get back on the saddle and pedal a few meters, before stopping again. *Tonight, I will sleep here!* The idea is too tempting. On the shady side of this giant, I find a suitable space, and before setting up camp, I check out the surroundings. Nobody is going by, either on foot or by motorcycle. It seems a safe place to camp, with the scrub hiding me from the road.

During previous bike trips, I have learned that the ideal place to camp must meet certain requirements. The scenery usually comes last. First of all, I need a place where I am sure to be out of sight, or, instead, fully in the public eye. After that, it is necessary to evaluate whether the selected position is sufficiently protected from the elements: wind, floods and so on. Lastly, if possible, I choose a pretty view and the tent's entrance facing the rising sun. There is nothing more delightful in the morning than being caressed by the first rays of the sun. That evening, honoured by the presence of the baobab, I found a perfect corner all for myself.

I wander around the tree, with the saucepan full of pasta in one hand and a spoon in the other. The profile of this savannah is dominated by several giants, relatives of my elderly friend. In the silence of that pale sunset, their presence only holds my interest.

When I lie down in my tent, I invoke the omniscient Google, who tells me a bedtime story:

"Once upon a time there was a spring and a lake as smooth as a mirror. Here, a long time ago, the baobab stood [...] The baobab stood near the water and raised the top to the sky. He could see other trees with leafy hair, soft bark, thin trunks. Everything sparkled with colour. The baobab saw all this in the mirror and was unhappy because its branches and leaves were tiny. Its trunk was enormous, its bark dull and wrinkled. It looked like the skin of an old elephant."

The skin of an old elephant... I think back to the moment I ran my hand over it just before. Yes, it's true—hard and wrinkled skin.

I resume reading: "*Then the baobab called out to God and complained to him. But God created the baobab and was pleased with his work. The baobab was different from all other trees, and God loved the diversity. He loved the hippopotamus, beautiful in his eyes. He liked the cry of the hyena, pleasing to his ears. Likewise, he was fond of the baobab, which was not like the others. But as the baobab continued to look in the mirror and voice his complaints to God, he got angry, got down, grabbed the baobab, picked it up, and replanted it upside down. Not seeing himself anymore, the tree stopped complaining. Everything was back in order.*"

In the morning, I wake up with a slight headache and feel somewhat sluggish. *Strange. Last night I slept well.* It takes a moment to recognise that these are not the effects of the previous day's fatigue. Since I left Guelmim a month earlier, I have only had a few days off, and fatigue has built up, slowly but inexorably. I need a good, long break, not the usual three or four days.

Thies is not far. I have found a reliable contact in the town of Thies, la Signora Ginetta, from Bologna. On the phone, her friendly tone and unmistakably Bolognese accent instil me with confidence. It dawns on me that I am longing to get there. For the first time since the beginning of the journey, I don't want to pedal that morning.

The following days turn into a tiring race to reach the town, a place where I can rest my mind for a while. I am not even interested in the local culture. After Morocco and the desert, I am entering a new dimension, so-called black Africa. People are friendly to me on every occasion. I stop in a village to ask for water, and some smiling kids accompany me to the well. I ask for hospitality for the night, and they offer it to me without expecting anything in return; furthermore, they add a plate of rice to their willingness. Yet I feel distant, aloof; I do not have the mental strength to interact and converse beyond the bare minimum. It wouldn't be the best thing to show up at Ginetta's house in this mood in two days.

Evidently, after turning all the baobabs in the region upside down, the good Lord has decided to cheer me up. He introduces himself in the shape of a young man driving a car on the national road I have chosen to reach my destination as quickly as possible.

The young man stops a little ahead of me and with one arm gestures for me to slow down. "Hey, man, where are you going so loaded up?" I could ask him the same question since his car is jam-packed inside and a load of packages are tied on the roof.

"Thies. But there is a lot of traffic, and this road is dangerous."

"And why don't you go along the coast?"

"Ah, is there another road?"

"No, no. It's a beach track. Turn right here, and in about twenty kilometres you'll reach the sea, and from there you skirt it. If you want, you can reach Dakar, like this."

"Ah." *Cool.*

The decision is instant. The smile is back on my face, and I thank my advisor several times.

I pass Lompoul and reach Lompoul sur Mer. The road ends at the port, but some motorcycles tracks suggest that I can continue without hesitation.

I meet several scooters going from one village to another along the coast. They are fishing villages, often reachable only by sea or from the beach. The abundance of fishermen and fishing boats makes me think that this is a very prosperous coast.

I follow the motorcyclists' tracks. I quickly learn that where the wave stops, just before it flows back, the sand has a compact consistency, and the wheels roll fast, as if on asphalt. I play with the waves, avoiding their splashes, but then, at times, getting stuck in a dry sandbank, which reduces my speed drastically. Then nothing can save me from getting wet!

Through the salty air, I see great excitement a few hundred meters in front of me. Two horse-drawn carts loaded with fish are moving towards me. The driver greets me smiling, and I reciprocate with a nod.

Apparently, I arrived in a village at the moment of maximum activity, when the boats come back from fishing, and each person carries out their task. The most robust men unload crates full of fish from the colourful boats. The ladies take the goods and immediately shout out the price at the customers who hurry up to find the best deal. A multitude of colours and smells mingle on a strip of beach. And the cycle traveller? He moves through this crowd, carefully studying each action. He politely asks "can I come through?" while fishermen interrupt their activity to stare in surprise at this alien with a bike on the beach.

The scene repeats itself shortly after reaching Mboro, the village that will take me back to the Thies' road. It's time to taste the Senegalese national dish: *thiebou dieune*, rice with fish. I eat in a run-down restaurant on the beach, and, in the late afternoon, I look for a quiet area to pitch my tent not far from the houses. Convenient dunes run parallel to the sea and provide a clear separation between a peaceful palm grove and the beach—the ideal place. I can't see the sea, but neither can others see me from the beach. In any case, I will wait for sunset to set up the tent on the comfortable sand; I expect a restful night.

I take a nap in the cool air of the late afternoon, but a chorus of rhythmic screams wakes me up with a start. "Wuuuu hoo, wuuuu hoo, wuuuu hoo." Thirty young people, or perhaps more—I can't see beyond the dune where they come from—are pulling on a massive rope. Still leaning against the trunk of the palm, I see the first of the young men running past me in this surreal scene. They give me a questioning look, but don't stop pulling the rope. *What is a toubab[2] doing*

---

[2] *Toubab* (in Malinké *toubabou*, in Wolof *tubaap*) is a word used in various parts of West Africa to designate a person with white skin. Various hypotheses lie about the origin of this word. It could be a deformation of the Arabic word *Tabib* (doctor), or

under this palm tree, alone? This is what I read in their eyes. To answer this obvious question, I get up and, without a word, join them in a dreamlike tug of war. From time to time, the boys change places so that the first ones, who pull more vigorously, can slide to the back, where less effort is required. In this way, I meet everyone's eyes.

"What are we pulling?" I ask the boy in front of me, but he doesn't seem to understand.

"*Le bateau?*" He nods his head, yes.

A little later, I question another guy. "*Le bateau, c'est un grand bateau?*" A doubtful expression arises on his face. "*Ce n'est pas un bateau? Poisson? C'est poisson?*" Another nod. *Oh well, I give up.* Wuuuu Hoo.

At least a quarter of an hour later, everyone drops the rope, in sync. The game is over. *Did we win?* Smilingly, they accepted me as one of them and a boy gestures to me to follow him to the beach.

With three other ropes in the distance, I and at least one hundred other workers we have just finished dragging a massive net, full of the previous hours' catch, to the shore. A horse pulls a cart on the shoreline, and some people are loading the net on it.

The boys invite me to the village with them. That evening I dine in numerous company; fish, obviously.

Entering Thies is disheartening. Near the airport hundreds and hundreds of meters of land are strewn with garbage, on both sides of the road. There is so much of it that you can't even guess the shape of the earth below. Tires, bottles, bags, containers. *Plastic.* Plastic everywhere.

I pedal on, disgusted by this squalor. A herd of cows is grazing amidst the waste, together with several goats not too far away. They munch on shreds that they imagine being food and then spit them out. Several shacks have been built on the edge of this landfill, and some

---

a Wolof verb meaning *to convert*, with a strong reference to the first (white) missionaries who approached these lands.

children wander around nearby. Kids with their legs buried in plastic, probably looking for something to scrape together a couple of bucks.

With this vision imprinted on my mind, I pedal absent-mindedly to the market square. It's a charming, noisy market with an abundance of goods on display. In an instant, I forget the horrible sight. Ginetta lives not far away from there. It's time to rest.

I knock on the door and wait. Shortly, Riccardo, Ginetta's son, peeps at the door. He looks friendly, with dreadlocks right down his back.

Riccardo takes me into the welcoming inner courtyard. Theirs is a modest home, yet, in the following days, I will learn to love this place, so intimate and calm. With Ginetta, there is an immediate empathy. She is very jovial and welcoming; I am at home.

She and Riccardo have visited Senegal several times. Here they both found serenity and well-being. Hence the decision to move here permanently. And the town of Thies is a kind of big village, where everybody knows each other, not a busy metropolis like Dakar.

I spend these relaxing days doing the dullest activities. I wash my bicycle and my clothes. I have some clothes to mend, some errands here and there, and above all, I have a pedal to repair. The inner bearing is gone, and the pedal is loose. Better to change it now, rather than in the middle of the savannah.

I travel with a range of tools, but nothing with which to unscrew the pedal. Asking around, I find a mechanic—a guy who takes advantage of a roadside tree with enough space below it to park a car—and I ask him for help. I sit in the shade while he starts work. As often happens in these parts, the mechanic is not alone: at least three other people are there to chat, and I join the group.

Despite intense efforts, the pedal seems stuck. A muscley guy gets up and approaches the bike. "Let me do it." Nothing doing, the pedal won't budge.

"No problem. We'll saw off the pedal, weld a bolt on the pin and unscrew it, easy-peasy," suggests the mechanic.

I stare at him, unsure if he is joking or serious. "It can't work, the weld will break on such a small surface."

"No, no, don't worry." The spectators, all obviously professional mechanics, agree. *Okay, let's go to the welder.*

Despite the midday heat, I shudder as I watch the welder sawing off the pedal pin. Voilà, a nice severed axle now comes out of the crank arm. He welds it. He lets it cool and then tries to unscrew the bolt. The weld fails. He glances at me. *I told you so.* But I shut up. He tries again, welds, let cool down, tries to unscrew. The weld fails a second time. He watches me. I am losing my patience, but now the damage is done. "Oh, brilliant! What are you going to do now?" I ask the smart guy.

"Let's go back to the workshop; meanwhile I'll have a little think," the mechanic replies worriedly. We go back to the workshop. I walk behind the wretch, mulling over an effective way to remove the severed pin.

The muezzin sings in the distance. "Sorry, I have to go to prayer. I'll be back after the break, in a couple of hours." And he vanishes with his friends, leaving me there with the unusable bike.

Now I'm really pissed off, so I head back *à la maison*. On the way home I pass a small workshop, whose sign reads: *"Réparation Vélo."*

It can't get any worse. Let's try. I go in and explain the problem to the boy.

The mechanic takes a wrench, and with only a slight effort, removes the pin. He looks at me triumphantly. I mumble something, but no convincing excuses come out for my apparent incompetence, so I thank him and leave.

Under the *sapoti* shadow in Ginetta's courtyard, with a full stomach and a refreshing *bissap* in the glass, I think it through. As the hours passed the temperature rose so the aluminium of the crank arm must have expanded sufficiently to allow the steel pin to be removed. Let's toast!

Lara, a very dear friend of Ginetta's, arrived a few days ago. She is also from Bologna. She too has an immense love for Senegal.

It is late morning, and in the shade of the *sapoti*, we are quietly conversing, Lara, Ginetta and I. Talk turns to Saint Louis, a city where I didn't want to stay for more than twenty-four hours, full of dirt and the smell of rancid garbage. Lara disagrees, she loves the city and its *decadent* charm.

"Lara, all those children on the street, begging... they are even here in Thies, but Saint Louis is full of them."

"That is a big problem in Senegal, and further afield. They are the *Talibé*[3]. Those kids go to Koranic schools, but instead of letting them study, the marabouts[4] send them out on the streets to beg. Begging is part of the training, but it often takes up their whole day."

"So, these individuals use minors to make money?"

"And if kids don't fulfil a certain quota every day, they get mistreated, maybe they are left without food, or they beat them."

"Poor souls. But are they orphaned children? There aren't any orphanages here, are there?"

"It's not that," Ginetta replies angrily, "here women give birth to ten children, and then don't have the money to raise them. So, kids are entrusted to these marabouts, so the family doesn't have to feed them, and they may even learn something."

"And are these schools found exclusively in Saint Louis?"

"There are loads of them all over Senegal. Few are real Koranic schools; most of them are in the hands of self-proclaimed marabouts. It's a mess!"

Three weeks later, in the swimming pool of a hotel in Kolda, Southeast of Senegal, I will meet a state official. During our conversation, I will have an ideal continuation of this topic. As he sips a Martini

---

[3] From the Arabic, *Talib*, *student*.

[4] From the Arabic word *marbut*, meaning *ascetic*. Some marabouts are venerated as saints, at a local level.

Bianco, he will tell me that he works for the state, supervising some Koranic schools in the region. Since the previous year (2017), the government has been engaged in a programme to remove children from schools that do not meet the minimum safety standards and modernise existing schools, including French in the curriculum.

"The fact is, when these kids finish school, they don't have any skills. We want to ensure that these children have a stable future when they grow up."

"Well, that's admirable. Do you think it is working?"

The official puts the martini on the table, leans forward and confesses: "*Pas beaucoup*. But we are working hard on it."

Bonne chance.

The Senegalese coast is busy and dirty, but above all is geared up for tourism. Probably, it wasn't a good idea to take this route, but I stick to the itinerary because I intend to visit the Saloum Delta National Park, a hundred kilometres south of Dakar.

But first I stop at Fadiouth, an islet covered with shells where there is an unusual village. Shells abound on these beaches. They are so common that they are used instead of gravel in the conglomerate of road asphalt and house construction. The spirit of tourism starts right from the parking lot. Guides assault me, offering me a tour; children stand behind them, waiting their turn to ask for some *argent*, and then there are plenty of street vendors selling the usual tourist stuff. Annoyed, I give up the idea of visiting the town and instead take a secondary road, which leads me to the cemetery. Here, too, shells are everywhere, from the ground to the tombstones. This cemetery's peculiarity is that around a large white cross on the top of the hill rest, under the baobabs, Christians, Muslims, and animists together.

A few hundred meters inland, the lagoon is dry at low tide. Crossing it, I can save myself a few kilometres of asphalt and shells. Luckily for me, the surface is coated with hardened salt. The rear wheel barely sinks, and I can keep on pedalling in this unique environment. The asphalt runs over there, on the horizon. Instead, I find myself pedalling on this precarious beach alongside the mangroves. Enchanting.

I reach the village of Fadial at the right time to ask for hospitality for the night. The peasants are returning from the fields, and the village is in full swing. Can't say it's the cleanest one I've ever been to. Around the first circle of houses, piles of garbage, to be burned or already incinerated, welcome one to the settlement. A multitude of chickens and goats roam the streets, tracing their path with excrement. *How can people live in such unhygienic conditions? And why doesn't anyone want to organise a clean-up day for their village?* I'm pretty sure that the ticks I found on me a few days later came from there.

I await the village chief's return sitting on a low wall in the courtyard of his house. Word of my arrival has spread. Numerous little children look at me shyly, some from a corner of the house, others from the door and yet others come up to the wall. A wrinkly old man comes towards me. He is wearing a rumpled cloth suit, and his back is bent over his stick. A group of kids follows him a short distance away. He presents himself as the chief, and the kids are eager to hear what I have to say.

It doesn't surprise me that the indigenous people answer affirmatively to every request of mine. The Malian writer and anthropologist Hampâté Bâ identified four characters to whom refusing something is considered an inviolable taboo. This was true for his community and common across all of West Africa. You can't say "no" to your parents[5], the village chief, the spiritual teacher and, finally, to the stranger, who is sent by God. Despite knowing this is both a tribal and religious obligation, I still feel a perennial sense of gratitude

---

[5] Especially to the mother, to whom a strict moral code is linked. The mother is "the divine laboratory in which the creator works directly without intermediaries, to form and bring to maturity a new life".

Touré, A. and Mariko, N. Amadou Hampâté Bâ, Homme De Science Et De Sagesse. Bamako: Nouvelles éditions maliennes, 2005.

because I, the stranger, am welcomed into their family. It's as if I were a great friend or family member. Once again, that evening the elder endorsed my request with a powerful, serious handshake.

It is the evening of the World Cup semi-final. There is no electricity in the village, so the TV would be useless, but there are some radios. In the courtyard, we are all seated around a tired, crackling radio broadcasting the match commentary. At a certain point, the radio goes silent and, while his friends look angry, a boy tries to reinsert the batteries. Despite this, the device seems dead.

I take my phone out of my pocket and see if the game is being streamed. The signal is low, only two bars out of four. Ah, here it is! Almost beside ourselves with joy, we can finally see the game. My guests often get carried away in lively discussions about how the match is being played. I am asked my opinion several times. Although I understand little about football, my every comment generates nods of approval on one side and friendly disagreement on the other. In Senegal, as in much of Africa, football is serious business. In the end, Croatia beats England two to one. The discussions go on for a few more minutes before everyone goes back to their homes, leaving me alone in the courtyard. Here I set up the tent, blissfully unaware that the roosters and goats were preparing to keep me awake for most of the night.

It is interesting to note that football is the topic that most helped me relate to the locals. If I claim to be a Juventus fan, for example, whoever I am with will tend to take a comradely attitude or make fun of me, but will rarely remain impassive. Immediately, distrust of the unknown disappears, friendly contact is established, and any cultural distance is overcome.

In its own way, religion helped me too. But starting from the acknowledgement of our differences: you are Muslim, I am Christian. Let's get to know each other. Even so, this is a topic to be addressed with more caution than football. From that evening on, I keep track of what is going on in the different championships, to always have a joke up my sleeve that I can use at the right moment. It turned out to be a good choice.

GAMBIA

*I'm at home, with my wife and children.
That's what matters.*

AMADOU

July

Cashew is business. It is the recurring slogan on many of the road signs, along with the name of the village that deals in it. Amdallai, Fassa, Keer Jatta. Each town on the road to the capital has its own sign. Cashew is business. I will soon discover the importance that this product has for the country's economy.

Cashew comes from the Greek word *kardia*, heart, since its shape and colour make it look like a human heart. The nut is an odd-looking growth attached to the lower part of the fruit. If you come across a cashew plant whose hanging fruit is colourful and attractive, resist the temptation: the shell contains a caustic oil, which, if not cooked, is not only dangerous for the body but potentially lethal.

Passing through mango and cashew plantations and rural villages dominated by towering baobabs, I head for Barra's town where I can catch the ferry to the capital. As per good African tradition, one of the two boats that cross the seven kilometres of water, the Gambia River, has been defunct since time immemorial. Luckily, the interminable queue of people and vehicles suggests that the surviving boat is about to arrive.

It's just after 3 p.m., and the sun is burning the air. While waiting, I try to keep cool in the shade of a parked truck. The truck driver and his mate are dozing under the chassis, lying on prayer rugs. I sit on the ground, leaning against the tyre. The man opens his eyes and nods his head at me in greeting. I nod in return. A half-hour later, he wakes up and comes to chat with the white cyclist.

I try to avoid the usual old conversation about me and focus on him by answering his questions with ones of my own. "What are you carrying?"

"Cashew nuts. They'll go to the port, where they'll be shipped abroad."

"Where will they go?"

"The boss is an Indian, so I think they will be going there." He tells me that all national production goes abroad. The raw cashew is exported to India for processing and then to Europe and America for consumption. Globetrotting cashews, lucky them! This explains why, much as I have searched for them, I haven't been able to eat a single nut in the week I've been here in The Gambia. I can only find the red fruit, but as it is delicate and difficult to transport, it is not cheap and is often thrown away.

Thanks to a steady increase in selling prices in recent years, the buoyant cashew sector is helping to improve incomes and alleviate poverty. Similarly, it is contributing to neighbouring countries: Senegal and, above all, Guinea Bissau.

The hours go by slowly. The only movements are those of the kids who pass by to sell refreshments in the form of an ice lolly with *bissap* or ginger and of the sun slowly approaching the horizon, disappearing behind the port company's building.

Suddenly, everything comes to life. The ferry has docked, and a minute later, a packed, multicoloured crowd is noisily and chaotically disembarking. People, goats, and vehicles form a single line snaking down to the exit of the port.

The fatigue of the day adds to the build-up of exhaustion of the previous days, and as we cross the river, I almost nod off on the port railing, lulled by the waves and the soporific rumble of the engines as we approach Banjul.

I spend four days resting and getting my strength back at the Catholic parish of Kololi. It's located near the Atlantic coast, in the modest district of Serekunda, the mainland continuation of the capital, Banjul. I was brought here by Eku, a guy a little younger than me, with whom I had made contact a few weeks earlier.

We spend Saturday afternoon on the beach with some of his friends. The atmosphere is playful and relaxed. The whole city today seems to have moved out here, by the sea. Thousands of people get together on the sand, at the water's edge and in the numerous bars, whether they be elegant buildings or tin shacks.

The low tide has uncovered lots of football fields. The goalposts work in both directions: they are valid for one pitch and also for the one immediately behind. We walk beside—or in the middle—of these temporary pitches for more than a kilometre. The sidelines are not defined but are left to the players' imagination. Ronaldo and Messi's shirts are running around in every direction. A single open-air stadium houses a large crowd watching all the games simultaneously, while some boys warm up on the sidelines—or on the pitch, again based on the imaginary lines.

With a coke in hand, we approach a crowd of excited and exultant young people. Beyond this human barrier, a large number of athletes are challenging each other in the traditional fight. *Boreh*, they call it around here. Here in the Gambia, as in most neighbouring nations, wrestling is the national sport, more popular even than football. Not a sound comes from the wrestlers, just short, firm breaths. I stop and look on in admiration.

Eku suggests we have a friendly fight. "Let me finish my coke, then we'll wrestle." *Great excuse.* Gradually the losers leave the ring, and in the end, only two athletes remain. Everything is ready to begin: the final match. The two wrestlers, both slender but with powerful bodies, are preparing for the fight. Sand sticks to the sweat worked up in the previous fights. The tension among the audience is at its peak. In the meantime, I eke out my coke to avoid the risk of making a fool of myself in a physical confrontation with my friend.

The two athletes move towards each other until they are at arm's length. They dip their hands in the sand to remove the sweat and make it easier to get a grip on their opponent, and then start with slow movements, still sizing each other up. Their bodies lean forward, their heads touch. It's a game, but there is a tense silence in the crowd and in the ring. The hands of the two athletes move in search of a good grip. With a sudden movement, the taller of the two dashes behind his opponent; with one leg gets him off balance, lifts him up, and throws him onto the sand. Game over.

The audience's excitement fades, as does the heat of the sun, which has almost finished its daily journey. Slowly, the crowd begins to disperse. Eku seems to have forgotten about our fight (phew!) and suggests an aperitif at a friend's bar.

I leave the main road to take a decent red clay track as I cycle towards the east. Dense vegetation alternates with cashew plantations. Sometimes it stops abruptly, giving way to large stretches of uncultivated land, where extraordinary earth structures stand out: termite mounds. They will be a constant for the next few months. But these natural masterpieces, red castles that dominate the view in this open land, are unique, and I stop to take some pictures. Some are over three meters high: to reinforce their structure, termites have built them around a tree trunk, thus creating a single entity.

Half a day later, I am again beside the Gambia river. How beautiful African rivers are! Languid, deep, meditative watercourses, with their undefined banks. They are so vast that they look like lakes, and in the distance, the water merges with the sky.

The cycling day comes to an end. Often, I don't have daily targets to reach, and in that case, I like to stop at least an hour before sunset to have time to wash and cook before the light fades altogether. Rarely do I have trouble finding a place to spend the night.

In front of me, the first houses of a village come into view. Actually, these few houses with their walls of dried earth and roofs of *tôle ondulée*, corrugated iron, make up the whole village. It's no different from the previous fifty villages or the next fifty, I would hazard to say.

From the door of a cottage, a man is waving his arms to get my attention.

"Hi," he shouts loudly, as soon as he notices my head turn in his direction. Now he's waving me over.

What does he want? To my dismay, in Senegal, I had learned that when someone calls me persistently, it is often to ask for a favour or sell me something. *Okay, for the last time, I stop and take the opportunity to ask where I can camp.*

"Hello, good evening."

"Welcome to Batloto."

Mmmh, it's not a bad start.

"I'm Filippo, and I'm an Italian cyclist."

"I'm Amadou. Pleased to meet you. How come are you passing this way? You lost?"

"Yes… that is, no, not really."

Several times in the previous months, I have tried to explain my philosophy. I often travel to get lost, intending to discover new things. And each time, I've been met with frowns and evident incomprehension. Tonight, I try to lead the discussion back to less philosophical levels. "I'm on my way to Jangjangbureh, but I'll probably get there tomorrow." There is a short pause. "Right now, I'm looking for a place to spend the night."

"I figured, that's why I called you," he replies with a smile. "Come, come, and I'll introduce you to my children."

Four faces break into smiles as I approach them. They greet me, and the oldest runs up to me to take the bike and lean it against the wall.

Amadou watches me, obviously proud of his children. He gestures to me to enter the house. This is the worst time, the late afternoon; the air in these houses is suffocating, hot and heavy. There is no ventilation, and the sheet metal on the roof helps keep this furnace burning.

"Listen, Amadou, I'll pitch the tent outside in the courtyard, if you don't mind. I don't want to disturb you. I mean, this is your home, and I wouldn't want to intrude."

Agreed; great. The mighty mango tree in the centre of the courtyard will be a worthy substitute for the Gambian sauna.

While I wash, my hosts place a bench under the mango tree, next to my tent. I take the opportunity to sit and observe village life at this late hour. However, I am worried about a huge spot that showed up on my thigh a few days ago. It's hard and reddish. Tonight, it's formed a head, and as soon as I squeeze it, some whitish pus shots out. I keep pressing. *Strange, there seems to be something solid inside.* Here it is, peeping out.

Gross! It's a larva! I slowly extract it and show it to Amadou, who checks it out, vaguely interested. "Oh yes, that's a fly larva; it's common around here. Don't worry, it's nothing serious." That may be so, I think as I try to keep the expression of disgust off my face.

Amadou turns out to be a wonderful host and invites me to dinner. Experience has made me aware that these are not strictly invitations but friendly orders. You are our guest; we will not leave you without food. As soon as we have finished a tasty rice dish of rice with the inevitable *sauce arachide*, the youngest son silently approaches his father, who looks at him lovingly before picking him up and sitting him on his lap.

We pick up where we left off, but Amadou has decided that it is time for a more intimate conversation, and he wants to tell me more about himself and his family.

"One evening, three years ago, I announced to my family and to my wife that I was going to Mali in search of a job. I didn't tell her, however, that I actually intended to reach Europe. People make money there, they say. But my family would never let me go because the journey is dangerous, and she and my father knew it."

At that moment, the curtain on the house's entrance moves and his wife comes out with the dirty plates in her hand. Amadou glances up and smiles at her, waiting for her to move to the back of the building, where she won't be able to hear us.

"I worked in a gold mine for about nine months to raise the money for the second leg, to Agadez, Niger. From there, a good contact would have got me onto a boat. They were hellish months; the heat and fatigue weakened me physically and in spirit." He pauses for a few seconds on this last sentence, perhaps reliving those days.

"One morning, I received a call from my mother to tell me that my son was about to be born. At that moment, I understood what had to be done. It was not my destiny to risk crossing the desert and the sea, but to go home and be with them."

A few moments pass, and I let his words settle while he starts stroking his son's hand.

"And now, almost three years have passed since that day. How do you feel? Do you regret not continuing the journey?"

He looks up at me as his lips stretch into a serene smile. "I'm at home, with my wife and children. That's what matters."

The fire has now gone out, and only the reddish glow of the embers remains. I get up, and after saying goodnight to my host and the young boy almost asleep on his lap, I go back to the tent for a well-deserved rest.

In Senegal, the recurring refrain was *"Toubab! Toubab!"* which was sometimes followed by the verse: *"Donne-moi l'argent!"* Presumably, every child was aware of this nursery rhyme. And what about in the Gambia?

In the Gambia, the people I met were genuine and hospitable. At times, too much so, even to the point of offering their daughter's hand in marriage.

I have just come to the end of a dirt track. It had led me through enchanted woodland, an English garden with herculean baobab trees soaring above all other foliage. In the late afternoon, I arrive in a pleasant village.

I approach two elderly gentlemen seated under a mango tree and ask where I can meet the village chief. One of the two points to a low mudbrick wall, beyond which laughing children play football between a group of houses.

The tallest of them calls the chief; I guess he is his son. A girl is sitting on the ground with her back resting on an old woman's legs, having her hair braided into cornrows. If today I think back to a recurring scene across several regions of Africa, I recall this one. Women of all ages devote a lot of time to hair care: combing each other's hair is a maternal gesture and an opportunity for undisturbed conversation.

The boy has probably already told the old man about me because he comes out with open arms, smiling when he reaches me. "Welcome, welcome!" The pleasantries are short, and he offers me two accommodation options. The first house has a floor covered with excrement, with a pile of straw in a corner. The next? An empty room, which looks okay. However, with its typical tin roof, the temperature inside reminds me of an Arabic *hammam*. No, thanks.

The village chief agrees to let me pitch my tent in the courtyard, even though he does not fully understand why. Hens and goats roam noisily through the yard. *Tomorrow, I'll have a very early wake-up call, once again. Damn goats!*

In the meantime, he has called what I think is his eldest daughter. Aisha arrives looking pretty, with freshly-braided hair from forehead to nape and a big smile on her lips. "Ask her anything; she will help you."

She is short and sturdy, with full lips and a well-proportioned nose between her dark eyes. I notice, which is unusual for me, that she has changed her clothes. Shortly before, Aisha was wearing a multicoloured *pagne*, tight at the waist, and a white vest. Now she's looking comfortable in another dress, also colourful but more elegant. This covers her whole body, leaving only her arms and ankles bare. Although apparently more chaste than the previous one, this dress enhances her breasts and the curves of her hips. *What am I looking at! She can only be about sixteen!*

Aisha helps me set up the tent. The audience of young children finds it hilarious when I sit and pretend to leave all the work to her.

She wants to wash my clothes. "Oh, thank you, but there is no need." They have the muddy and earthy colour of the trail. She stands by as I cook pasta with pesto and sits bum-to-bum with me while I satisfy my hunger. I have also prepared dinner for her, but after a few forkfuls, Aisha puts down her plate and entertains me instead with exciting stories about her family. Out of the corner of my eye, I notice her mother, still sitting where I found her upon my arrival. She's with two of her daughters, exchanging whispered comments and giggling.

Aisha is gentle and caring. As soon as I finish eating, she takes the pot and cutlery from my hand and goes to wash them at the well. I grab the chance for a quick walk in the village, and I am chatting with an assortment of cousins/brothers/relatives when the older boy, the one I met first, calls me. "My father wishes to have a few words with you." Wow. "Okay, let's go."

I find him sitting alone on the porch, and he beckons me over to keep him company. "You have a nice family, you know? Here everyone is big-hearted and welcoming to me."

"Oh, thanks." He is visibly pleased with this compliment. "I'm glad you are enjoying yourself."

"Yes, sure! Your daughter has been helping me all evening. Now she has gone to wash my dishes, although I told her I would do it later."

"Her mother is proud of her." A moment of silence, he loads the ammunition into the barrel. "Do you like Aisha? She is of marriageable age now."

Oh god! I suspected everything had been prepared. Now, I have to be careful about how I answer, considering the etiquette of hospitality. A firm "no" doesn't exist in African culture. I beat about the bush. "Yes, she is lovely. But I'm too old for her, I'm thirty-one, she's what? Sixteen?"

He chuckles. "Oh, no, no. She is of age now. There are no problems." I still have some doubts.

"Do you know what? At the moment, I am on this long journey. I would like to get to Guinea and perhaps continue further. I cannot commit to marriage right now." It sounds as if I have accepted.

"Then will you come back to the Gambia?"

"Yes, it would be wonderful to come back. I love it here."

"That's fine then, come back and visit us," and he lets the matter drop.

Two relatives join the conversation, which turns to football, the government, and its total indifference to anyone who doesn't carry money in his pockets—this includes pretty much most of the population.

I thank my guests and go to my rooms. Aisha is waiting for me next to the tent. "Good night!" she says in a melodious voice. "Good night, see you tomorrow," I echo her tone. I close the zip of the tent and watch as my betrothed walks away lightly.

GUINEA BISSAU

One can know a man from his laugh,
and if you like a man's laugh
before you know anything of him,
you may confidently say that he is a good man.

F. DOSTOEVSKY, THE RAW YOUTH

August

"*Branco pelelè, branco pelelè,*" the children who are playing barefoot by the roadside chant in rhythmic voices. As soon as I cross the border, they make it clear that Portuguese is spoken here.

I have always been fascinated by the first few kilometres in a new country: they are the trailer for the film of the next few days. In a short clip, they give me a brief idea of what is to come. *Are the people hospitable? What are the roads like? Will the police mess around with the traveller, or will they behave professionally?*

In Guinea Bissau, the first rides evoke dirt, abandon and great human warmth. As well as the presence of tons of *cajú* nuts lying on the baking asphalt to dry. I will soon discover that this first impression is absolutely true.

Bissau is the country's first surprise. The colonial city welcomes me with its pastel colours and the unkempt atmosphere of a small capital abandoned by westerners. I've seen many examples of neglect during the trip. No effort is made as far as upkeep is concerned.

Hence, the once elegant buildings of Bissau *Velho* now have a listless air. The windows are boarded up with wooden planks; electric cables hang low over the alleys and are often used as clotheslines for drying the washing; ivy and mould fill the gaps left by fallen plaster. The elegant tree-lined boulevards that I saw in a photo from the 1960s no longer exist. In many parts of the city, the worn asphalt has reverted to a sandy track. Here the shared taxis, tired white-blue Mercedes, and *Toca-Tocas* (minibuses travelling loaded at least twice their capacity) run up and down.

Walking through the streets of the centre, I meet a guy who says he saw me arrive a few hours earlier. Felipe is very forthcoming and, since we both have free time that afternoon, he invites me for a tour of Bissau *Velho*. We walk through the narrow streets or run across the big, busy roads while discussing football and politics.

It is almost dusk. After he has shown me the harbour, I invite Felipe to have something to eat with me. He has brought me to one of the poshest places in town. I've had a few rough days, and a tasty fish meal can only help.

I try a delicious and spicy *Sigá*, a shrimp soup with piri-piri, while Felipe tells me about his country's difficulties: corruption, lack of humanitarian aid and, finally, drugs.

Felipe went to Senegal to study but then had to return to be with his sick father. I admire his capacity for analysis, and he tackles the subject meticulously.

Guinea's coast features a thousand and one inlets, into which an intrusive ocean penetrates. And, off the coast of Bissau, a few hours away by boat, are the Bijagos Islands. A natural paradise of uninhabited islets that could be a great asset for local tourism, as Felipe points out. Instead, ships and planes land here with loads of drugs, mainly cocaine, from South America. The airspace is not controlled, and there are hardly any coastguards on patrol. Let alone satellites to track activity.

Bissau has now become an international nexus of illegal business. As a result, kidnappings, murders, and threats have become common in a country where organised crime was previously unknown.

By the time the goods arrive in Guinea, thanks to the porosity of the borders, it is easy for the drug traffickers to get drugs across the frontier. They often pay Islamist groups, who now rule in the Sahara, to protect the shipments as they cross the desert.

This is a rich source of cash that enables terrorists to keep their activities going. The narco-traffickers, in turn, have often used this method because, on the coast, the rough terrain makes it easy to hide the movements of the goods. Besides, the police and customs often turn a blind eye, especially if sweetened with a lavish bribe, or even two. The amount of money involved is so significant that Guinea Bissau is considered for all intents and purposes the continent's first narco-state.

Felipe shares this last morsel of information with a hint of sarcasm. This strikes me as unusual, as the local humour tends to be more earthy and direct.

After this sad revelation, Felipe goes back to his soup, indicating that the conversation is over. The rain starts to fall again, and the sound of the drops on the roof now mingles with the background music of the restaurant. I finish my coke while I watch a group of girls dancing sinuously to the tropical rhythm of the rain, waiting for it to clear.

There are not many roads in Guinea Bissau, and since I have always been welcomed everywhere, I would like to extend my stay and explore some of the hidden corners. Studying the map, I discover a large green area in the south of the country, the Dulombi national park, with only one road running through it. Most of the route runs along the border with Guinea before returning to the main road. Perfect, let's go.

At the village of Contabane, I leave the asphalt and head towards the park. After a few kilometres, it becomes clear that it will not be an easy ride. The track, two metres of loose earth winding through the lush forest, is interrupted several times by large puddles. Crossing the first one, I keep to the edge, where the water level is lower. These are deep puddles, and the consistency of the ground makes the edge steep and slippery. The front wheel plays an unkind trick on me, and I get stuck. I fall to the ground, or rather, in the water.

I get up again. When I reach the next puddle, I try a new approach by going through the middle, where there is less slope. The front wheel sinks into the quagmire, and I come to a complete stop. I then try to make my way through the tall grass beyond the edge of the road and the water. Here the track is very muddy, and the wheel sinks; I pedal hard, but despite this, I advance slowly, too slowly. Out of instinct, I put my foot down. Where does it land? On the edge of the puddle. *Splash*. And again! Any spectator would be laughing his head off, but I'm alone, there's no one around, so it's just me that bursts out laughing, still lying in the water.

I advance unhurriedly. And in silence. No noise can be heard, other than the wheel occasionally breaking through the water surface and the call of a lonely monkey in the distance. Sections of impenetrable forest alternate with meadows of tall grass.

Several grey earth structures draw my attention, about half a metre high and with a curious mushroom shape: a trunk that gradually narrows and a large hat on top. I spot many of them along the road. It will be a passer-by I met in the following days who will enlighten me on the mystery. They are termite nests, with a hat to protect the structure from the rain, so abundant in this region. Nature's ingenuity leaves me speechless once again.

In the late afternoon, the sun is already hidden beyond the vegetation, while I still haven't found a suitable (i.e., not flooded) area to pitch my tent. But luck is on my side today: a clearing opens up unexpectedly on the right-hand side of the track. Here five round huts stand out, not arranged in a particular order. The wooden structure is unevenly covered with mud, and on the top lies a conical roof, covered with thick, well-woven straw to protect it from the incessant rain. A burnt-out termite mound towers over the clearing: it has been stormed by the goats who have made it their fortress. I see misery and extreme poverty in the environment.

Some kids are sitting on a felled log, chatting. An old woman is beating a pestle in a large mortar, and a naked little girl with a swollen belly is playing on the ground, not far from the fire. Her belly button protrudes: umbilical hernia, so common among African children.

None of them speaks Portuguese or French. However, even in this godforsaken corner, I find a family who welcomes me as if I were their own son. Intrigued, they help me set up my tent and teach me how to grind millet in the mortar in the most efficient way. There are three of us around the mortar. We beat the grain into flour with a large pestle, one blow each. A boy starts up music on his mobile phone, and the act of preparation turns into the funny mortar dance. The younger children roll around laughing as the branco moves completely out of step, slowing down dinner preparation.

Men sit around one bowl, the women another, all eating together in the darkness, interrupted only by the bright, small beam of a mobile phone, while a croaking radio plays music from neighbouring Senegal. Little by little, everyone heads for their huts and I for my tent.

I try to send a message to my parents, but there is no signal. A young boy sees me and realises my problem; he takes me to the base of the termite mound, pointing to its tip. By now, the goats are asleep, so I climb undisturbed to the top. A small signal. Yeah! On top of the mound in this clearing in the forest, with one arm pointed up towards the sky, I'm at the summit of Everest.

I return to the tent and close my eyes, but keep my ears wide open to listen to the frogs singing songs to the star-filled ceiling.

Today, no words were needed to forge unbreakable bonds with my new brothers and learn a great lesson in humanity from these people. Whether Portuguese, Creole, Fula or Mandinka, verbal communication has proved more complicated in Bissau than elsewhere. But it is not always necessary if you are armed with a good smile.

Smiling. That's the key to people's hearts. It is a universal language; you don't need to know the other person's language. There is no need for words when you can smile and laugh. Entire conversations are transmitted in a few moments. With a smile, you can express an infinite number of emotions, but *that* smile, at *that* moment, directed at *that* person, has a unique meaning. And empathy, that amazing and absolutely human capacity we have, translates that smile for us.

I pass a child on the path; it's just the two of us. He is tense and does not know how to behave or what to expect. Maybe it's the first time he's met a white person and, moreover, on a bike. I give him a broad, friendly smile. The tension melts away immediately, and we're the same, we're friends now.

An elderly woman is bent over as she works in her fields. She sees me pass, stops working and raises her arm in greeting. Despite her fatigue and hunger, she smiles. It is a discreet and serene smile, but it fills us both with courage and energy.

It is almost dusk. As I pedal along a narrow path, two burly men approach, both carrying machetes. One of them carries an axe on his shoulder. All three of us slow down. Tiredness can lead to misleading interpretations of reality in these cases. I stop, move the bike to the side of the path and smile uncertainly, accompanying it with a slight nod. "Please, do pass." They reciprocate. We wish each other a good rest and continue on our separate ways.

I arrive exhausted in a village, and it is almost dark. A mob of excited children is chasing me. The women are sitting next to the fires and cooking dinner. They watch this strange traveller pass by with curiosity. Under the big tree, there are the elders. I cycle over to them. I brake, stop, put my feet on the ground and smile. A tired but friendly smile. And they smile back as if to say: "Hello, welcome to our village. This evening you will be our guest." Words will come later, but they do not add any meaning, as the essential has already been stated.

I cycle through valleys submerged by the constant rains and through battered passes between the highest mountains in Guinea—one hundred and seventy metres, the highest point in the country. Finally, I reach the edge of the park. Here, I go through one sad village after another. There is a sense of isolation and neglect in the air. The locals confirm that the government does not look after this region at all. As I have found out, the roads are challenging to travel along, and during the rains, these people are almost cut off from the rest of the world. Some cattle and crops are all they have.

A few kilometres from here, on the hill near the village of Lugajol, is the place where Guinea Bissau's independence was proclaimed in 1973. One hovel remains, in a state of complete dereliction and full of excrement.

Beyond the mountainous area near Boè, the road gradually flattens out. In this natural basin, the ground is so saturated with water that it cannot absorb any more. The whole route is just a lake, and I pedal on for one kilometre in a surreal environment—the frogs and me. The sporadic rays of sunlight make the vegetation glisten bright green. And finally, I reach the Rio Cocolì.

On the opposite bank, a pirogue is unloading passengers and slowly returns to this side of the river. I feel dazed. I have been on another planet for two days, and the boy who is paddling in my direction has the task of bringing me back to Earth. In the province of Gabu, to be precise. The young ferryman is also an excellent businessman: a thousand CFA[1] or nothing. I try to bargain, but he doesn't give up. Heigh-ho!

I sit on the bank to grab a bite to eat and recover my strength before the last stretch of road. But a sudden clouding over and gusts of wind announces the arrival of yet another rainstorm. Not far away, a cloudburst rises up to touch the dark thunder clouds.

---

[1] The Franc of the French Colonies of Africa, the current currency for fourteen West and Central African countries. 1000 CFA corresponds to 1.52 €.

In the opposite direction, the few houses of the village of Andebe welcome me. The first drops fall, and a woman, shouting, invites me just in time to join her family on the porch. A few moments later, the cloudburst explodes—buckets of water, as always. The woman who had invited me to the shelter runs into the house and comes out with basins that she places in the collection points under the roof. Cascades of water flow from the corrugated metal sheets; it is impressive how quickly the containers fill up. I try to communicate my astonishment to the lady, but the deafening roar of the rain on the roof makes this impossible. So, after the second attempt, I give up and go back to watching the rain falling violently.

The woman's children are now in the courtyard dancing, running, and playing to the rhythm of the raindrops banging on the roof. Water is a blessing: *baraka*, the Arabs say, in the local language I don't know. I am entranced by this primaeval dance, as the children enjoy the water streaming down over their bodies. The words of a poem I read recently come to mind:

and dance again in the floods
what is the summer storm for
if not to remind you
not to stop dancing?[2]

The spectacle of the African rains lasts a few minutes, then gives way to a drizzle that is soon chased away by the strength of the sun. And life resumes, after it, too, had been paused to admire this explosion of nature. Birds are always the first to notice that it will soon stop raining. When they start singing on the tree again, you can be confident and put your umbrella away. Then come the cackling children, jumping in puddles. Finally, adults. The men return to their

---

[2] Gio Evan, *E fatele queste cazzate*.

meeting places, the women resume their activities. Until the next downpour.

I am shocked by the panels placed next to the signs with the name of each village. Guinea Bissau has been the focus of humanitarian organisations because of its poverty and lack of infrastructure. Every village, or small town, has its sponsor: the European Union has funded a school; USAID has created a hospital... and so on.

I find it hypocritical. I imagine that farmer walking to the field every day past that sign that reads: *UNICEF - Against hunger, malnutrition, and poverty*. If he could read, what would he say? Is it necessary to remind those people that they are poor and that someone wants to help them? What is the purpose of these signs? It gives the organisations a return on image, but what's in it for the locals? Although extreme poverty has been eradicated, these people still have barely enough money for one meal a day.

I don't want to be rhetorical. If you look at the data, people still go hungry. 70 per cent of the population lives on less than two dollars a day. According to the International Monetary Fund, the country ranks among the world's worst performers in economic and social development indices. Since independence, there has been no leader in Guinea capable of creating the structures necessary for a democratic state to function. The fact that there have been fourteen successive governments in just a few years, hampered by four coups d'état, is not an excuse. All past governments have pocketed billions in international aid that have simply vanished and then reappeared in some tax haven account.

This is why even the structures financed by willing NGOs, including hospitals and schools, are abandoned. There is no money for teachers and nurses, no money for maintenance and equipment.

In Guinea and other countries, I have often slept in school classrooms because "there are no teachers anyway, there are no lessons tomorrow." This sad sentence reveals the difficulties that these countries will have to face in the coming years. The young people will not be sufficiently prepared to face the challenges of the modern world.

Mind you, almost all the children in these countries are more self-sufficient and capable of looking after their little siblings than our youth is. They can manage a herd of cows. They still maintain a strong bond with nature and with each other, to the benefit of society. Our school system does not teach all this, showing its shortcomings.

African countries, and indeed most developing countries, are aligning themselves with Western models. This requires more and more technology, engineering, and online business and so on. However, it is clear that the current weaknesses of the education system will slow down this development. It is not up to me (us) to judge whether this kind of development is good or bad. At the moment, it is what the more enlightened governments are looking for, and many young people are also clamouring for. Some countries have understood this, with great benefit for the general well-being. Other leaders, however, prefer to line their pockets while they watch their backs waiting for the next coup.

Thinking about these thorny problems, I reach the border between the two Guineas. Coincidentally, an hour earlier, I had asked for directions at the police checkpoint, and they told me that I could get my exit stamp at their station. Had I not done so, now that I am at the river, I would have had to retrace my steps.

It hasn't rained today; in fact, a fierce sun has stifled everyone's activities. I feel the heat on my skin, covered in sweat and red dust. Soon I will cross the river and be in Guinea Conakry. In some ways, I am a romantic traveller. The idea of entering another country aboard a narrow, unstable pirogue, a hollowed-out tree trunk, in the heart of the forest, evokes in me images of olden days, adventurous stories of ancient journeys. I am deeply moved, and my tears flow down to join the steady, peaceful flow of the river.

GUINEA CONAKRY

Education is the most powerful weapon which you can use to change the world.

NELSON MANDELA

August

I still haven't got over all the excitement when a young man on a bike draws up alongside me. He is coming back from the field, carrying a large basket full of vegetables on his rear rack. He has a broad, welcoming smile. "Where are you going, my friend?"

"I am going to Conakry[1], but it is still a long way to go."

"On that bike?" For months they have been saying this to me. "You'll never make it; it's too far!" People travel by bike, but only to go to the neighbouring village or their vegetable plot. Just saying the name of a village over ten kilometres away is enough to trigger local disbelief. Whether it's ten, a hundred, a thousand kilometres away, the reaction is the same. "On that bike?"

"Yes, but very slowly."

"You need at least two days," replies my friend.

"You go fast, don't you? With all this stuff, it'll take me at least two weeks to cover seven hundred kilometres."

"You must be tired today. Tonight, you will sleep at my family's house." The sun is setting over the cornfields, and the last rays are gilding the roofs of the houses, so I am delighted to obey his orders. We cycle side by side along the short stretch of road that separates us

---

[1] Guinea Conakry capital.

from the village. When we get close, the boy races on ahead to reach the small square before me. After hinting at racing him, I just let him go. I've got too many kilometres in my legs to manage a sprint today.

The victory has brightened his smile, and here he is now joyfully calling out to me from the courtyard of a house. After introducing me to all the relatives, he gives me a bucket of water to wash myself and insists on offering me "the best roast chicken in Guinea". I could eat two whole chickens this evening. I'm so hungry.

It's still dark, maybe four o'clock, but the inexorable rooster alarm rings. I roll around in the liner for a while until the goats are let loose in the yard. They have to compensate for the inertia of the whole night, so they run and bleat and butt each other. There is no respect for a tired bicycle traveller.

I am in a new country, but if it weren't for the language, now French, previously Portuguese, everything looks the same.

Guinea was a French colony until 1958 when it declared independence, and Sékou Touré was elected president. At that moment, a unique event occurred in the history of former French colonies in Africa. For other countries, independence meant a formal recognition of the new nation, while the economy and finance remained in French hands. Touré wanted complete autonomy. The colonial elites were furious, and when the colonists left Guinea, they wiped out everything of value to the country. Schools, hospitals, public administration and research institutes, machines, everything was destroyed. Farm animals were killed. The food stocks in the warehouses were burned. This clean slate caused a meltdown in the already weak economy of newborn Guinea. The new currency, the Guinean franc, was enormously devalued.

The message France wanted to send to the other colonies was explicit. Either you are with us, or you are with us. Fear spread throughout the former French colonies, and to date, in 2019, no other country has achieved total *independence* from France. Moreover, pro-

French presidents are still in government in most cases. In the past, some presidents have tried to improve the situation by raising their voices and cooperating with neighbouring countries. But Paris has always been extremely smart at manipulating local politics. They have often supported coups d'état, openly or tacitly, or intervened in defence of pro-French regimes when the situation could be detrimental to their interests.

In the Republic of Togo on January 10, 1963, Sylvanus Olympio, the first elected president of the newborn nation, decided to abandon the CFA franc. He wanted to solve a crisis in the economy, which was on the verge of collapse, and he began printing a new currency. Three days later, a squadron of soldiers, backed by France, went into action, and a former sergeant of the Foreign Legion killed the president.

History repeated itself in Mali in 1968, when President Modiba Keita was assassinated by Moussa Traoré, a former lieutenant of the Foreign Legion. And again, two coups, on January 1 and 3, 1966, in the Central African Republic and Upper Volta (now Burkina Faso).

More recently, the French government intervened at gunpoint in the 2010 elections in Côte d'Ivoire. France supported Alassane Ouattara, a friend of Sarkozy, who went on to become president of the country. This led to the removal and arrest of the *outgoing* president Laurent Gbagbo, who had been at loggerheads with France since Chirac's time. This is a story worth exploring.

The last major manoeuvre took place in Libya in 2011. For years, Gaddafi had been advocating the creation of the United States of Africa, an idea based on Pan-Africanism as a recipe for wealth and stability for African countries. He would have stockpiled substantial gold reserves necessary for a new African currency[2]. This would have led to the economic independence of the former French colonies in

---

[2] More detailed overviews can be found everywhere on the web. I suggest this article: https://www.econopoly.ilsole24ore.com/2019/01/24/macron-franco-cfa-colonie/.

Africa. The subsequent events, which took place from March to October 2011, are well known.

It would take at least a chapter to carry out an in-depth analysis of this subject, but that is not the purpose of the book. Let's go back to Guinea, which today is a country in serious difficulty. It's plagued by violence, social unrest and growing tension between the population and the government, with constant outbreaks of violence in different parts of the country.

When I reach the first town, I wander around the market, intending to change money: I sell *franc CFA* and buy *franc guinéen*. The largest denomination of banknote available in the country is ten thousand—one euro.

In no time at all, it becomes known that a foreigner wants to buy a million francs, one hundred euros. All the moneychangers in the market are rushing in with wads of notes in their hands. Ten thousand here, twenty there, and, shortly, I find myself with a pile of cash worthy of the best American films and with plenty of eyes on me.

I hole up in a restaurant nestled in a side street to quietly stash away the money, and in the meantime, I order a plate of rice. The choices are somewhat limited: *"poisson, ou viande."*

A bowl of rice with meat costs two thousand francs. Twenty euro cents. I still have all the cash in my hand, and I'm looking for a banknote that matches the amount. The lady looks at me and snickers: "I don't have change for all that."

"I eat a lot, ma'am."

Thinking back on all the landscapes I've been through, West Africa doesn't offer much. Entering the *brousse* or the forest, I can ride for months without seeing an end to it. The view is blocked in every direction, and the horizon becomes an abstract concept. For this reason, I decide to cross the mountainous region of Fouta Djalon, in the North-west of the country. At least for a while, I want to soar above my surroundings and set my sights on the distant horizon, to dream and not lose my motivation.

On the main road, the traffic is sparse. A few motorbikes pass me with a nod of greeting from the riders. Occasionally a *sept-place*, a Peugeot 505 from the '80s, passes by, loaded to the hilt. Almost all these vehicles have a rear tow bar reinforcement, which I imagine is because they often get stuck in the mud or break down. Officially, there are seven seats inside, while on the roof, the car carries its equivalent in weight of luggage, goods, goats, and passengers. I stare at them in amazement, and they stare back with equal curiosity.

The climb begins, and the asphalt suddenly stops. For the next forty kilometres and thousand metre climb, a strip of mud and stones hinders the ride. Under a torrential downpour, my sweat mixes with the rain as I make my way up what was the road, now a stream.

Some abandoned trucks lie along the way. They are unsuitable for this type of track, as they are over-loaded and only have smooth tyres. Two *sept-places* are broken down, parked by the side of the road, and a strong smell of burning mingles with the scent of rain. "*Avez-vous besoin?*" "*Non, Non. Le mécanicien est en route,*" replies the driver. It doesn't matter when. These people wait, knowing that the mechanic will arrive. The breakdown is not unexpected; the breakdown is part of the journey.

Time doesn't belong to us; how we overvalue this concept! For the West, time is money, so time then makes our lives stressful - we are squashed into "twenty-four hours". As we try to own time, it loses all value for us. To own often means to be owned; one thinks it's the active form, but no, it's passive instead. The paradox occurs when we make time free. When we become aware that we cannot dominate it, then it goes back to giving us its richness. To be able to stop and contemplate a line of ants crossing the road; to have a whole day to visit a friend who lives far away; to sit on a bench at the quay and admire the fishing boats returning at the end of the day... that is its richness. I have time for it. I don't own time.

Cycling during the rainy season in this region is not at all easy—or perhaps wise, but what can you do? This is the call of the mountains; that's what I love. I spend the next six days under the rain, a furious downpour or an accompanying drizzle, along paths that are often destroyed and flooded. The few shops with supplies and the incessant rain tested my will.

Sometimes, with a little luck, I find a dish of rice with okra sauce or fish in peanut sauce. But both of them are unfortunately rare. In the villages and the countryside, people often only have breakfast, rice, or bread with beans; the rest of the day's meals for me consists of biscuits, or *beignets*[3], or nothing. Many people in poorer areas eat only once a day: they have no money for more.

This was not what I needed right now. My motivation has gone right down, flooded in the soles of my shoes.

During this time, friends send me encouraging messages on WhatsApp. Some of them ask me how I manage to ride in such a hostile environment: first the desert, then the rainy season in countries with no essential services.

The problem, if I can call it that, is not the physical struggle of pedalling. True, there are still tough mountains passes to cross and rough and challenging trails, but that is not what tires me out in the long run.

There are two ways of experiencing this continent. Either by passing over it, simply watching the wheel turning on the asphalt as you go from one country to another, or by letting it absorb you without putting up any resistance. And when the latter happens, you are part of it, and you also contribute to making it what it is, Africa. In the long

---

[3] A mixture of flour, sugar and yeast deep-fried in palm oil. It is widespread in most of the continent.

run, *this* is mentally exhausting. I want to give my all; I bond with people, with their stories. And selfishly, I don't want to miss anything; I want to assimilate all I can of this land that is so different from mine but at the same time so authentic. *Why is everyone so friendly to me? How can they give me all this food if they don't have enough to eat twice a day?* I have so many questions. I meet tens, hundreds, even thousands of people by day and even by night. Every single day!

And I am alone down here. I rarely meet other westerners. I have a great friend named Ivan who, like me, is crossing these lands on his bike, and by talking, we manage to understand better every now and then. We often tell each other that we cannot change things. We are individuals in a sea of humanity. Yet, how can you pass by begging children, rubbish, and injustice without feeling powerless?

I feel as though I have been thrown into a tornado, on a rollercoaster of emotions; one minute I am sitting with other people by the fire eating with my hands from the same bowl, and when I zip myself into my tent, I think: *every damn day the same food, if the universe is kind with them. Otherwise, they don't eat at all.*

And how do you imagine I feel when a child approaches, perhaps barefoot and wearing a shirt that leaves more skin uncovered than covered, and asks me to give him a plastic bottle? Maybe the teacher told them to bring a full bottle to school so as not to waste time during lessons by going to the well. And they don't have the bottle, and they don't even have anywhere to go to buy it.

I can't get over these situations. I could *escape* to the coast, where tourists don't see this and enjoy an exotic holiday, where I could always buy the food that I want. Where I could detach myself from this reality and just go and *see things*. But I can't. Travelling to Africa without experiencing these realities would be a huge waste of time; it would just be pedalling.

What else can I do? I'm not in a position to fight these injustices, but I can become aware of them, and I have to accept them. Is it painful? Yes, it is. Later in the trip, I meet Victor, a Spanish cycle traveller. By observing his mannerisms and gestures, he makes me realise that the only thing that can help—help us—is giving our love, unconditionally and straightforwardly, to the people we meet. Until that meeting with Victor, maybe I did the same, or perhaps I didn't, but only then was I able to understand this fully.

Yet, the time always comes when you reach saturation point. Then the only solution is to put everything on standby, to shut yourself away, or to resume contact with an expat, or to devote yourself to the things you like: a good meal, a swim in the pool, or perhaps a visit to a museum. Not to forget, but to give ourselves time to internalise what is happening to us and maybe find a lesson in it before diving back into this exceptional, ordinary world.

And finally, I ask myself: those who live here, how do they do it? I don't have an answer yet. Perhaps they have simply given up trying to understand; they just accept. They accept what God has given them: a bit of cassava, a child, rain, life. Life itself is the *gift*. And if someone gives us something, we do not ask: "Why?"

To leave, to leave and not come back. These are the words I hear most often in this corner of Africa. Whether it is Senegal, Gambia or Guinea, the young are intent on forging a future far from home.

A reflection: there can't be many opportunities at home if they all want to leave. True. Almost without distinction, in every rural region, there are no real opportunities for professional and personal development. Okay, in the last five years, Africa has been inundated with Chinese and Indian motorbikes. Some young people have accumulated a fair amount of money by reinventing themselves as taxi drivers and moving people and goods between villages. Six hundred and fifty euros to buy the basic model and you can earn up to ten euros a day in the city—a little less in the countryside. Apart from this, today's youth can choose whether to continue their parents' work in the fields or try their luck in the big cities. And little else. As teachers, there is a high risk of not getting paid. There are some shops, all identical, with the same goods on display. That's why, when they speak, I often hear talk of Europe, football, and money.

I've been cycling for several days in the rain; I am exhausted, and I'm feeling under the weather. My feet are constantly soaking in damp socks, and sores are forming on the soles, which makes walking painful. I have just completed the crossing of the Fouta Djalon massif, with a significant expenditure of energy.

I guess that the sun has just passed its highest point when I reach the village of Konkouré. The sky, which is always grey at this time of year, is getting dark again. Since I woke up, it's been drizzling with occasional quick sunny spells.

In the village, I stop for lunch, but there is little on offer. On a porch, I see some pots side by side on a table, and some people sit on the benches around—here is my restaurant. The woman who runs it is drowning *beignets* in a cauldron of bubbling oil.

Madame sees that I am approaching and, sensing my hunger, lifts up the pan lids, releasing a mixture of aromas into the air. "*Ici c'est le riz, sauce arachides ou foutti. La bas c'est le poulet.*"

"*Merci madame, riz avec foutti et un morceau de poulet,*[4]" I order as I remove my gloves and sit next to a little girl with her hands dipped in a bowl full of rice. Perhaps her daughter.

The dish is soon served, and two chicken legs are floating in the sauce. "Don't worry; the other one is a gift." She anticipates my comment.

Hot, well-cooked rice and delicious sauce, if too spicy for my taste. I really needed this. "Madame, what's in the *foutti, c'est tres bon.*" As often happens, I ordered without knowing the ingredients of the meal.

---

[4] "Here is rice. Peanut sauce or *foutti*. Over there is chicken.
"Thank you, madam, rice with *foutti* and a piece of chicken."

"You like? I'm glad. I made it this morning. It is made with okra, aubergines, onions, tomatoes and Maggi.⁵"

Reader, I apologise. When it comes to cooking, I often get distracted. We were talking about young people and their desire to emigrate. The culinary interlude was useful to introduce the restaurateur's son. He is waiting for me to finish my meal to sit next to me and chat. He is a smart boy and confides that he likes studying very much.

In the meantime, it starts raining again; a part of me was waiting for just this as a reason to ask for hospitality in the village, even though it is only three o'clock in the afternoon. Alpha, the boy who has just sat down next to me, asks his mother, and in an instant, they find me a place in the courtyard under the roof of the communal hut. It's still drizzling, and the gentle dripping of the water on the roof makes for a pleasant rest.

I awake with a shiver when darkness has already fallen. The temperature has dropped, so Alpha and some friends are sitting by the fire. As I put on an extra layer of clothes, the guys burst into gales of laughter. I hurry over to them, intrigued. "Hey guys, hello everyone!"

"Hiii" echoes the merry bunch. Alpha introduces me to his companions, and, as always, I haven't had time to memorise the first name when the round of introductions is already over.

One of the youngest, about ten years old, gets up to give me a seat on a large log. "Well, what's so funny here?"

"What's going on here is that this afternoon while fetching water Sidy tried to kiss Fatoumata... but it didn't go very well!" The boisterous laughter resumes, and I smile, trying to recognise the unfortunate Sidy among those present. It's simple: they're pointing at him and patting him on the back in mockery.

---

⁵ Okra is a green vegetable native to these regions. *Maggi* is the nickname given to the soup stock cube, after the brand name that is popular throughout West Africa.

"And got a big slap in the face too!" SLAP! Adds a friend, imitating the sound with his hands. The cackles reach new heights.

Sidy looks upset. His shoulders are slumped, and his eyes downcast as he pushes away the friendly hands. Actually, he, too, is giggling about what happened. Little by little, the laughter dies down, and the boy of the slap asks me: "Philippe, how come you stopped by Konkouré?"

"Well," I make myself comfortable on the log, ready to tell the story "I'm travelling by bike, and I'm going to Conakry."

"No, sorry, I mean, why are you in Africa and not Italy. There is a lot of work there." The concept of cycling for pure pleasure and no economic purpose is alien to most, so I try to sidestep the topic.

Silence has fallen over the group. Only the flames seem uninterested in what I'm about to say: "Mmmh, maybe. How do you know there's so much work in Italy?"

"Well, many people we know are there or in France. Some are from here, from Konkouré. One is *mon frère*," Alpha replies.

In the meantime, his little sister has approached us, and I lift her onto my lap. She looks amused and rests her head on my chest. I stroke her cheek, and she lets out a childish giggle.

I pick up the thread of the conversation: "Wow, they've been through quite a journey. I guess through the desert and across the sea?"

"Yes, yes, but they are there now and make a few bucks."

"Not bad! They were lucky, Alpha. The crossing is arduous, and so is finding a job." A moment of silence, and then I continue: "What do they do?"

Now the silence goes on a bit. "I don't know. But they told me they earn some money."

"And do they manage to send money home?"

A few of them exchange glances, and one boy replies: "Nothing so far. *Mon frère* says he has to pay for some documents and the rent since he has only been there a short time." He doesn't seem to believe his words either.

I have had dozens of conversations like this in this part of the world. Families raise capital to pay for the trip of one of the sons, usually the eldest or the most capable. They tell me they have to scrape together an average of $5,000, which is a ridiculous amount for their lifestyle, based on a monthly income of one hundred dollars or so.

The bulk of the money is not for the ride. When these boys reach the Sahara, they are transported to places like Agadez and Dirkou—in Niger—before crossing to the coast of Libya. Often, army soldiers demand a bribe as a toll, or worse still, the migrants end up in the hands of the Bedouin tribes who sell them to other militia groups. And these groups demand ransoms for the release of the migrants. This money must be paid by the family or by the migrant himself through forced labour.

And once these people arrive in Europe, how do they feel? They cannot disappoint their families' expectations. The financial sacrifice is too great to tell their parents that they are in a shelter for migrants waiting for who knows what. Nor can they tell the families they are sleeping on the street or in sheds crammed together with others who have suffered a similar fate. At home, they must receive positive messages, optimistic about the future. Like the photo of a friend shown to me by Alpha. It shows a man in a Sampdoria shirt kicking a ball around a football pitch. "You see, he plays in the Serie A. He made it."

I try to push a little more: "Alpha, I don't believe that it's all a bed of roses in Italy, as your friends make out. Nowadays, it is almost impossible to get into Italy without a proper visa[6], let alone find a job. Even if they get a three-month tourist visa, they still can't work."

He reflects for a while and replies with stubbornness: "But I know people who have made it, have a job and send home a lot of money. You should see what nice houses their families have now. And they

---

[6] At the moment of narration, the Conte/Salvini/Di Maio government has just been elected in Italy. The direction that the policy on migrants will take is evident from the first days.

always have food several times a day. Here, you can see with your own eyes; we don't have anything."

After this statement, I don't feel like prolonging the conversation. Alpha now lives on this hope of travelling to Europe. He probably doesn't believe a word I say because for him, as for thousands of other adolescents, Europe is paradise. The news of shipwrecks and deaths at sea reaches here too, but those who die are few; those who make it are many more, they tell me.

And who am I to smash their dreams? On several occasions, I have tried to tell them the truth, my truth, about what is happening in Italy and the great dangers of the crossing. But then, as Alpha tells me, I look around, and I see a harsh life, with no future for these youngsters who have no hope of a trustworthy government. Maybe I understand them: if I were in their shoes and saw a European coming who could afford the luxury of travelling for a year without working, what would I think?

I am slowly but surely making my way back to the coast, a month after leaving the sleepy shores of Bissau. It is not raining in the morning, and I shake off my hitherto damp mood as the sun begins to shine again. Past the village of Kollet, the trail begins to descend, and the wheels roll fast through the lush meadows. The gloomy thoughts have evaporated with the dry weather, so I can lose myself in the beauty of the landscape.

"*Chinois, chinois!*" some children in chorus call my attention. *Who's Chinois?!*

"*Chinois!*" In the village, yet another little girl on the side of the road calls out to me. Her sister, a few years older, is at her side. I put my bike on the ground, and a group of young men of all ages surround me.

"*Mes amis!* I'm not Chinese; I'm Italian. The Chinese are short and yellow and have eyes like this," I say as I lower myself to the supposedly average Chinese stature and pull at the corners of my eyes.

They burst into roaring laughter and imitate me in this game of mimes. Some run to their mothers jumping from one foot to the other, now that they have become real Chinese.

The mystery is soon revealed. A little further downstream, a massive dam is under construction, obviously with Chinese labour. The Kaléta dam should be finished later this year. So far, the section on the left bank is completed, and the skeleton of the remaining section is being built.

The road crosses a bridge a little further downstream before going through the dam construction site. The soldier on guard is unwilling to let me pass. "*Monsieur*, this is a public road and open to everyone. If you want to close it, put signs at the beginning. I'm not going back now. It would take me several days on my bike." The authoritarian tone might have its effect, but the stubborn soldier doesn't want to let me pass. "You have to pay to get through." *Ah, l'argent.*

"*Monsieur*, you are wrong to ask me for money. I am the *Engineer*." I put a lot of emphasis on the last word, so it echoes in his ears. Not bad for nonsense, I chuckle to myself.

"Ah, I didn't know that. Excuse me, Sir. Please go ahead."

"*Merci.*"

In this way, I crossed the bridge, had a chat with a Chinese engineer who was proud of his work, and finally headed for the coast.

I enter the region inhabited by the Susu ethnic group. *Djarama*, which mean *hello* in the Fulani language, has worked well until now. Here, people reply with *inouwali*. With the best will in the world, it is challenging to keep up with every African dialect. Sometimes two completely different languages are spoken in two adjacent villages.

In the late afternoon, I am greeted by the elderly head in a village made up of just a few huts.

A swarm of children keep an eye on my every move, and as soon as the old man agrees to let me stay with them, they joyfully come up to me. Theirs is an honest joy to see me and have me there. They start to dance; I join in them while they laugh. For a moment, I, too, become a child.

The adults, attracted by the clamour, come closer and clap their hands in time. Some try out a few dance steps. It all seems so surreal now, writing this. But this is Africa. Don't put obstacles or limitations in the way; don't ask yourself why. Join in, and go with the flow of events. Then this continent will reward you.

I accompany a lady to fetch water from the well at the nearby school. The building seems abandoned, and a quick investigation confirms that it has never been used due to a lack of teachers. Funded by the European Union.

In each country, I find a different type of well. Here in Guinea, water is pumped through a piston worked by foot. The girls improvise jumping dance steps to apply enough force and pump some water. Cement has been poured all around the well to prevent contamination of the aquifer. Financed by Saudi Arabia.

A young boy shows me a rickety wooden structure surrounded by four metal sheets. It's the shower. With a bucket full of water and a smaller container to pour it into, I set off. I undress and hang my clothes on the top of the sheets. As they are quite low, they only cover me up to the chest. A little way off, with some on the ground and some on chairs, the village kids are watching me: it's the *White man and the shower* show! Roll up, roll up! Privacy! Forget it!

In the evening, we are sitting around a cheerful, crackling fire, lit more for the smoke to ward off the mosquitoes than because of the cool temperature. It has not rained all day, and the sky has remained clear even at night. I catch a glimpse of the first stars rising above us while the radio plays a dance song, similar to all the big hits I hear every day in the shops and cafes. The small kids are still running around in the courtyard and on the deserted street. The men and boys are conversing about... I don't know what. They are speaking in dialect.

However, I am fascinated by the sound of the words, and I pay attention as if I were able to make out even a single syllable.

Otherwise, I concentrate on their faces and expressions: a raised eyebrow or a pat on the knee; the tone of their voices, sometimes high, sometimes low; on the lively energy that accumulates in the space between us and vibrates, tickled by the laughter and the glow of the flame. Is it necessary to understand the meaning of their words when so much of the conversation is there before my eyes? As I am juggling with these thoughts and feelings, they begin to question me. They ask about: Italy, migrants, football. Then they talk about: hunger, unemployment, the state.

"But we Africans have one value that we will never lose. The family." And that evening, I am with them as part of the family, as I was part of a family the night before and will undoubtedly be the next. By now, I feel at home, in this battered and forgotten Africa.

In the tent, I have a song going round in my mind that goes something like this:

> and makes you want to live until the last moment.
> where the music plays
> In the land of men
> where you also find a place for those who
> Smiles at you from a corner[7]

With this verse, my eyes close, and only the chirping of the crickets and the warm glow of the ashes remain.

The poetry of that evening stops there. Heavy rain keeps me awake in the first hours of the night, while goats, cockerels and dogs kept me company in the hours before sunrise. At this point, the women start sweeping the courtyard, but I am already ready to go. However, I want

---

[7] Jovanotti, Lorenzo. *Terra Degli Uomini*. Backup - Lorenzo 1987-2012, 2012.

to wait for the chief and the others to wake up, to thank them. I wait a good half hour for them to appear.

I need to thank these people. They are so cheerful and always open-hearted towards me, which is extraordinary. Without this West African love and solidarity, I'm pretty sure I would have thrown in the towel a long time ago. Travelling in these countries alone is no small thing. I am still on the road thanks to their smiles and cries of encouragement which make me feel like a member of their family.

The etymology of humility comes from *humus*, which means earth. And it is in this red soil and mud that I rediscover the richness of simplicity. I can easily take away the superfluous, material objects, but above all those complex emotions and feelings that are useless and harmful here. A journey by bicycle, but above all, a journey through these lands that we conveniently call Africa, teaches me that to live with dignity, you need to detach yourself from pride and ego. I could not face this journey alone; you cannot be self-sufficient; the presence of others is essential. And these others, who are none other than our Brothers, teach me about sharing. It doesn't matter if there is little food. We are sitting around the same rice bowl, so what is theirs is ours. When it comes to preparing food, the ladies do not simply make enough for the number of people in the family. They prepare more, in case someone drops by who does not have any food that day.

And observing my Brothers in this and other daily chores, I have seen that through their humility, they have come to have great Humanity. It is not an accident that the word human also has its origin in the word *humus*, in the earth.

I pedal while meditating on all this. After a few kilometres, I stop on the crest of a hillock. The grass is still wet from the night's rain, and a faint sun reflects off the droplets. I close my hands around a long tuft and slide them upwards, in the same way I would make a ponytail of hair. I pass my damp hand over my face, rinsing away the tiredness of a bad night's sleep, and unexpectedly find myself smiling—a great act of love and intimacy with nature.

You never get used to the traffic in big African cities. Each time seems worse than the last. Each time I pray to merciful God that I reach my destination safely, get my visa and escape from the mess.

Undoubtedly, Conakry can claim first place on my personal podium of chaotic, busy, and run-down cities of Africa. Conakry is a tongue of land protruding from the coast into the sea for almost forty kilometres. *La Ville*, the city's beating heart, is in the Kaloum district, where most of the offices, government facilities and banks are located. As well as the embassies. Kaloum is at the bottom of this strip of land, forty kilometres from me.

The sight and sound of the traffic are shocking. And my feelings are heightened since I am back in a city after a month spent in the forests and mountains, encountering only a few harmless little towns here and there. What's more, my phone has run out of battery, and I can't use the navigator. I ask passers-by for directions, and after putting together four or five indications, I discover with relief that I just have to keep on the same road all the time, without turning off. *Easy, straight ahead, with eyes wide open.* A deep breath of smog, and off I go, feet on pedals.

It's a multi-sensory experience that I haven't really had before. Travelling along the edge of the road initially seems the safest option. I soon discover this is wrong. The column of stationary *autosaurs* is overtaken by motorbike taxis. Bikers make up their own rules as to who has right of way in every situation (they do) and zig-zag between one car and another, often crossing my *safe* lane. At intersections, the number of pedestrians increases dramatically. Of course, they also walk on this thin strip of asphalt. Street vendors wander among cars, dodging motorbikes and potholes. But they are not as intrepid as the motorcyclists who spin into every gap between vehicles. And then there are the cars coming in the wrong direction. With two wheels on the tarmac and the rest on the dirt shoulder of the road, these vehicles advance slowly, but inexorably, towards me. My frantic gestures that they should move aside are in vain. They claim the right of way, and I have to squeeze myself onto the other side of the traffic jam, in the middle of the road, which turns out to be where I have the best chance of survival. Breathing the air made heavier by humidity and exhaust fumes, I make my way through a symphony orchestra of horns and grumbling engines towards the edge of the suburbs. Here a few major arteries separate from the aorta on which I am travelling, and the traffic regains a more bearable appearance for a few minutes.

The journalist John Gunther visited Accra during his travels in Africa and described it in these terms: "[...] a jumble of tin shacks mingles with crumbling buildings of beams and masonry and miserable little shops under crumbling arcades. A viewer's first impression is of almost despairing squalor.[8]" Observing the outskirts of Conakry, I find many similarities with the capital of Ghana, which the author visited in 1954.

Almost every district has its own market, either large or small. As I get closer, bus conductors shout out their destination from the always-open doors of their vehicles. "Medina! Medina!" comes from one bus. "Bambeto!" echoes another arriving bus. They bang hard against the side, or on the roof, adding to the din. They do their best to be heard over the racket of the horns, which blare incessantly. Next to the market, buses and taxis stop, so passengers can get on and off by the roadside. Everywhere, it's the same noisy story. In one place, the roadway closest to the market is taken up by a pile of garbage, burning and stinking in the still air of the city.

I have been pedalling for about two hours through traffic and have not yet reached my destination. I am worn-out and find it hard to stay focused on pedalling with all the distractions that compete for my attention. There is a road sign to a Salesian institute. A pause to say hello is obligatory, as I am originally from the village where Don Bosco

---

[8] Gunther, John. *Inside Africa*. Plainview, N.Y.: Books for Libraries Press, 1955.

was born. What's more, by chance, it's August 16, the anniversary of his birth. Excited by this stroke of luck, I go into the courtyard. I am welcomed by an oratory with several boys playing football and a statue with the kindly face of Don Bosco.

I knock on the door indicated by a boy and go in; the parish priest sits behind a desk cluttered with papers.

"Good morning Father, my name is Filippo, and I've come from Castelnuovo Don Bosco on my bike."

He lifts his head, stares at me with interest and, bursting into a toothy smile, exclaims: "Don Bosco has come to visit us!"

We talk a lot. He tells me about his trip to the Shrine in Turin and his visit to the Basilica of Don Bosco. We both fly in our imaginations to those far off places. The joy of his memory and my nostalgia mix together in the air until the deacon enters and summons the Father for a task.

I say goodbye to him and continue on my way towards Gloria's house, a girl from Cuneo who will host me for the next few days. As in other capitals, the wealthy districts are full of white governmental or NGO Land Cruisers. Conakry is no exception.

Gloria is still at work when I arrive at the apartment building where she lives. "You can wait for me by the pool. I'll be there soon," says her cheery Whatsapp voice message.

The pool, what a luxury! I lean my bike against the wall and limp over to the pool. My shoes have been soaking wet for days and blisters and sores have appeared on the soles of my feet. I collapse on the deckchair, take off my shoes and let my feet enjoy the hot, dry midday air.

In the meantime, I get a voice message from Ivan:

"Oh Fili, you see I'm back, eh! When shall we meet up?" Ivan had interrupted his journey but now is back in Dakar, ready to resume it.

"Iiiiiivan! Welcome back. Well, I'm not sure how that is going to work out! You're two months behind, and you're really slow," I reply, pulling his leg.

"Put the brakes on a bit! Slow down, or find yourself a girl maybe, and one for me too. So, come on, let's go crazy. And we will never get to South Africa. Ha-ha, wicked!"

He always manages to put a smile on my face. What a guy! We're going to meet up, but who knows when or where. And I'm slowing down, starting right now. I really needed this break in Conakry. I must recharge body and soul before going on to Sierra Leone. There is no better way to do this than by switching off my thoughts with a swim in the pool.

A few pages back, I wondered how indigenous people can mentally cope with living in such miserable conditions, in filth and with little food, always the same food.

What are these miserable conditions? What are the criteria?

If I look back over the whole journey up to here, I have never seen anyone starving. Quite the contrary. The men often have enviable physiques, and the women, too, are strong and muscular from all the weight they carry every day. And people smile, wonderful, infectious laughter. And yet, it would be hypocritical to say that everything is fine. But, if you use criteria that are not exclusively economic, who is better off? The person who looks for happiness through buying a new car or new clothes? Or he who has just enough to live on, and has time to spend laughing and joking with friends in the shade of a tree? Is there not a greater social dignity in the respect they pay to the elderly and the less fortunate?

But these traditional values have been eroded in recent years. The smartphone has come into African lives. I am not saying it is evil. People have the right to call a distant friend to find out how they are doing. However, the smartphone is transmitting an ideal of beauty and well-being that distorts their way of life, their beliefs. You can see it in every music video on local TV: money, nice cars, and women.

And even those who live here start asking themselves: "Why?"

SIERRA LEONE

September

What makes a journey a Journey? The way I see it, I am Travelling when body and soul are both active and receptive, and when I am mindful. My five senses are engaged: I admire the colours and pick up the expressions on people's faces; in the silence of the forest, I hear the soundtrack of Life; the scents and fragrances of the market saturate my sense of smell; I savour the sweetness of a freshly picked mango; I embrace a brother.

And in all this, my soul is present. It joins with all the other souls of this world in a great dance, and I can no longer tell it apart from a myriad of other fluttering souls. Then yes, I am Travelling. My soul feels most at home in the great African dance, which welcomes me in and enfolds me within the great Oneness. So far, Africa is where my soul belongs.

Everyone with experience knows (and others can easily imagine) that Travelling requires a great deal of energy. Constant focus, concentration and participation require a lot of motivation, dedication, and sacrifice.

In the last month, I've been exhausted. I have lost some of the motivation, the initial drive, to keep going with my life in the saddle. My soul has been the first to give up, to stand aside. I lose interest in giving time to a relationship with a brother; *he is just one of the many I will see today and then never again.* I pedal on, thinking only of the destination, where I will sleep tonight. I have started counting the days to figure out how to divide the stages, and here I am, without even noticing, in Sierra Leone. But I am not really there; I am crossing this country without taking it in, and without leaving any trace of myself as I go.

In the three months it took me to write this book, I could not write even half a page about the days I spent in Sierra Leone. I thought about faces, tried to remember the events, but few came to mind. A daring crossing of the capital at night in the pouring rain, beers by the sea with a friend, the resilience of a Sardinian NGO in managing a hospital, painful inflammation and little else.

How arduous it is to travel, how easy it is to fall into the trap of just moving on, no longer Travelling.

Maybe Mick Jagger was right, telling me on a rainy afternoon in the saddle that "you can't always get what you want, and if you try sometimes, yeah, you just might find, you get what you need."

Maybe I needed this kind of Sierra Leone experience, even if it wasn't what I was looking for, and all I had to do was keep going and not give up.

Perhaps these days were decisive and gave me another wonderful year on the road.

LIBERIA

Paaaauteeeeeeer[1]

ELIO RIVA

October

On a cool evening in Thies, Senegal, I received a phone call from a friend. My best friend.

In a few lines, here's how it went:

"Hi Fil, where will you be in October? I'll catch up with you, and we'll ride together."

"Hey Fred, great! I might be in Liberia in October, but it's not the best place, maybe. I'm expecting some tough days, and there will be a lot of mud, as it will be towards the end of the rainy season. Don't you have another good holiday period? In July, I'll be in Guinea; otherwise, I'll be in Sierra Leone…" I leave time for the last words to travel through the ether.

"No, no. Liberia sounds very attractive to me. I'll check with Elio too. Talk later."

And so it was.

I found myself strangely attracted to three countries: Mali, Angola, and Liberia. I cannot explain how or why, but they really fascinated me. It was enough to read their names, and they sparked the desire for the unknown, for exploration. Unfortunately, I could not get to Mali:

---

[1] An exclamation that connects *pauta*, mud in Piedmontese dialect, and *powder*, fresh snow of excellent quality in the skiing jargon.

a large part of the country, where I would have liked to spend my time, is off-limits, in the hands of jihadist groups. Angola was the highest, most seductive point of the trip. And Liberia was no different. It was an essential moment in the journey, a turning point.

The way I see it, travelling by bike together with other people is challenging. You have to compromise often; you have to make sure that your actions, but above all your thoughts, are aligned. It can often be restricting and hard work, especially when you are tired and it's easy to let off steam and offend.

Not with Elio and Fred. They are mountain buddies. In this environment, whether skiing in deserted valleys or climbing cliff faces, I only go with people I trust. When you have a good relationship with your buddy, you can raise the bar, knowing you can count on your companion at all times. Fred knows that it's enough to keep my stomach full, and I would follow him anywhere. The mountain makes a selection, strengthens bonds. That's why I knew with the two of them, I would have no problems.

Let's unroll the time now, until the beginning of October. The heavy rains are now over, and I am recharging my batteries in Monrovia, the Liberian capital. Here Elio and Fred join me with a long-awaited gift: a new rear wheel, impossible to find in African countries with that size of tyre. Several cracks had opened up on the rim, weakening it. I would not have got very far without their intervention.

On the first day of our journey together, we travel along a paved road, which is really busy as far as the airport. In fact, we pass hundreds of cars parked in its vicinity on the roadside. Entire families and groups of young people walk towards the airport. There is a joyful atmosphere, with laughter and singing cheering the people on their way. Numerous police and military patrols ensure that order is maintained.

I go up to a policeman standing by himself: "Good morning, Sir! Excuse my question, but what's going on? Where are all these people going?"

Visibly pleased with my interest, he replies: "The president is about to land; he'll be here in a minute. All these people are here to welcome him."

It is George Weah, the footballer president who has dedicated his whole life to human rights. He is famous for starting his speeches by chanting "*Amandla!*" and the audience shouts back "*Awethu!*" "Power to us." After leaving the football fields, in recent years, he has built a dizzying political career that has led him to the presidency.

The situation in Liberia is, dare I say it, disastrous. Decades of troubled political life have been sandwiched between two civil wars that left two hundred and fifty thousand dead. The Ebola scourge from 2014 to 2016 and the almost total absence of roads, hospitals, and schools, leave the country at the bottom of the world development rankings.

As soon as he came to power, the president rolled up his sleeves to start emptying the water from the sinking boat using a bucket. After a year, it's clear that this bucket is too small. But the Liberians I have met have repeatedly emphasised their confidence in his means and decisions, hoping that Weah will lead them out of the mud and on the path to a long-lasting development.

And if I were the president, I would start by taking an interest in the roads. I can confidently say I have encountered the worst roads in Africa here, in the Liberian rainforest.

The tarmac ends one day's ride by bike from the airport in the port town of Buchanan. At the edge of the city, where the forest trail begins, there is a house where you can find refreshment and shelter for the night. Four large vehicles with heavy-duty tyres are stationary in the middle of the road. The dirt road begins in front of us, and mud is

---

[2] An incitement borrowed from South Africa's fight to overthrow apartheid.

everywhere, so we opt for a pitstop based on bread, eggs and mayonnaise, and a refill of water while the convoy sets off. "The vehicles never travel alone here. The next few kilometres of the road are *pretty bad*, and they often get stuck in the mud," a man who has just left the building informs us, emphasising the words pretty bad. He is more interested in the convoy than in our presence and stares at the column as it moves away.

He was right. It's only a few kilometres, maybe less than three, but I've never faced so much mud on a bike, or in a car, or on foot... in short, never.

We leave the tarmac, the first hundred meters are flat and in decent condition, but reaching a small rise, we are forced to get off our bikes. There is a muddy pool ahead of me. Making an error of judgement, I set off on foot, pushing my bike towards where the mud seems liquid enough to allow me to get through. With every metre, the mud level increases, up to my knee. Each step becomes even slower and heavier, and finally, my foot gets stuck in the deep mud.

I yank my leg, but my foot comes out without my shoe. It's stuck at the bottom of the pool. I take a deep breath, and I turn towards my friends. I don't get worked up. On the contrary, being in their company makes the episode funny. For some perverse reason, I'm comfortable splashing around in that mud.

"Not this way!" I shout to Elio and Fred, who are enjoying the scene from a roadside clearing. Here the two have found a reasonable way through with little mud, albeit slippery.

A motorcyclist passes me by. He is also clearly struggling on his overloaded motorbike, but looks at me as if to say: *he who hesitates is lost*. He continues slowly and unsteadily until he escapes from this hideous muddy pool. When he has already moved away, I plunge my arm into the mud where my shoe is supposed to be and, trying here and there, I finally fish it out.

I gather all my energy to pull the bike out of the mud and lift it above the level of the quagmire. If possible, I sink even deeper than before, but with a final effort, I reach the track my friends are on. "If it's all like this, we'll die here, crossing Liberia," I gasp with exhaustion, as I catch up with them while they giggle, grateful for this comic relief.

As the days go by, we go deeper and deeper into the jungle, in its grand splendour at the end of the rainy season. The roads are also at their prime after five months of torrential rain. However, the soil is not too clayey, so the numerous pools, some of which are quite deep, are 95 per cent water and only 5 per cent mud. The villages are fewer and farther between, so not many people travel here, and the few motorbikes on the road in the past few days have become even rarer.

On the third day, the roar of the motorbikes disappears, leaving only the forest and its original inhabitants as the soundtrack to our ride. *Strange, we are on the main road of the region, how come there is no traffic at all?* Even the fairly good road surface suggests that fewer vehicles use it, as the greater the traffic, the muddier and more damaged the roads become until they look like ploughed field. On the other hand, in this part of Liberia, our bike wheels zip along the clean surface, and only a few puddles slow us down.

This is not the only good news of the day. The forest also grants us a precious gift. Countless swarms of butterflies are resting in the sun in the middle of the track, and as we get closer, they take flight, allowing us to pass through. They are black, with multiple shades of blue that change with the movement of their wings and shine by reflecting the sun's rays. At the tip of the wings, a linear series of dots echoes the bright cerulean colouring. An enchanting sight that I gladly stop several times to photograph.

In the late afternoon, we meet a man walking along the side of the road, probably on his way back from the field, and we ask him what lies ahead. "The road is broken, an hour's walk from here."

I study the map. About six kilometres away, there *should* be a bridge over the Timbo River. I give Elio and Fred a quizzical look and shrug as if to say: *what do we do?*

The farmer deciphers my look and continues: "When you reach the village of Gbap, you can ask someone to take you across in a pirogue. But you will have to walk a bit to get back on the road.

We thank our impromptu guide, who walks away at a brisk pace in the opposite direction to ours. There are more unspoken questions in the air. If we have to retrace our steps and take another road, the journey would take at least two days longer.

"Let's carry on, get to the village and decide what to do tonight. It's late now, and we won't get anywhere else before sunset," Elio suggests. That seems the most appropriate option for the situation. Elio is the most impulsive of the three of us, but, despite his young age, he's full of wisdom.

Going gently downhill, our wheels bring us to the village of Gbap. The first buildings we come across are the school and the church. They are located at the edge of the town, as often happens in these regions. They are the only concrete structures, but with corrugated metal roofs, obviously.

The next scene sees three cyclists surrounded by an intrigued crowd. Cut. Meeting with the chief of the village. Cut. The three cyclists set up their tents inside the church.

A few minutes later, a man approaches and offers to accompany us to the other side of the river in his pirogue the next morning. As is the case with any vaguely interesting discussion in these parts, kids and adults have gathered around us and are listening with great interest to the conversation. However, the bargaining is quick and listless: we have to continue, and he is interested and eager to lead us.

It has rained during the night, but only a few drops to get rid of the day's excess humidity. I love the gentle pitter-patter of light rain on the metal sheets; I find that it calms my thoughts or sends me to sleep. The rainy season is now at an end, and the violent downpours have now receded into but a damp memory. After packing up our luggage, we leave the church and, quite predictably, a crowd of onlookers is already waiting for us, ready to study our every move.

The procession sets off towards the river with the village chief's son and the three of us in the lead. We walk along a rough path that penetrates the forest, crosses a marshy area, and ends on a steep bank by the restless waters of the Timbo River. A substantial group of people has accompanied us: three white men with bicycles who want to cross the river by pirogue pass by here once in a blue moon.

From the moment they woke up, Elio and Fred were excited about this new different way of travelling. In the previous months, I had already used numerous boats to cross rivers in the forests, so I didn't really think about it. Yet, as soon as I see the pirogue, I become worried. Low and narrow, the boat does not have a high enough hull to lean the bike on.

I am the first one to risk a bath in the waters of Timbo. Two young men steady the pirogue on the shore. With quick steps, I move along the wooden boat, which immediately begins to rock despite their efforts. Two other boys lift the bike, and I help them to get it on the pirogue. As soon as I tilt the bicycle towards the hull, the side bags plunge into the water. The bike would have followed them if we hadn't been able to hold on to it. This is not going to work.

Kneeling on the river bank, a boy suggests something to our Charon, who niftily picks up the bike and lays it down crossways, so it is resting on both sides of the boat. One of the side bags is full of water, but it seems a good compromise solution. He is satisfied.

With his hand, he signals me to crouch down on the bottom of the hull. I obey, but rather nervously. Every movement seems to rock the boat, however controlled it may be. The boys on the bank, on the other hand, are watching the scene with amusement and exchanging a few jokes in dialect before bursting into laughter. I look at them and smile too, trying to relieve some of the tension, but at that moment, I can't manage a convincing laugh.

The river current is particularly strong, yet centuries of experience have shown the locals the best place to get on board. As the boys release the pirogue, it sways lightly and lies motionless in the sheltered bend. I lie down on the bottom of the pirogue while the boatman, sitting at the stern, starts rowing against the current along the bank. Here, the water flows slower than in the middle of the river, so less effort is needed.

The river banks are covered in lush vegetation, but when I look at the boatman, he nods his head to point out the landing place, twenty metres further on. He continues to paddle upstream, with slow but steady strokes, before turning his bow towards the centre of the river. He does not utter a word as we cross the current, and with millimetric precision, the hull reaches the docking point on the other bank. I stand up slowly and turn around, ready to take one step into the water and the next on the bank. Amused, Charon stops me by grabbing my arm, and his dive into the dark water gives me an idea of the depth. It would have been a comical faux pas followed by a clumsy fall into the water. He helps me unload the bike, and while two ladies get on the boat, I put the money in his hand, plus a little extra. He closes his palm without further words, lifts his chin in greeting, and sets off to pick up with my two companions.

Well, that's another obstacle overcome. So far, it's more of a gymkhana than a bike ride, but that's what makes it so interesting. What's next for us? Fred checks the GPS: there are two kilometres as the crow flies between us and the road, beyond the point where the bridge collapsed.

The path goes into the dense rainforest and winds hesitantly, dodging around obstacles. The air is saturated with humidity. So, when I brush against the leaves, all the drops of water that had settled there during the night fall on me. After a few steps, I start sweating profusely again while we struggle to push the bikes over the uneven ground.

I lift the bike to cross the first stream I meet, but the next one proves to be more difficult. Charles, a friend of the boatman, is guiding us through the tangle of the forest, and with a detour, shows me a tree trunk suspended like a bridge between the two banks. Crossing it while pushing the bike requires the skill of a tightrope walker. The moss and the wet wood made it even more challenging. Elio and the boy chance their luck on the trunk with the bike looking precariously unstable. Oh, how I miss those lovely red dirt roads I cycled along over the past few months...

Two hours have gone by since we disembarked, and, finally, the forest opens up in front of us, revealing the road. I am exhausted, my throat is parched, and an itch on my arms brings together all the scratches I've got along the narrow path; my friends are in no better condition. Two kilometres as the crow flies; never was information more misleading.

Over the next two days, the road situation is better. Wide dirt roads, repeatedly bordered by an impenetrable vegetal barrier, lead us through a hilly landscape dotted with small, crumbling villages.

Despite my long stay on the continent, I can't help but be amazed by the immense number of children in the villages. With adults often working in the fields or at the market during the day, these villages seem to be run independently by children. Our interaction with them is repeated five, ten times a day, always in the same way. As soon as the nearest kid to us notices the three foreigners on the saddle, he runs to call anyone within voice range. Many smiling faces pop up from the back of the houses or from their shelter under a tree to say hello and study us. At this point, the friendly pursuit begins. Until their breath fails them, they run after us at great strides, but it is often a steep slope that weakens even the most tenacious who, having reached the top, continue to shout joyfully in our direction, shaking his arms in case one of us turns around. A few kilometres later, a new village, a new chase.

In the late afternoon, a village about ten kilometres away appears on the GPS map and, reassured by the decent condition of the route, we decide to reach it and ask for hospitality. And yet, the forest is preparing a not-so-funny joke for us. A sharp turn to the east, and in a few minutes of pedalling, the road turns into a muddy strip that bisects the otherwise impenetrable forest. It's a different kind of mud from the previous days: the soil here is clayey, and the rains have turned it into a mortar suitable for building, not for travelling over. This fatal combination of mud and pebbles begins to stick to the wheel, and in a few rotations, becomes so thick that it touches the rear part of our bike frame. The wheels stop turning, and we have to drag the bike, which, covered in mud, has now doubled its weight. The progress is exhausting. A few steps, then I have to remove the dirt to allow the wheels to move for a few metres, at least. And repeat.

At the beginning of a climb, my morale sinks even lower. It's now clear that we won't get to the village by light at this pace, with two kilometres covered in an hour. Heat and humidity pervade the still air, so much so that one would sweat standing still; imagine yourself making such a huge effort. Sweat drips incessantly on my eyes, which burn from the constant rubbing, and my glasses are constantly fogged up so that everything looks misshapen and blurry. Our water reserves are almost gone, which poses another major dilemma.

Finally, defeated by the environment, the proposal is to stop, pitch our tent as soon as the terrain permits, and the next morning with new strength, we continue on to the village. The sky is gloomy, and in the distance, we hear the sound of thunder.

These are tense moments. Elio would like to continue through the night, while I would like to be somewhere else right now. In twenty minutes, we are at the top of the rise, which would usually have taken only a few moments, while the light fades more and more. Another day comes to an end, and today we are unprepared to face the night for the first time.

"Enough, let's pitch the tent," Fred concludes. He puts the bike down, starts walking and shortly afterwards calls us in a loud voice; Elio and I set off with the bikes, and we reach him in a rough clearing of a few square metres stolen from the forest. Puzzled, we look at each other, and without further comment, we beat the ground with our feet, to flatten it enough to make a tent fit.

If we had been in a film, what would have happened next would have been the typical twist, turning the plot upside down. Sometimes it happens in reality too. Two people come on the scene from a hidden path in the forest, carrying sacks on their shoulders.

"Hello, guys! What are you doing there?" the older man begins.

Briefly summarising the latest events, we explain to them that we are preparing to spend the night here. "We won't be able to get to the village in time, and we're without water, so it's a pretty shitty situation."

"Farther down on the road, there is a building under construction. And some water."

The drums roll. We exchange fleeting glances; we don't even need to talk. None of us wanted to spend a night in the mud, under a storm.

"Come on, we'll give you a hand with the bicycles," the boy continues before we've even posed the question as he leans the sack against a fallen log. "I'll pick this up in the morning."

A surreal conversation in a surreal setting. There are now five of us, pushing three bikes: we have a numerical advantage, good. With their help, despite the approaching darkness, we reach the house of our salvation, located a few dozen metres above a lagoon of stagnant water. We thank our two saviours, who set off towards the village and disappear into the night. We look at each other for a moment, all three of us exhausted.

"Great, we have shelter for the night, and now let's make a big plate of pasta!"

"Yes, but where's the water?" retorts Elio. I check around the house, but there is no well nor a cistern.

"I haven't found anything... Guys, what about that pond we passed earlier? What do you think of it?"

"Don't even joke about it. We'll catch all the viruses in Liberia if we drink that water."

"Listen, let's boil it, and we can also use Elio's purifying tablets. You said you have them with you, right?"

"Yes," he replied uncertainly. Besides, we've been without water for hours, and we're all exhausted. We must drink something, or we won't even be able to eat, with our mouths so dry. I offer to go down to the pond, but it takes me twice as long to retrace the same steps as it is now dark.

It's time to test in practice all the purification methods we know: in succession, carbon filter, boiling and tablets. The latter take at least thirty minutes to work, and, adamant on this point, Elio sets his stopwatch. Fred goes down to the lake to clean the mud off himself while the two of us remain seated, with little energy left. We look at the bottle, then at the clock and at the bottle again. It's frustrating. "I would have drunk it straight from the pond. I'm so thirsty, Elio."

Fred comes back with another guy—how much traffic is there in this forest at night? —who tells us that he's also stuck in the mud on his motorbike. He still has a long way to go to get home, and when he saw the lights of our headlamps break through the darkness, he stopped.

"Do you have any water?" We exchange distressed looks, but let's not defy karma. Two strangers appearing out of nowhere in the forest have just helped us get here. It would be at least inappropriate not to help this guy. Therefore, we watch as our bottle of water empties relentlessly into the motorcyclist's stomach. He didn't even wait for the half-hour to elapse.

The sun is shining in the morning, and our morale is back on track after a night of profound rest. We have a quick breakfast and go down to the pond to clean the hardened mud off the gears and wheels. None of us has commented on the yellowish colour and cloudiness of the water we drank the night before.

We laugh a lot when we see the last stretch of road: not a puddle of mud, smooth and easy all the way to the village. Here we are warmly welcomed by the usual group of curious kids. They inform us that the only place where we can get something to eat and fill our water bottles is at the health centre. A couple of them take us there and introduce us to the nurses.

With a hundredweight of boiled plantains for breakfast and bottles full of water, we are lying on the lawn, ready to go again. Each time, I marvel at how little the body needs to recover: a short rest, adequate nourishment, and it's back in great shape. We live in a fantastic body, a real masterpiece of nature. You can drain it, require it to make exceptional efforts, and drive it to the point of exhaustion, yet all it takes is a little care and, above all, respect to get it back working perfectly again.

The unexpected beauty of the path that leads away from the village and back into the forest amazes me. It's narrow enough to allow one motorbike to pass at a time and clear enough of brushwood to allow us to let our bikes run wild as we lose height, lulling us along the winding, elegant path that takes us to Gwen Creek. A couple of "Yeaaaaah" break the otherwise monotonous melody of the forest.

On the other side of the bridge, we enter Nimba County, and the vegetation changes abruptly. It is no longer the gloomy rainforest of the previous days but a pleasant woodland interspersed with palm trees and banana plantations. One village quickly follows another. At first glance, they are all similar, but there is often something that allows us to distinguish and remember each one.

We have reached the village of Yeagoan, which consists of about fifty mud and palm-leaf huts scattered here and there in the dim light of the sparse trees. The village chief welcomes us with open arms, the villagers rush to meet us. A young boy hands us each a coconut, as his way of welcoming us. This sweet liquid rehydrates the body and alleviates fatigue. While we drink, the boy is already cutting up three more nuts with his machete. They show us the village, we pick up some bananas here, some oranges there, everyone wants to give us a present. It seems that they don't want to let us go anymore, or maybe it's us who are attracted by the authenticity of the place. Here I feel a great sense of harmony between man and nature, and also among the inhabitants.

I have few regrets, that's not how I am, and those few are almost always short-lived. And yet, among the unsaid and *un-done* things that I happen to think about in later moments, not having stopped for longer in a village is perhaps at the top of the list, which is rather meagre, to be honest. On the trip so far, my breaks have always been in the city, either to relax or to get a visa. If I could, I would go back to that village to stay, for a week or more. I remember the hugs of the people, the warmth of the smiles. It was one of the most pleasant and meaningful moments up to that point. I was at home, here, among these people in the Liberian forest. But a journey of this kind is made up of an endless succession of places and situations, which become stopping points and dwellings, or as Magris writes, "fleeting stops and roots that make you feel at home in the world.[3]" The welcome they gave us, but above all, the energy and positivity that these people transmitted to me, had lasting benefits, and I will not forget them.

We finally reach Tappita Town. On paper, it was a three-day journey. On the mud, it was twice that. At first, it was a dot on the map, then as time passed and we went through remote villages, our fantasies about Tappita had thrived. It would be a pleasant town with a few bars and a supermarket to refresh us. The locals whetted our appetite by extolling the big town. The last few kilometres of the road flew by, buoyed by anticipation.

---

[3] Magris, Claudio. *Journeying*. Yale University Press, 2018.

Tappita is a small village, not much bigger than the previous ones; on market days, the surrounding province's population gathers, hoping to find a few more luxuries on the stalls than in their own villages. There should be electricity in Tappita, but a fault caused by the rains has interrupted the power supply indefinitely. The hotel owner where we are staying guarantees that as soon as the generator is repaired, he will turn it on and we will have light in our rooms. We leave four days later, and the technician still hasn't turned up. In Tappita, there is a large hospital, the largest outside the capital. But to get there, one has to take the high road, which is only accessible for cars with four-wheel drive during the rainy season. So, the sick get to the hospital on the ubiquitous Indian and Chinese motorbikes. In Tappita, we didn't get as much rest as we had hoped.

We are not far from the Ivory Coast border: forty kilometres on the high road and a dozen on a secondary track. The main road turns out to be an obstacle course, with constant ups and downs that have created natural pools in cahoots with gravity. Mud pools, of course.

The incessant passing of vehicles has carved deep furrows, making it back-breaking for cyclists and even more so for cars to travel along the road. At the end of one long climb, the trench is so deep that a lorry has plunged all the way into it. We push our bikes through the vegetation at the side of the road, but the traffic is blocked in both directions. Will they pull him out? I don't know. For the time being, some young businessmen from the nearby village have arrived with a stall and are taking advantage of the small crowd of motorists to sell sachets of water and biscuits—home delivery service station.

Unexpectedly, the last few kilometres to the frontier are in better condition than the previous roadway. In less than an hour, we could be at the border, except that some hustle and bustle in the bush attract our attention. Beyond the first line of trees, a clearing opens up on our right, where dozens of people are hard at work. We have stumbled upon one of the many illegal gold mines scattered throughout the region.

In spite of our arrival, almost everyone is still working, except for a young man who approaches us in a friendly manner and says his name is Opon. The life of these people is tough, needless to say. They work up to sixteen hours a day with ready-made equipment, and with a bit of luck, they might find a few golden grains. A gram would already be a lot, which would earn them thirty dollars. Otherwise, they will go home with empty pockets.

Liberia has always been one of the biggest exporters of gold, along with neighbouring Sierra Leone, Ghana, Mali and to a lesser extent Burkina Faso. With the end of the second civil war (2003), numerous foreign investors arrived in a few years, led by the Chinese. Large investments have been made in the construction of mines, thus providing many jobs for the local population, as well as for people from neighbouring countries. Alongside the large multinational mines, smaller, unofficial ones have sprung up; there, lots of people go to seek their fortune.

Like Victor, a thirty-year-old who came to the area because of the favourable hearsay of his compatriots who had got rich doing this work. Now Victor stands at the bottom of his pit, it's five metres deep. He has a protective helmet in his hand, which he uses to remove the water that fills the pit. I can only wish them good luck as they search for a golden needle in the haystack.

At the entrance to Côte d'Ivoire, the roads are once again in good condition, and the last few kilometres with my friends fly by. What was it like travelling with them?

They helped me a lot by joining me at this point in the journey. First of all, because of the difficulties I was encountering. Alone, it would have been much more complicated, and sometimes the spurring on of a friend can make all the difference. We were stuck in the mud in the forest, the night was approaching, and the storm was coming fast in the distance. A shout and some encouragement helped to pull me out of the mud.

Crossing Liberia proved to be one of the purest and most intense moments of the whole trip, and I am happy to have lived this adventure together with them. Sharing thoughts, smiles and impressions improved the experiences, taking the sense of Journey to a higher level. It becomes a simple, pure Journey like the one we read about in those books that make us dream. There are no expectations, no more plans or *things to see*. There are three friends, a forest, and a road. All that we have encountered along the way becomes an inestimable wealth. Intimate and lasting.

Happiness is only real when shared... is this true?

IVORY COAST

Je vous remercie mon Dieu, de m'avoir créé Noir,
Je porte le Monde depuis l'aube des temps
Et mon rire sur le Monde,
dans la nuit
crée le jour.

BERNARD B. DADIE,
JE VOUS REMERCIE MON DIEU

October

Man is an unusual town, at least in these regions. It lies among green mountains, in the *Dix-huit Montagnes* region, and has a relaxed and jovial atmosphere. Looking north, among the luxuriant forests, Man's Tooth stands out. It's the mountain symbol of the city, which with its two twin pillars quietly observes the flow of life at its feet.

My friend Ivan and I chose Man as our meeting place. He is now facing torrential rains in northern Guinea and is one cycling week from the border. I can't wait to hug him! After a virtual relationship that has lasted six months, we will finally meet. In recent months our calls increased, and a pause on the roadside became a good opportunity to send a WhatsApp voice message. I could transfer any event, thoughts, or emotion into a message to him without the need for filters or censorship.

The desire for these chats grew little by little – there was no better dialogue. It could not be any other way. We shared the same dream and basic needs, and our common desire to explore and get completely engaged created this intense friendship. I was having similar experiences as Ivan. By talking to him, we could have two visions of the same event. Sometimes it was not even necessary to relate the whole anecdote, but, expansive as he is, Ivan loves to recount. In his stories, I find all the minutiae as well as his own insights, which he colours with a strong Umbrian accent. His kilometre-long voice messages became my favourite podcast when I was in the saddle.

Getting to know him was a joy. How nice to have a friend like him, he is a person I don't really know, but at the same time, he's so close to me. My behaviour often depends on the person in front of me or the environment I find myself in. With one guy, I can't joke about something; with another, the relationship is not deep enough to talk about other topics. I do things because of variables—sometimes unconsciously—dictated by a previous story, by moments lived together or thoughts already shared. With Ivan, it doesn't happen. Ours is the story of a great friendship written on a clean sheet, which so far has no boundaries. Our relationship in the first months was an anomalous but exquisite experience. It seemed I was travelling in parallel, once on my own journey, and secondly on his journey. In some way, we travelled together. Despite our bodies being thousands of kilometres away, the souls pedalled side by side. Ours were solo journeys, but travelled together.

I take advantage of the wait to visit the city and its surroundings. Walking through the streets, I come across some weaving and handicraft workshops, where the famous traditional masks are produced, as attractive as they are frightening. Besides the masks, jewels and accessories of various kinds are exhibited on the stalls; the artisans explain they are often used during ritual dances.

On the roadside, vast carpets of drying cocoa beans can be seen. This is the leading business in the city, but, as often happens when the money starts to circulate, several problems have arisen. These affect not only the *Dix-huit Montagnes* but the whole Ivory Coast.

It's important to understand that this country is the largest producer of cocoa in the world. Over the years, driven by this profitable business, more and more farmers have started growing this crop, drastically reducing the area covered by virgin forest. Some reports cite an 80 per cent reduction[1]; these are alarming numbers. Around Man and throughout the West of the country, there are several protected forests and national parks. Yet, incited by large profit margins, farmers have also taken over these lands, destroying the vegetation, or at least part of it. The cocoa plant does not like direct light and grows well in the undergrowth, sheltered by the forest giants. Walking in the mountains, away from the more touristy paths, I came across several plantations of this type, invisible from the outside.

Once harvested, *pisteurs*[2] carry the cocoa pods to the collection centres, including Man and other nearby towns. Here, intermediaries handle sales directly to the big chocolate companies, and through the port of San Pedro (and Abidjan), the cocoa is exported all over the world. Unfortunately, the price of cocoa has fallen considerably in recent years, reducing even further the income for growers, whose average salary is now about fifty cents a day.

Cocoa brings with it another great problem. As I wrote before, the lands for cultivation are limited, and the cocoa tree needs the shade of the forests for profitable growth. Thus, the *slash&burn* technique is becoming unviable. Farmers increasingly grow cocoa land that has already been cultivated, and which needs fertilising and replanting. This leads to a higher demand for manpower: more and more children are involved in cocoa plantations. It is estimated that two million children are working in this sector[3], scattered between Ghana and the Ivory Coast. They're not only Ivorians and Ghanaians but also migrants from neighbouring countries, mainly Burkina Faso.

---

[1] Mighty Earth. *"Chocolate's Dark Secret"*, 2018.
[2] Literally *bloodhound*, they are those who transport the fruit from the plantations to the collection centres.
[3] ILPI. *"Child Labour in the West African Cocoa Sector"*, 2015.

The week waiting for my friend and future colleague to join me passes quickly, between a walk in the mountains and a visit to the city's excellent pastry shop. I found a room in a Catholic centre, a secluded place at the base of the mountains and away from city traffic chaos. Mine is a small room, but my tent would fit in it at least four times, so by my standards, maybe it's not that small. There are two beds, two bedside tables, a washbasin, and a wardrobe. A dusty Bible sits on the bedside table. I pick it up and open a page at random. I don't read, I hold the book up to my nose and inhale. It smells like all the other Bibles in the world, with the whiff, albeit muffled by dust, of a used book. Yet I remain with my face between the pages for a long time. I don't remember the last time I had a book in my hand, and yes, I'm one of those people who sniffs books before reading them.

The back door opens onto a small balcony with a shower, which in turn overlooks the woods. The city begins a few hundred meters further on. I can catch the sounds if I pay attention, but a breeze of wind is enough for the leaves' rustle to cut me off.

I can get to the entrance by following a path of stepping stones placed on a well-kept lawn. The hard stones are like a bridge spanning a green lake. But I soon get off the stepping stones and walk barefoot on the lawn. I love the prickly sensation of freshly cut grass, and I don't dare tell you about how heavenly it smells. This is another first in a long time. I am sure that the last time I walked on a lawn was at my parents' house. I don't forget these details.

On a damp evening, where the cold grass bends under its own weight, and some blades stick to the soles of your feet and between your toes, Ivan arrives aboard a 4x4, with the bike in the back. I recognise him from a distance: he is wearing an aerodynamic cycling suit; a fisherman's hat covers thick curly hair and an un-aerodynamic beard of a similar length. He is weak from a high fever, and to avoid his visa running out in Guinea, he got a lift here. Ivan now needs a lot of rest.

We share the room, which is not small even though there are two of us now. Ivan is still ill three days later. Moreover, I get sick too. There they are, the two West Africa bicycle *conquistadores*, stuck in bed with a raging fever and a headache that muffles sounds and colours. The days go by slowly. Each one is lying in his bed tossing and turning, looking for relief from always lying in the same positions of convalescence.

Finally, Ivan gets better. One afternoon he shows up aboard a jeep on his return from an excursion to the city. He is clutching a tray of pastries: cream doughnuts, *pain au chocolat*, and other delicacies. "Ivan, my friend. Who is this guy with you?"

"Search me, Fili! I asked for a ride, and he came back here to eat with us."

Thanks to the custard and sugar therapy, I am also beginning to regain my strength. It's been over two weeks since I arrived in Man, and it's time to move on. Yet, our bikes need urgent care, and we are still weakened by the after-effects of our illness. What to do? We decide to go to Abidjan, the main city, by bus. There, we can fully recover and repair the bicycles.

We spend another week enjoying the vices of the city: a beer, a real Neapolitan pizza, and a few days at the beach. Now, after this long pause, our legs are eager to get on the pedals, so are our minds.

On the eighth day, I am done. I need to get going. I go to Ivan's place—he is staying with someone else—to inform him of the imminent departure, but I find he is a *prisoner* of his hosts. She is out on errands and has shut Ivan in the house by locking the metal bars that keep the flat safe.

Ivan can only speak to me through the bars, but I infer that he still wants a few more days of rest before resuming. I can understand, we both have cycled for a long time in Guinea under the rain, and I imagine the tiredness that still wears him out. Looking at him on the other side of the bars, I remember my days of complete idleness in Conakry. I say a sad goodbye, and we hug, the two of us plus the bars of the cell. It is just a matter of days before we'll meet again, but it seems we are going to be apart for ages.

Going through the Ivory Coast towards the north, the traveller has the pleasant sensation of a gradual return to the savannah. We can imagine this country as made up of many horizontal bands of different vegetation but blurred outlines. Dense forests and endless banana fields accompany the view for a hundred kilometres. Gently, imperceptibly, the tallest trees thin out more and more. The vegetation is dense, of course, but the treetops are closer to the ground.

A mighty tree stands out in this dense forest, a relative of the baobab tree: *Monsieur Le Fromager*. Unlike the sacred plant, this oddly-named tree has not quarrelled with God, and its vigorous branches are stretched to the sky fifty meters above the ground. Impressive buttresses sweep towards the soil from the mammoth thorny trunk: these are the roots, coming out of the ground even for a few meters like large blades and giving stability to this giant of the forest.

The next band to the north is the *brousse*, the bush. Here, trees no more than ten meters high intertwine their trunks with thorny shrubs, and the shades of green fade as the traveller proceeds to the north. The shrubs on the edge of the road are red, red like the clouds of dust from passing vehicles. Slowly, that vibrant green of the southern forests, so luxuriant at the end of the rainy season, vanishes.

I return to cycling on a dirt track after several weeks of tarmac and forced breaks. I feel at home again. This is paradoxical, considering that I have just left a house after twenty-five days, and, from today onwards, I no longer have a real abode. Yet on that red earth road, through wild vegetation, where sudden clearings announce traditional villages, I feel at ease. I have gone back to doing what I like best.

At the edge of a rubber plantation, two kids play with sticks on the track in front of me, brandishing them like swords. As I materialise out of the *brousse*, they stare at me, scared, before running away. They run at breakneck speed until they disappear into the courtyard of a house.

I ride into the village and find the two kids now sheltered by their mother's skirt; she is rightly worried by this vandal who has terrorised her children. Actually, the vandal is smiling and greeting the lady and all the other inhabitants he meets on the way.

The fearless kids now take up the chase with great howls of laughter until they catch up with the cyclist. He is now leaning his bike against the well and filling his water bottles. He drinks the whole bottle in one gulp and now extracts something from the bag hanging from the handlebars. What will it be? He says these are called dates. The two kids don't know them and are tempted to refuse what the cyclist is handing them. "Try them; they are good. They grow on palm trees." The older one takes them, divides them, and gives half to his little brother.

His teeth brush against the fruit's glossy surface, nipping off a morsel that would not feed an ant.

The expression on his face is uncertain. Somewhat reluctantly, however, the kid gulps down the date.

"You like?"

"Mmmh," laconically comments the older brother. For the western palate, a fruit rich in sugars like the date is tempting. But for the villagers, who feed on tubers, grains, and leaves, it has a strange flavour, which they are not used to.

"Here, have some more." This time the kid takes them but hands them over to his buddy, and then runs away.

In the next village, shortly after passing a school, some elders sitting in the shade of a majestic tree invite me to join them. I travelled a few kilometres only, but the overwhelming heat again forces me to another stop. Furthermore, the elders are entertaining themselves with palm wine, and they promptly offer some to me.

"Where are you going with this loaded bike?" one of them asks me with an affectionate expression. He seemed glad to give me a bit of a break as I clearly looked exhausted.

"*Moarè oh[4]!* I'm going to Yaffo, to the market." *And heaven knows if I'll be able to find some fruit.*

I must have seemed quite savvy, and expert of these countries as the old man leaves me flabbergasted: "And what are you selling?"

I have an overloaded bicycle, and I go to a market. I think back to the rare cyclists I met on these roads, so far away from the big daily markets. Here, today I could be one of those merchants who pass from village to village on a bicycle, full of bags and fabrics and sometimes with a pallet used to display goods. What could I go to the market for except to sell something?

Here comes a horde of students running towards us. The cheering crowd surrounds me. The teacher behind them calls them back: "Go back to class, go back to class!" But at a nod from the elder—as if to say "let them stay, everything is okay"—he falls silent, indeed, says hello.

These children are tremendously curious. "What is this for?" "What is this?" "Can I play the trumpet?" "Will you leave me your bike?" and so on. I take several photographs of this well-meaning assault, and they sing me a lovely welcome song. Only then do they obey their teacher and go back to school, satisfied by this break.

Sitting at a small restaurant counter on the side of the road, I am fascinated by the tall girl with a shiny *90 per cent dark chocolate* complexion, my favourite, while she sautées strips of *viande de brousse*—game—for me. If it is common to find pheasant, hare, or wild boar meat on your plate in Italian cuisine, it is equally common to taste antelope, porcupine, rat or pangolin in African cooking. It is often better not to ask and hope that it is well cooked, whatever meat it is.

I am lost in her bare shoulders, beaded with sweat from somewhere under her long black hair, when a little girl peers out from the counter, probably her daughter. The little one will be three years old, more or

---

[4] *Good morning*, in the Baoulé language.

less, two big black eyes and two round cheeks that I can't help but pinch. She looks at me and laughs. She laughs out loud. Every now and then, she opens her eyes, shiny with tears, she stares at me and starts again laughing. "Machetteridiii?[5]" I say jokingly with a strong Roman accent—a contagious laugh. Her mum is cooking, and she sometimes observes me, with an expression that includes embarrassment, amusement, and heartfelt apologies.

Pampered by this family atmosphere, I think that the Ivory Coast has won me over in a few days of cycling, with all its simplicity and serenity. The ride goes ahead relaxed, without particular hitches and therefore so enjoyable.

I reach the village of Babakro as sunset approaches. It is usually a good time, people have already returned from the fields, and I can meet the village chief. But this evening, he has not yet returned, so a boy invites me to sit in his courtyard waiting for him.

We chat for a few minutes, and the elder shows up. The tools of his work still resting on his shoulder. I get up to shake his hand, hardened and made calloused by the daily work with the hoe. He does not speak French, only the *Baoulé* dialect, which is widespread throughout the country's central region. Kodissou, the boy who welcomed me, volunteers to be my interpreter to keep things simple. I thank him very much for his offer, especially after my long day in the saddle.

We move towards the communal hut. The elder, like every labourer of this region working in the *brousse*, wears rubber work boots. I regularly hear stories of attacks: the cobra, the black mamba and even the fascinating green mamba all inhabit these lands. We arrive in the big hut, and the old man sits on his chair, pointing to the bench in front of him. All around the building, many from the village gather and chat loudly, both adults and children. The elder begins to speak, and thirty people fall silent instantly.

---

[5] Pronounced in Italian, it triggered further laughter from the little girl. It means: *What are you laughing at?*

Why do I spend my afternoons looking for the village chief, sometimes waiting for hours for his return? Out of respect or cordiality?

The organisation within traditional societies is based on a complex network of relationships, structured into groups, with the *family* at the basis. Taken as a whole, all these family ties make up a *clan*. Several clans which share the same dialect and similar traditions make up the *tribe*.

Each group has a leader; the father will generally be responsible for the family[6]. He is the guarantor with the chief of the next group up, and so on. Going up the hierarchy, the power of tribal leaders becomes more and more generic, while at the extended family level, the chief has more specific powers according to the context. Hence, a village chief has authority over the land and resolves any disputes on land use or exploitation; he oversees the economic management of the group's assets; he acts as a judge in family disputes and, if necessary, imposes sanctions to control the behaviour of all members. He is often joined by elected elders to help him manage the village.

The village chief is also a judge who enforces specific laws. Which? Unwritten rules, obligations handed down orally for thousands of years, that have been able to keep abreast with the current context. "It is customary that...," not: "the law says that..."

I find the administration of the law (what we call *The Law*) interesting. *The Law* did indeed come to African countries under colonialism, but it did not wholly eradicate traditional law. Nowadays, especially in rural societies, *civil* and *customary* law coexist. Almost always, however, the latter is applied first: after all, it is the legacy and enlightenment from past generations.

A fundamental aspect is, in fact, its conciliatory nature. The village chief will attempt to guide both parties to reach a peaceful

---

[6] The ancestors also belong to the family, as do those who have not yet been born. The surviving members must not forget the deceased, because they support and guide them. Otherwise, misfortune could befall them or their relatives.

compromise, thus preserving social balance. Sometimes, however, sanctions are applied; in the most severe cases, they can exclude the *criminal* from the community.

Therefore, the chief must be aware of whatever happens in his region of responsibility. That's why the traveller will pay homage to the village chief and then ask for authorisation to stay for the night in his region. From that moment on, the responsibility for the actions and the traveller's safety are in the village chief's hands.

That afternoon, I am sitting in front of Koffi, this is the chief's name, waiting to present my case. I speak, Kodissou translates, the old man listens and nods, all the others are silently waiting for his response. *Who knows what Koffi will decide? This foreigner looks like a good guy. I'd let him stay.*

I've never received a refusal, as a matter of fact. Hence, for me, it's a formality, yet there is tension in the air: it seems a crucial decision. "Yes, sure, you will sleep in the big hut in the square, where we met before, okay?" Kodissou translates the old man's words. Nods of approval also from the stands. The wanderer breaks the daily monotony of the evenings here in the village.

I get up, Koffi gets up and offers me his calloused hand and, with a friendly smile, welcomes me. "*Bienvenue*," in French. "*Amun khwa*." Thanks. The laughter following this exchange of pleasantries welcomes me into the family.

In the meantime, the mosquitoes appeared, the bastards! Fighter-bombers on reconnaissance attack your feet, ankles, hands. Wherever they can find a little flesh to penetrate with their sting. After a year of travelling, I still haven't learned how to foil their attack. So, for the whole year, I have been slapping myself here and there until I give up. It's time to put on long-sleeved clothes and pitch the tent. I go back to get my bike; the group follows me.

The preparation of the encampment always arouses great interest, especially when I build *la maison*. I like to ask the kids to help me. Those I invite are often too shy and don't come. But there is always someone more curious who steps forward. And then even the others join us, as we work under their friends' curious eyes.

At nightfall, the women are preparing dinner. They are sitting on a chair in front of their houses, with the fire lit under the stockpot resting on a tripod. The women do not move away from their pot, except when I take the gasoline stove out of my bags to cook. Then, some get up and approach. It is probably the oldest who suggests I don't need to cook, as they are already preparing dinner for everyone. Menu of the evening: *foufou avec sauce claire*. Yam polenta with aubergine sauce. I put my stove back.

While we eat, illuminated by the lights of mobile phones, I ask Koudissou if the village chief's name is actually Koffi. He reeled off a list of names, which I'm not sure I understood and memorised. Kodissou repeats his full name; I forget it a few moments later, but Koffi is on the list. Good, I didn't make any gaffes. "In our tribe, the *Baoulè*, Koffi is a name given to a child born on a Saturday."

"Interesting! What about your name, then?"

"Kodissou means: *If the good Lord wills*. Mum lost two children before me. Now I am the firstborn."

If the good God wills, I'll sleep well tonight, even if I'm in the village square.

But I guess God got distracted that night. There was a constant coming and going of people who came to say hello or just to peer, even after I had holed up in my tent. Koudissou is at home, his music blaring. I recognise several of the songs that are played. The Ivorians love music, and in every *maquis*[7], they broadcast the latest hits, over and over again. Koudissou's is not a *maquis*, yet the CD runs all night, on repeat. I look at the time, it's almost two o'clock. *When does he go to sleep?*

I go knock on the door, but nobody answers. "Koudissou, Koudissou!" Nothing. *Could he really have fallen asleep with this music?*

---

[7] Open-air restaurants where you can enjoy the basic dishes of Ivorian cuisine, or simply sip a beer while listening to good music.

Lucky old him! I return to the tent and continue the sleepless night. Miraculously I manage to sleep, but it doesn't last long.

In fact, at five o'clock, the muezzin shouts from the mosque: "Wake up. Prayer time!!!" More elegantly and formally, but the meaning of the chant is that. The music is now silent.

In the unexpected silence of the morning, men drag themselves out of doors towards the mosque, exchanging whispered greetings. But the damage is done. The goats are free. Roosters crow. With the first lights, women and girls come out into the courtyard to sweep the ground; lastly, the kids appear. My dark circles and I wriggle out of the tent when the kids are already gathered around there, waiting. I dismantle the encampment quickly, and before setting off to greet the village chief, I look for Koudissou. "He is asleep," declares his mother.

I go slowly along the trail that winds elegantly in the low forest, enjoying the pleasant morning coolness. A few hours later, I emerge from the half-light of the thick bush and look out into the great emptiness and dazzling light of the savannah. It is a vast steppe and reflects the white light of the midday sun.

Moving north towards the Sahel, the temperature has increased more and more in recent days. The early afternoon is no longer suitable for cycling. A handful of houses overlook the track. Not a soul is around, given the time. Nonetheless, I find a restaurant. Inside, two old men are sharing apparently funny stories, bathing them in beer. A girl with generous curves and elegant features, with a baby swaddled on her back, looks into the room. Beans or beans, what do you prefer? *Up to you.*

The restaurant is a shack with walls made of wooden planks alternating with empty spaces. They guarantee shade and adequate ventilation. Now satiated, I lie down on the bench with the idea of resting for *five minutes*, and crash out instantly.

Upon awakening, there is silence in the room. Considering all the delightful din of the previous day (and night), it is an enchanting silence. A soft breeze cools the room. The pretty girl who served me is now lying on the floor on a mat, resting. The baby, with his buttocks deliciously in the air, sleeps next to her. I love the quiet of the siesta, everything is still, but there is no tension in that inertia. It is a pleasant stillness, which satisfies the spirit, transmits tranquillity.

One of the two elders is left in the room. When he notices I am awake, he nods and continues to weave fibres. He is creating a small basket. For a long time, I look at him, captivated by his movements' precision and repetitiveness.

The baby has awakened, and his crying breaks the spell. I put on my cycling gloves, say goodbye to the mother who is now breastfeeding the baby, and step into the Ivorian furnace.

Going along the torrid savannah, I try to imagine what a bike trip in these regions could have been like a hundred years earlier. Probably an encounter with some wild animal, if not with an elephant, would have been quite normal. Today, a traveller only meet cows, squirrels, and chickens. As the name suggests, the Ivory Coast has been one of the major trading points for ivory in past centuries. The latest sad estimates point to a residual elephant population of just a few hundreds. Only in recent years have policies been deployed to preserve these remaining specimens.

Here we are. Ivan will finally join me! I reach the mission of Dabakala in the middle of a parish feast; a tipsy priest, Father Raul, comes to greet me. He was called by a young man in a suit that's supposed to be stylish, and shouts, so his voice carries over the music: "Let's talk afterwards, come to the party now, let's have fun."

It seems to be the same CD that my friend Koudissou played. The songs are so similar. The square is full of people dancing while under the white awnings the same number are chatting and drinking, but still keeping a close eye on the dance floor. Father Raul introduces me to all the guests and invites me to stay, sitting next to him. Bock beer, my favourite around here. It may be the tiredness, it may be the beer, which I was no longer used to after a year spent in Muslim countries, but my head is now spinning to the beat of the music. I remain seated until the end of the party, enjoying the chaotic bustle of people and confused conversations blurred by loud music.

For me, the Catholic mission is the Grand Hotel: a quiet room, a comfortable bed, good food. If I'm lucky there also is a washing machine, or else someone always willing to wash my dusty clothes. This is the ideal place to rest seriously after a week in the *brousse*, I think, as I lie on a comfy mattress and shielded by a mosquito net, fixed with a hook to the ceiling.

Ivan joins me on the following day. In front of an appetising dish of *garba* with a side of *attiéké*, fried tuna with a fine cassava couscous, he tells me about the adventures of the day. "A py-thon! You cannot believe how big. Two meters. He was there, right by the roadside. Crazy. Oh, Fili, I was shitting myself. You can't imagine how much!"

I love listening to him when he starts talking in that strong Umbrian accent. He would make a normal day-in-the-office seem exciting, let alone his close encounter with a snake in the bush.

Tomorrow, we start pedalling together. Two Italians, conquering the savannah!

But on the first day, we don't conquer much. We advance slowly. Although we have been talking to each other every day for a year now, we have so much to tell each other that the landscape takes a back seat. Around noon, we notice a problem on his bike: the bike's internal hub gear is leaking oil. Ivan would need a wrench to tighten the nut. *No bueno.*

At Bandarama village, we ask for a mechanic. A guy has some tools, and he could fix the problem. I have no worries now but hunger. "Is there a restaurant or a *maman* who prepares something to eat around here?" I ask the clerk of a booth.

He exchanges a glance with the other people sitting on the front porch of the shop, and with an apologetic tone, he replies: "No, unfortunately, there isn't."

What happens in the next moments is another of the numerous examples of African people's greatness. Hardly a minute passes, and a boy who had witnessed our arrival returns with a bowl full of *fufu* and peanut sauce. Shortly after, he comes back with another pot, *viande de brousse* stew. Ivan and I look at each other, amazed. We know it is the food prepared for him and his family, although he denies it. "*No, no, ça c'est pour vous.*" After a year, this continent still knows how to surprise me. And it will do it countless other times. This is also why I am here. Such sights fill my memory with wonder.

A great heat accompanies us on the path between cashew plantations and cotton fields. I haven't seen cotton before. I find it funny to imagine that cotton wool is made from these plants, one meter tall or so. The plant is widespread mainly in the pre-Sahelian belt, in countries such as Benin, Burkina Faso and the Ivory Coast, which is the third African producer.

We pass by the side of a yellow cart loaded with cotton. A little kid is pressing it with his feet to squeeze it. I cannot help myself but laugh out loud, associating the image with that of Adriano Celentano treading grapes in the film *Il Bisbetico Domato*. The young Celentano gazes around absent-mindedly and continues dancing while friendly greetings resonate from the field behind him.

Regardless of the midday heat, this family continues the harvest without stopping. The price of cotton is volatile, but at the moment, a kilo of cotton is worth about € 0.40. Over a whole day, they gather five kilos. The whole family participates in the harvest, including a mother with a newborn baby in the sling on her back. She is drenched in sweat dripping from her forehead. She gives us just a fleeting glance without interrupting her picking of wads which she throws into her jute sack.

The other family members smile as Ivan and I improvise a scene and pretend to collect cotton with them. *Aaah, les touristes!*

Ferkessédogou welcomes us with its colours and scents. The next morning Ivan will continue to Korhogo and the border with Mali while I will enter Burkina Faso. Goodbye has come too soon.

The city streets are even more animated in the evening than during the day. Shops and stalls are open till late, and Ivorians love to stroll or go to the *maquis* to have a beer and listen to good music. Walking on the main street, an intense aroma of roast meat makes my nostrils open wide.

"Ivan, how about a nice *mouton*?"

"No, Fili, I'm not hungry. But if you want some, I'll just take a small piece to keep you company."

Following our sense of smell, we reach a grill with several pieces of meat roasting on it. Just the fragrance makes my mouth water.

"Listen, I'll take the thigh, and we can share it?"

"Okay, but I only eat a small piece of it." It's probably more than a kilo but, in an instant, it disappears down our stomachs, and only the bones with a few shreds of meat remain on the plate. Exquisite, I lick my fingers before taking a sip of beer. In the open-air *maquis*, some laughter resounds among the notes of a dance song.

"Encore?"

"And you really need to ask, Fili?" It's so rare to eat so well!

I'm sad this morning, and I suppose Ivan is, too, I gather from his unusual silence. Getting together in this way, two travellers, moreover Italians, sharing a wonderful world like this, was an immense gift for both of us.

We leave the mission that hosted us for two days, and we have a hearty breakfast. Sandwich with spaghetti, eggs, beans, and mayonnaise. "Give me two, thank you." The time to say goodbye is coming; it is at the end of the sandwich. It is an intense and prolonged hug. We transmit tons of energies to each other and many unspoken words. I take a step back; Ivan has shining eyes. How I would like to continue cycling with my brother!

I turn and jump into the saddle. Ivan does the same. After a few metres, he stops and shouts: "*VIVA L' ITALIA!*" *It's a goodbye until the next time, Brother, we will meet again soon.*

It gives me strength to know that, around the world, there are other members of this small *sect*, the cycle travellers. They are all tracing large brushstrokes around the globe; inevitably, they will end up crossing each other sooner or later. Each has his own journey, each different. But always with one element in common. That delicate moment at the beginning of the trip, perhaps the most unpleasant, when they jump in the saddle, one or two strokes of pedals to find the balance and they turn back, while their families, and their friends, are there watching them go away. We say farewell to them with a smile and a wave of arms, which often hides a tear. We discover the richness of the world, but at the expense of momentarily leaving behind us an even greater resource, our loved ones.

And when those brushstrokes finally cross, in an explosion of colour and emotions, the members of this bizarre sect find themselves telling each other about all the amazing treasures discovered during the journey. About how lucky they are to be able to enjoy the world from the saddle of a bicycle, but above all, of the inestimable wealth that awaits them on their return.

And that invigorating and energising moment gives us colour and energy, and as if we had wound up the spring of a toy, we start tracing brush strokes on the globe until, perhaps, we cross another line of colour.

BURKINA FASO

If women lowered their arms, the sky would fall.
AFRICAN PROVERB

November

The prosperity, at least apparent, that I sensed in the Ivory Coast stopped at the border. Immediately beyond, I encountered shabby roadside stalls, a few goods piled up, and a lot of dirt. Yet the entrance into Burkina Faso did not do justice to all the goodness and genuineness of the Burkinabé, the country's inhabitants. Every day and on every occasion, everyone I have met has shown me this trait of theirs, this kindness that sometimes borders on subservience.

Instead, I am thrilled by all the bicycles passing by. Men, women, children, the elderly, everyone uses this means of transport to carry goods and water. For once, I don't feel like an alien, and I don't have to put up with the astonished looks of everyone. Here, the bicycle is the means of transport par excellence.

The first track I take, leading to the town of Sindou, is a jewel. A green savannah of low bushes is interrupted by this wide strip of red earth. Scattered along the way are a few small villages with earthen brick houses and pointed thatched roofs.

Numerous cyclists ride along this track. They are farmers returning from the fields with their tools on their back, a young boy accompanying two children on the rear rack, and some girls.

Ah, the women of this region. They make my head spin, literally. A beauty on a bicycle comes from the opposite direction, we pass each other, and I turn my head to look at her as she rides away, *ognuno là per là, la testa girerà e allegro canterà¹*. Like most girls from these regions, she has a slender figure, which I can just make out under her traditional dress, and fine, elegant features. Their bearing is always elegant, whether on foot or on a bicycle. These ladies walk with a slow, measured stride, their torso erect and their shoulders back. They look like queens—every woman in Burkina is a queen. Every woman in Africa deserves to be a queen. In this continent, women take care of everything. After childbirth, they quickly go back to work in the field or in a chaotic village market; they raise and look after the children, prepare food for the whole family and fetch water from the wells. What would Africa be without women? Women are the vital energy of Africa. Africa is a woman. The woman is queen. Although she is well aware of her position in society, she accepts it with profound dignity and maintains it by living it to the full.

A great writer once said: "The continent is too large to describe. It is a veritable ocean, a separate planet, a varied, immensely rich cosmos. Only with the greatest simplification, for the sake of convenience, can we say 'Africa'²". I have made this sentence of Kapuściński my own, and I confirm its truth every day.

And yet, when I reflect on what all the countries I have visited so far have in common, I think of women. Women who travel many kilometres every day, a fabric pad wrapped around their head, carrying something on it. Whether it is a sack containing goods for the market, lumber for the fire, or a heavy bucket of water, everything is carried in this way, with skill and balance. And when I see this familiar silhouette in the distance, I feel reassured because I have arrived in the vicinity of a village.

It should not surprise me that in Burkina, too, women carry objects on their heads. It surprises me instead because they often do it on bicycles. I will never forget a mother I met during my first days in this

---

¹ Pampanini, Silvana. *Bellezza in bicicletta*, 1951. "everyone there and then, their heads will turn and cheerfully sing."

² Kapuściński, Ryszard. *The Shadow of The Sun*. Allen Lane, 2001.

wonderful land, with her baby in a sling on her back, a daughter on her rear rack and a basin full of water on her head. I followed her for several minutes along the road, the liquid visible inside sloshing slightly, not a drop spilt.

Moving away from Banfora, the second-most populous city in the country, I head east. A few sharp changes of direction, first north then east, north again and finally east, will take me to the capital in a week's journey. As far as the village of Ouo, the asphalt road runs pleasantly under the wheels, and a light headwind accompanies me, although it doesn't hinder my progress. Leaving the village, a possible shortcut through the *brousse* shows up on the map. I don't think twice about it and take the track. But after a few moments, I discover that the track doesn't exist anymore; it gets lost in a courtyard or in the brushwood. A quick investigation shows me a path that goes more or less in my direction and can only be followed on foot or by motorbike. And by bicycle, of course. I consult the map, which is blank on a uniform grey background. *Hic sunt leones.*

"There are borders beyond which one is not allowed to go. God wanted it to be written on certain maps: *hic sunt leones.*[3]"

But Jorge, the character of Eco's book, did not know these regions. The path, although bumpy and sandy, makes its way enthusiastically among the shrubs, offering great cycling satisfaction. I pass through miserably poor villages, and yet the people greet me joyfully. In every exchange, I have always noted a great dignity in the Burkinabé, even from those who are poor, sick or alone. It is a population I have learned to respect greatly during the journey.

On the crest of a hill, the path forks. The main trail continues along the ridge, while a secondary path, more well-trodden, descends to the

---

[3] Literally, "here are lions". Eco, Umberto. *The Name of The Rose*. Mariner Books, 2014.

foot of the hill. *Heads or tails?* I choose to go right, the most likely direction to continue northeast.

Soon the path gets busy. A continuous coming and going of burly men and boys, with a dusting of white powder on their bodies and clothes, who step aside for me to let me through. Some are pushing wheelbarrows; others are carrying spades or hammers on their shoulders. About fifty metres from the crossroads, I come across what appears to be an illegal mine. A big guy comes towards me with a menacing air. In jeans and a shirt with sleeves rolled up above the elbow, he alone is well dressed and without dust on him. He's probably the boss.

"Where are you going?" No greeting, but straight to the point with his booming, confident voice.

"I'm going to Djassara and then Tiankoura," I reply uncertainly. I can't decipher his mood and manner. He might be annoyed by my presence. He scrutinises me for a long time before saying: "go that way, and in a couple of kilometres, turn left," and then goes back into the dusty worksite. I'm not sure, and it doesn't seem the right moment to ask questions, but I believe it's one of the country's many gold mines. I take an indiscreet look inside before walking away—big holes in the ground, some machinery and water pumps. Everything is covered in a layer of white dust.

Following the big man's directions, I find myself crossing a village of shacks that are dilapidated or just made out of a few planks and bits of fabrics, certainly not built to last. In the midday sun, the ghostly, blindingly white atmosphere of this village in the middle of the bush is disturbing. Those who have stayed in the village are lying inert in some patch of shade out in the open. It is probably impossible to stay in the hut at this time of day. The dust hanging in the air makes me sneeze. I try to hurry and find my way out, but every street is identical to the next, and several times I have to ask for directions. Despite the village's isolation and ramshackle appearance, I come across a few small shops, a mosque and even a hairdresser. In this place, people come and go seeking their fortunes. Only the shacks stay behind.

When I go online for information, I discover that these are actually gold mines. Since former president Blaise Compaoré deregulated the gold rush, there has been a significant proliferation of mines, which now employ a million people. In this region, people dig deep holes in the earth's bowels, even a hundred metres down, hoping to find a vein of gold. Once they find it, they continue to dig horizontally, following it. In a hellish environment, the rocks are broken with pickaxes and dynamite and then brought to the surface, often by teenagers, to be ground up. That's where all that white dust comes from, which the wind blows over everything. In a country that is often subject to periods of drought, even during the already dangerously short rainy season, harvests are often at risk, threatening the survival of families. This is why people choose the sacrifice of working in the mines, hoping for a few nuggets of gold.

In the evening, I am welcomed to the village of Djassara with great honours. I meet Amadou, a polite seventeen-year-old boy who accompanies me here and there, introducing everyone we come across and helping me with all my needs. While I am sitting on the bench of a roadside restaurant, eating a plate of spaghetti, many folks look for an excuse to come up and examine the foreigner. I then spend the night in a tent in Amadou's courtyard, in the company of roosters and goats. It's a cold night, or at least cool, compared to the previous months, and after one year, I dust off my sleeping bag, which until now had no reason to be part of my equipment.

In the morning, a concert for rooster's crow and goats announces the dawn and the advancing daylight. Amadou should go to school but is not worried about being late. We push our bikes calmly along the village's main street, stopping to greet all the people we met the previous day. They ask me if I had a good night and if I will speak well of their village. I dedicate a line in this book to declare that yes, it is a village of extremely warm and friendly people.

In the meantime, Amadou and I make another stop at his uncle's bar for a Nescafé and a plate of beans.

"Amadou, but it's almost nine o'clock. Didn't you tell me that school starts at eight?"

"Yes, but don't worry if I'm late. Eat slowly. Anyway, when we get to school, you're going to talk to the teacher, aren't you?"

"...about?"

The sly guy is carefully studying the coffee grounds in the cup and doesn't answer.

After paying for the two breakfasts, I turn around and see Amadou shyly standing next to my bike.

"Can I try it?"

"Only if you let me try yours," I answer, smiling.

The scene is embarrassing. His bike, with its thin wheels, sinks into the sand, and with the crooked handlebars, I make acrobatic gestures to keep going, or rather, just to stay in the saddle. He, much smaller than me, can barely reach the pedals. We are the village clowns, and everyone watches with amusement as the odd couple ride away.

The school building is a little outside the village, and we reach it in a few minutes. Parked in the shade of the trees are several dozen bicycles, which I note with pleasure.

"Come on, let's go inside."

"Amadou, I can't go in there. I have a huge tear in my trousers. What am I going to look like? Look at this!" I attempt a tactical escape, showing him the rip in a sexy/embarrassing position on the crotch of my trousers.

"No way, they'll all be very interested in your story!"

"Whatever. I'll take them off then. Wait."

"And you'll come in only wearing your underwear? Come on!"

"They are bicycle trousers!" I protest, uselessly. By now, he has already dragged me into the classroom. The teacher greets me, and hundred-odd students look at me. They are all full of curiosity, some silent and a few whispering.

"Good morning, Sir. I apologise for Amadou's delay, but he was with me and..."

The teacher interrupts me before I can come up with some super bullshit: "Hello, welcome! What brings you to Djassara?" *And why are you walking around in torn trousers?*

I told these students about my trip, some anecdotes, the reasons why I'm travelling. All this with a tear in the crotch that doesn't go unnoticed. My only hope is that I've enthused them enough to get their full attention.

"Do you want to leave a message for the boys before you go?" the professor asks me.

I thought for a moment, and now I am pretty satisfied with the message I gave them on that occasion. "Always pursue your studies and dreams. In this way, you will never stop dreaming, and learning."

Once the questioning is over, I stay on with the boys and follow an intriguing mathematics hour with them.

On leaving the classroom, Amadou says goodbye by saying: "*On est ensemble.*" I reciprocate in the same way and hug him. During the trip, I learned and internalised this excellent concept. It is not just a way of greeting each other. *We are together*, it is a philosophy that embraces the whole continent. When someone tells you that, it means they are expressing a feeling of solidarity, of support. I am because you are— *Ubuntu* in the Zulu language, which means recognising the humanity in everyone. Now we leave each other, but the day will come when you need me, and I will be there.

For a month now, I have been carrying around a nasty infection ever since my saddle was damaged in Sierra Leone. I still haven't found a replacement, and I'm riding with a pair of socks wedged between the seat post and the saddle to prevent it from over-bending. But still, it's not comfortable; actually, it is painful. From time to time, the infection recurs, and I suffer fever and feel very weak when it does.

The earthen track, well compacted and clean, runs straight through a low savannah. The sparse trees have just begun to hide the disc of the sun with their thick foliage. Here and there, the warm light of sunset reappears on the fields of millet shoots. When I arrive at the village of Bon, my fever comes back. I want to have a quick meeting with the village chief and pitch my tent far from the houses, perhaps in the wide uncultivated space between the few dwellings in the village. In fact, in this region of Burkina, the various households live far apart. Homes are built of raw earth with clay mortar. The man's house and those of his various wives are built around a courtyard surrounded by walls. Inside, each family has its own granary: a cylindrical structure raised above the ground, with a pointed thatched roof. Usually, a narrow round opening high up in the structure allows access to these granaries.

A group of small children greet me, smiling. "*Nassara! Nassara!*" they shout as they wave at me. I reciprocate with a tired greeting. Entering the courtyard of the chief's house, I am welcomed by a white-haired man. He is wearing overalls made of cloth and does not speak French. Issouf, who introduces himself as his son, acts as my interpreter.

When I ask to camp a bit away from the village, the chief looks at me in surprise. It can be dangerous to spend the night alone. Better to remain by the side of the houses, he says, pointing to a spot in the courtyard. I insist, mindful of many sleepless nights and crepuscular wake-up calls. Finally, I get my way. "*Barka,*[5]" I tell him getting up, and while I shake his hand, I try to show my understanding and gratitude with a slight bow of the head.

---

[4] Appellation for the white man, in the Mooré language.

[5] In Mooré language, it means *Thank you*.

His act goes beyond courtesy. In Africa, isolation and individualism are synonymous with misfortune and curse. A family is needed for a child's birth, but it takes a whole village to raise him, says the proverb. The newborn child will have to go through a series of initiation rites to be fully integrated into society; thus, he is also the son of the whole community, which endows the person with his cultural identity. Everything is shared within the family – a supportive group is the only way to survive in this hostile environment of the Sahel. A person who lives isolated from the community has often been kicked out of the group for a misdeed against the community or is the village madman. I am neither one nor the other; I have only developed a deep hatred of goats and roosters—at least the live ones. So, this time, I take no notice of the local tradition and let Issouf accompany me to the suggested campsite.

I would like to rinse off the day's sand, but my host recommends I wait until it gets dark to take a shower in the courtyard of the house. I clearly remember how some showers became a public event, and so I agree with the proposal. I take the opportunity to pitch my tent. Paracetamol before dinner gives me some relief. As always, the traveller enthrals the village children. However, this one is strange: he stays away from everyone, so it is better to study him at a safe distance.

While waiting for the water to boil, I do some stretching exercises, and my funny movements arouse the amusement of the public. With my legs apart, I tilt my chest forward and extend my arms to touch my toes. Peeking between my legs, I catch sight of some young girls at the well, who look back at me with the same curiosity. Still, with my head down, I greet them, causing shy laughter.

No way, I can't keep away from people. A little girl with a bucket appropriate for her size is trotting towards the well, passing inside the *red zone* around my tent. I turn off the stove and swing her onto my shoulders. When the girls see us jogging over, they interrupt their chatter.

Taking water from the well is a social event, as are many other daily activities, in different parts of the village. But the well is the meeting place par excellence where ladies meet and chew the fat. And since there are many of them and only one hand pump, they spend a lot of time waiting together.

Yet when we arrive, they step aside to let my young friend fill her can. She seems embarrassed by this privilege, lowers her eyes and shakes her head. Admirable.

While waiting for our turn, I chat with the girls. It looks as though they have lots of questions for me.

"Do women in Italy go to the well to get water?" a little girl of about twelve asks me.

"Well, we have piped water, so it's in every house."

"I knew it! It must be nice there. Will you take me with you?"

"Only if we ride our bikes there."

Her friends giggle at her answer, but she replies straight-faced: "All right, I'll take my brother's."

Another girl, a few years older than her friends, asks me about my portable kitchen.

"It uses petrol, but it's small, for two people at the most."

"What do you prepare?"

"Pasta, we Italians love pasta."

"But with what?"

"On its own, with tomato sauce only." From the way she wrinkles her nose, the answer doesn't seem to convince her. In African culture, pasta is a side dish. In Guinea, I found it in an egg and bean sandwich. In various countries, it is served with meat, but rarely on its own.

It is the turn of the little girl I accompanied to fetch water now. The other girls seem very interested, so they stay with us at the well, even after filling their *bidons*. It's now sunset, and for the second time, I help the little girl up on my shoulders and take her water canister. She pulls my ears to indicate the direction to follow and leads me towards her house. Her mother is leaning over the fire and preparing dinner. She is astonished when she sees us enter the courtyard, at the sight of her daughter raised two metres above the ground on the shoulders of a *nassara*.

After a satisfying night's rest, I wake up surrounded by grazing cows, and the fever seems to have gone. I get an early start, and in a couple of hours, I am on the asphalt road that will lead me to the capital. The road now leads me towards the east, and the Harmattan wind hits me with all its power.

After a few kilometres, I stop. The view sweeps over the immense plain, colourless and dusty. The Harmattan raises a large amount of soil into the air from the thirsty earth, drying out the lungs and making it hard to breathe. There are not enough trees to filter the air or obstruct its flow. I feel the constant urge to drink, not so much because of thirst, but to moisten my lips, palate and throat, which dry out with impressive speed. In one of his books, Percival Wren defined the Harmattan as: "A mist of fog and dust as fine as flour, filling the eyes, lungs, pores, nose and throat; entering the shutters of rifles, the mechanisms of watches and cameras, contaminating water, food and everything else, making life a burden and a curse.[6]" An apt description. Yet, it is a fresh wind, and it brings down the temperatures in this desert area. Despite this, the days that will lead me to Ouagadougou will be exhausting.

Ouagadougou is my favourite city, even before I set foot there. The name is enough to put me in a good mood. Round, booming. Legend has it that the leader of the *Mossi* conquerors was welcomed with great honours by the leader of the *Nioniossé*, the original population; so, he replied: "Thank you for the welcome," which in dialect sounds like *Gnam yelamé tid wa tid woogho do*, hence Ouagadougou, Ouaga to its friends.

---

[6] Wren, Percival Christopher. *Beau Geste*. London: Murray, 1927.

One element surprised me as soon as I entered the city, or rather, two. The first is the absence of chaotic, deafening traffic. Wide avenues, of a suitable size for the number of vehicles in the town, draw the main routes. Above all, the traffic lights are not merely Christmas decorations but are almost always respected. The chances of ending my journey on the bonnet of a car are certainly lower than in the other capitals I have crossed so far.

And the second aspect? The bike lanes. In Ouaga, there are cycle paths, well-marked and separated with road dividers from the central lane, low but practical. Okay, let's be clear. Today, the cycle paths are used as lanes for motorbikes, which run rampant through the city, as well as for street vendors' carts. And yet, this system dramatically reduces accidents by separating car lanes from motorbike lanes. The *Ouagadin* motorcyclist, in tacit agreement with all other motorcyclists in African cities, has created an alternative, unofficial road code in which he holds absolute power over the road. And so, cycle lanes come to the rescue of daring motorcyclists.

Why bike paths? For Thomas Sankara, *the President with the bicycle*, this means of transport was of enormous importance, as it is (was) for all Burkinabés. Before the advent of Chinese and Indian motorbikes, a large part of the population travelled by bicycle, the humblest means of transport, given the extreme poverty in the country. Sankara travelled around the city on his bicycle, just like a tailor going to his shop or a woman fetching water. Therefore, bike lanes were necessary during those years to increase people's safety and channel traffic. Now that pushbikes have been replaced by motorbikes, these lanes fulfil this new function just as effectively.

As I write, I'm simplifying things. Yet, it took me a while to understand this rule of the road code. Annoyed by all these scooters speeding past me, in protest, I started riding in the middle of the lane, which pissed off the bikers no end. "*Ici c'est pour le vélo!*", I say. "*C'est pour les motos aussi,*" they retort, often adding a colourful insult in local dialect. I take a photo of the third motorcyclist with whom I argued as he passed by the sign for the cycle path. A little later, I show it to a policeman. "They are allowed to use that lane."

"Oh, okay."

"Hey. Where's your helmet?" Time to get away, quick as the wind!

Now, reader, before reading the next few paragraphs, I invite you to take a short break and google *Thomas Sankara* to read about his life and his dream, which died with him in the coup d'état organised by his best friend, Blaise Compaoré. You will discover one of the most influential personalities on the African continent. Much has been written about this character, and he deserves more space than a few lines in this book.

Nigeria is the country that worries me the most due to the domestic instability and the difficulties in obtaining a visa. *Mission presque impossible, apparemment.* Soon there will be presidential elections in Nigeria, and the government, to avoid troublesome or embarrassing situations, has blocked the issue of tourist visas. The three embassies I visited in the previous months—in Guinea, Sierra Leone, Ivory Coast—all confirm this information: No, no and no.

But nothing is set in stone in Africa. In Burkina Faso and Niger, it still seems possible to obtain a Nigerian visa. Which is the reason for this detour of over one thousand five hundred kilometres back to the Sahel: to get my visa.

The Nigerian embassy, an elegant white stone building, stands on the outskirts of the city, in the residential district of Ouaga 2000. Sumptuous dwellings, wide, orderly streets and an imposing presidential palace give one the impression of having arrived in a wealthy European city. Considering the city's size and the central location of the building where I am staying, it is a pleasant fifteen-kilometre ride through traffic to get there.

It's Friday, and I have to wait two hours for someone to show up after prayer. Leaning out of a small window overlooking the car park, the receptionist denies me access to the building. "No visa if you're not a resident," he mutters.

"Is there no other way to get one?"

"Try coming back on Tuesday, talk to the visa officer."

It's now Tuesday, and the visa officer looks out of the small window and peers at me.

"Do you have all the necessary documents?"

"Yes, sir."

"Come in."

Noise of the electronic door opener. Clack. The door stays ajar.

"Good morning. My name is Mussah. And you are..."

"Graglia, good morning to you."

"Let's see your papers."

He is a small man in his forties, dressed in an elegant midnight blue loose-fitting garment. He is waiting for me on the other side of the metal detector, holding out an arm which means: only the documents pass. You wait.

I hand him the sheaf of documents. He leafs through them diligently, dwelling on every detail. In recent months I have learned to read people's expressions, to anticipate possible behaviour or thoughts. Mussah, on the other hand, is a sphinx from this point of view. His face remains blank. "Okay, it's all there."

"Good."

"Are you a resident here?" he asks as he hands the papers back to me.

"No, I told that to the receptionist."

"No visa then." A grin appears on his face. He enjoys the power he has. Damn him.

"But sorry, until last week, you were granting visas, and now nothing?"

He tightens his shoulders. "Hm mh."

"Aaaand, isn't there any other way?" the tone of voice hints at my blatant intention to gloss over the legal aspect of the matter.

"No, no." The evil laugh reappears.

This time I had made it as far as the metal detector before coming up against a brick wall.

I jump on the saddle and rush to the town hall.

"Hello, I would like to take up residence here in Ouaga."

"Okay, fill in this form and bring me a photocopy of your tax payment."

Easy.

I jump on the saddle and rush to the tax office.

"Hello, I would like to pay for my residency tax."

"Okay, fill out this form. It's ten thousand CFA."

Easy.

I fill it out. Under the heading: Address of current residence, I look around confused. A gentleman is sitting next to me, filling out the same form. For a moment, I revert to school test mode, stick my neck out and copy from him. The man notices me. "Oh, sorry, but I just saw that we live close by." I smile. He smiles.

Electricity account number. I tick the Other box. Specify: I am not connected to the electricity grid. Solar panels.

Water account number. I check the box Other. Specify: I have a well in my backyard.

Easy.

It's Thursday. Mussah looks at me seemingly benevolently through the porthole of the guardhouse.

"I'm here for the visa."

"You're not a resident. I can't issue it." A calm and irreconcilable tone.

"Yes, I am a resident now."

The grin fades. "Come in."

I pass the metal detector. Mussah studies my residence certificate before retorting: "I need a form certified by the police." A sneer and cynicism.

I go back through the metal detector and jump on the saddle towards the nearest police station.

I have to be careful; no messing around now.

I enter the office with shaking hands, a little nervous about my impending false declaration to a public official. I probably have it stamped on my forehead: *guilty*.

"Good morning. I need a certificate of residence from the police."

"Oh yes, your papers, please."

THUMP. A dull blue stamp appears on the document. *That easy?*

It's Tuesday. Mussah inspects me as if it were the first time I had been to that embassy. He takes the papers, examines them as if it were the first time, he hands them back. "Okay, I'll call you Saturday morning."

Easy. After only two weeks.

I am travelling on a smooth asphalt road towards the border of Burkina, a country that has given me so much and above all has confirmed the legendary goodness of the Burkinabés. The Harmattan is at the peak of its intensity these weeks, but luckily its direction now partly coincides with mine and relieves the fatigue of pedalling. With these distractions, I pedal up to where the carriageway narrows due to roadworks. Here the cars pass even closer to the bike, and I move even further to the side of the road.

A loud and repeated honk behind me. I don't have time to turn around but only feel the impact. The collision throws me into the air, and I slam onto the ground, hitting the asphalt hard with my shoulder. I roll a couple of metres down the ditch, where I stop. I am still stunned by the impact, and it takes me some time to understand what has happened: a large truck has just hit the handlebars of the bike. When I raise my head up and look around, I can see the truck moving away. I drop my head to the ground again.

By now, I am an expert. I know what I have to do. I carefully move my four limbs to check that everything is working and that nothing is causing pain. Even my neck responds positively to the assessment. I sink one hand in the sand to get up from the ditch, I'm all covered with dust, and I beat the clothes with the other hand to tidy them up. Ow! Pain in the palm of my left hand.

The driver has parked the vehicle beyond the bottleneck and comes running up to me, looking shocked by what has happened. "How are you feeling? Are you hurt?"

"My hand hurts, and my shoulder too. Now let me check the bike."

It's in one piece too, just the handlebars are bent, and some new scars shine on the frame.

I shift my gaze to the driver; he's staring at me worriedly. "*Putain*, where were you looking, driving with the mobile phone in your hand, maybe?" I attack him with words, perhaps more than necessary.

In the meantime, a small group of people have huddled around. The road workers have witnessed the scene and accuse him and shove him around. A boy brings me some disinfectant alcohol and gauze. While I clean the wounds on my elbow and knee, the driver and the other witnesses talk animatedly. I finish dressing the wounds. They don't seem to be serious, and the anger dies down a little.

The driver approaches me again and asks me if I need treatment.

"I'm afraid I may have broken something here, on my hand."

"Come on, I'll take you to the hospital." A few seconds to consider possible other options, then I accept. "Okay, but you'll have to load the bike on the trailer."

"I ask you to forgive me," he says as he climbs the steps to the cabin and slams the door behind him.

It is less than forty kilometres to the Togolese border, and we cover them in no time at all aboard the truck. There are three of us in the cabin. Between the two of us sits his mate, the guy who had just given me the gauze. All in all, I'm not in a bad mood, and I try to chat to distract myself from what has happened. But I ask to take a photo of his licence and vehicle registration, in case the health insurance company asks me for it to reimburse the hospital. Silence falls over the cabin. I look at the big man at the wheel. *Is he pretending not to hear me?*

"Can I take a picture of the documents, please? I don't want to press charges, but I need to have them." The apprentice lowers his head sadly. "Were you driving? And you're without a licence, I bet..."

Elementary, my dear Watson.

The truck driver interrupts my outburst. "Listen, I caused the accident, now I've taken responsibility, so I'll drive you to the hospital, and I'll pay all the expenses. That's how we do it here, in the *Land of honest men*[7]."

---

[7] The country's current name, Burkina Faso, dates back to August 4, 1984, when it replaced the old name *Upper Volta* under President Sankara. By combining two words in the country's two main languages, it takes on precisely this meaning. Burkina translates as *integrity, honour* in the Mooré dialect and Faso means *territory or homeland* in Dioula.

NIGERIA

If the devil exists, he is in Nigeria.

IVAN BIANCONI

January 2019

On the other side of the desk, the border officer is checking my passport. My hands are sweating with nervousness. I am about to enter Nigeria, and up to now, I have never been so tense as I am today.

One fundamental lesson I have learnt is not to hold prejudices. A situation arises, I try to assess it objectively and act accordingly. But Nigeria, well, that's another story. Ever since I started the journey, I have been thinking about this country. I have heard so many stories that, unfortunately, passed on many prejudices to me. "Be careful; they kill you there to steal one euro." "Nigerians are not like us. They are bad." "They only act for their own interest, and if they want something, they take it." "And corruption..." "And the pirates." "And Boko Haram." "Did you hear about that bombing the other week? One hundred deaths."

Another lesson I learned on the trip? That people love to talk. Often, they don't have direct knowledge of a subject but have heard about it, so they talk. And you know how Chinese whispers works. *So? Shall I worry? How should I behave?*

At the moment, I'm sweating profusely. It's not due to the thirty degrees, but the anxiety. I am holding my gloves, and I fiddle with them nervously. A light breeze wafts through the room and gently ruffles the papers on the desk. I focus on the refreshing feeling it gives.

"I like the Italians. I like them." The officer meets my eyes and smiles. He's young but looks like he knows what he's doing. He manages to put me at ease in a few moments. Contrary to what I've been told, he's not an "ugly, nasty alcoholic". The checks are strict, vaccine booklet, contents of the bag, stopping points and destination. Soon there will be elections, and they do not want disturbances on their borders at such a delicate time. The parliamentary elections in African countries are as important as the World Cup final.

A couple of hours later, I am out, free to ride wherever I want for the next three months. First rides in Nigeria. Sensations? It seems like a continuation of Benin, a country I crossed in a few days, except the people here speak English. Hardly a profound or philosophical thought, but it's enough to relax me. Money changers (off the book), SIM card, a coke. Repetitive actions that I perform at every border. As I move away from the city, I revise my old assumptions about this country, unique in Africa.

Nigerians number two hundred million. The Nigerian economy is the strongest on the continent, thanks mainly to oil and foreign investments. It's among the countries with the largest number of people below the poverty line in the world[1]. With a population growth rate of more than 2 per cent, by 2050 the population will have doubled to four hundred million. That is the background.

The current situation? As of 2018, it can boast the title of world epicentre of sea piracy. It ranks third in the world for risk of terrorist attacks[2]. Boko Haram in the North-east has killed more than twenty-five thousand people in ten years, and three million people have been forced to leave their homes. Continuing conflicts in recent years between Fulani herdsmen and farmers have resulted in four thousand deaths because of the introduction of firearms, and thousands more internally displaced persons. I like to have numbers at hand. They give

---

[1] World Poverty Clock, updated 2019. https://worldpoverty.io/
[2] http://visionofhumanity.org/indexes/global-peace-index/

objectivity to what people say—sad numbers, in this case. Yes, I had been not a little worried about entering this country.

And what does it mean for the local population to have to live in all this? I got my answer in the first few days: people live in terror.

As is my wont, I prefer country roads and paths through fields to wide asphalt roads where the life flows faster and more disengaged. Even in my first Nigerian days, I spent a lot of time in mostly rural areas.

On the third day, I am cycling along a peaceful path through fields of maize and cassava. I meet a few people that morning. After a slight bend in the road limiting my view, I run into a girl just ahead of me. She is wearing a typical coloured *pagne* and is walking barefoot. On her head, she is carrying a large basket with various kitchen tools inside: pots, knives and plastic plates. As usual, so as not to frighten those I meet by surprise, I call hello and smile. The girl hears me and turns around. And here is the unexpected.

Not a word, not a scream, but terror appears in her eyes. The girl lets the large basket crash to the ground, where it rolls over, spilling the contents. In the meantime, she runs away along the path. I'm bewildered; I don't know what to do. My instinct is to run after her, and I shout in English: "Wait, wait, I don't want to hurt you, I'm not dangerous. I'm a traveller!"

Without stopping, she gives me one last fleeting glance before running off into the bush. I can no longer see her. I put my feet on the ground, next to her stuff. I find myself filled with sadness, and in an instant, I am there, in the middle of the bush alone, crying. I still don't have a clear explanation. Probably it is the first time someone has been so terrified of me that they have run away. I feel a tightness in my stomach as if I had done something terrible that I regret. But I haven't. *Why, why did you run away like that?*

Let's do an exercise and try to imagine what went through that girl's mind when she saw me.

It's such a nice day, and it doesn't feel too hot with this breeze. I'd stop to relax for a moment, but I mustn't be late. I want to surprise my aunt for her birthday. I'll make her some excellent Jollof rice with the incredible chillies Dad gave me. Auntie will be so happy!

I'm almost at the village. Oh, I love the warm ground under my feet. Someone is coming. He has just called out to me. I turn around slowly; I don't want to drop all this delicious food I'm carrying. It's an Oyibo[3]! He approaches me quickly. The oyibo is wearing a hat pulled down over his eyes and sunglasses. And a scarf pulled up to his mouth. His shirt is open. It's all dirty. How scary he is! He looks like he's on a bicycle, but it's so big, and it's got loads of stuff hanging off it. What witchcraft is this?

Suddenly I think back to my brothers' conversation about the terrorists; they are in the north of the country, but they said they could come down here any day, now. They have killed so many of our brothers; have they come here already? I am paralysed with terror.

Fortunately, my instinct is to run away. I don't think about what I'm carrying. Everything crashes to the ground. Damn it. But I have to run, I can't stop. Oh no! He's following me, and now he shouts something in his own language. Stop, stop, go away! He's catching up with me; I have to hide. Here, in the bush, he cannot reach me. I run at breakneck speed, the branches are scratching my arms, but I don't care.

After a few minutes, I stop; my heart is pounding, and I'm out of breath. I turn around, but I don't think he followed me here. I made it. Did he steal everything from me? God only knows why he was after me. I'd better wait a little longer, then I'll go back to collect the pots and the food. Hope to find a brother on the way.

In the late afternoon, I arrive at the village of Igbimo. I stop by the side of the road, where some people are leaning a wall, chattering.

"Hello sirs, my name is Filippo. I am cycling to Onitsha, but now I am looking for a quiet place to spend the night."

"Hi. Nice bike," one of them answers.

---

[3] *White man*, in the Yoruba language.

The man at his side intervenes: "Listen, you can't stay here; we have no place for you." His tone seems friendly but distant.

"For example, a school, the church? I don't need a hotel."

"Continue to the next town, didn't you hear what my friend here said?" resumes the first one while still looking at my bike with interest.

"Whatever, thanks." Rejection can happen, not often, but it does happen.

Past a bend, I spot a church and approach the gate. A rusty padlock hangs from the bolt between the bars, and the building seems as if it's closed. "What are you looking for?" A thick-set man is approaching me. He may have been drinking, he doesn't look very sober to me, and his red eyes give him away.

"I'm looking for the priest. I'd like to ask him if I can stop here to sleep for the night."

"No, no priest here. There isn't one."

"A catechist to ask, maybe?" In the meantime, other people have gathered, forming a circle around me.

Bling. Alarm-bells. I'm starting to feel uncomfortable. "What's in those bags?" the big man asks me. "It's not dangerous stuff, is it?"

I try a joke. "No, no, I carry my house with me." It usually works, but nobody's laughing today.

"Listen, it's almost dark, and I have nowhere to stay." The sentence has no effect.

"Try to understand; it's dangerous for me to move around at night, especially alone."

A glimmer of hope appears: "Mmmh, check at the guesthouse at the end of the town, follow directions to Iluomoba."

"Thanks." Drained from the day and worried about the situation, I turn the bike around and get back on. The people around me comment on what's happened, as they move out of the way to let me pass. I nod at those closest to me and smile tiredly. "See you."

The sun is now closer to the horizon than I am to the next village. Make or break. I arrive at the guesthouse; *Home away from home*, says the sign at the entrance. The car park is empty, except for a motorbike parked near the wall. The place looks deserted, with no lights on. I'm about to leave as a boy, maybe fifteen or sixteen years old, comes out the door.

"Hey, do you need?"

"Hi!" I force a half-hearted smile. "Yes, I'd like to ask you the prices for a room. I'm on my own."

"Wait, calling my dad."

A few moments later, the father shows up, scrutinises me and declares: "There is no room; we are full. Bye."

The place is clearly empty. No customers. But I am not welcome here either; there would be no point in forcing the situation. "Thank you, goodbye."

I am about to leave the village, now in the dark, when I pass in front of the police station. An officer is on the doorstep, smoking a cigarette. One more try, come on.

"Hello Sir, I'm Filippo..." a much-repeated story ensues.

Give me your passport. What's in the bags? Why are you here alone? Okay, let's go back to the guesthouse together. I'll talk to Anthony.

That's it. I'm exhausted, but it's not physical fatigue, just mental. Like a zombie, I follow the captain. He exchanges a few sentences with the guesthouse owner, who still examines me doubtfully. I pay, go up to my room and throw myself on the bed. Home away from home.

The next morning, I get into the saddle early in the morning and set off along the main road. After a few metres, I hear the police captain calling me in a loud voice. "Good morning. Did you sleep well?"

"Yes, Sir, thank you."

"The village chief asked me to give you these." He says this while extending his arm. He's holding two thousand nairas[4] between his fingers. "These are for the hotel room. The Chief apologises for how we behaved yesterday in the village."

---

[4] Nigerian local currency. Corresponds to about five euros.

I am speechless again. This I didn't expect. "Sir, I can't accept them. Give them to the owner of the guesthouse instead."

He shakes his head, bringing his hand even closer. I stretch out mine. "Thank you, that's a laudable gesture from the community, Sir."

The morning starts off in the best possible way. *Today will be better, I feel it.*

Two hours later, while riding through a small town, the police arrest me.

Still in the saddle, I am following two officers on their motorbike. The pillion rider is keeping an eye on me, and the rifle in his hand is not an invitation to mess around. We leave the village and reach the police station on the outskirts: a concrete building, a large courtyard with abandoned wrecked cars and a big tree in the middle. A policewoman is sitting on a root in the shade. One of the two officers on a motorbike signals to me to lean my bike against a car and wait. Soon after, the highest-ranking officer appears. He introduces himself as the Captain of the station while keeping a considerable distance from me. Around him, all the officers keep their weapons at rest but still at the ready. "Who are you?"

"Captain, my name is Filippo Graglia; I am Italian. I am travelling by bicycle from Italy to South Africa." I could record the speech and play it back as needed, twenty times a day.

"Let me see your passport." He continues in an authoritative tone.

The passport is in the bag on the handlebars. I open it and take out the document. One step in his direction, and the officers point their guns at me. "Freeze!"

"Leave the passport on the ground and walk away. Officer, go and retrieve it," orders the captain. I obey. The officer obeys. The situation doesn't look too good, but I feel calm. I have nothing to hide, and my documents are in order. We'll see what happens.

The captain starts leafing through the passport. As he turns the pages, I summarise the whole trip. He asks me about the dates of my stays in the various countries. At which border did you enter Senegal? How did you get a visa for Nigeria? A full-blown interrogation. Time passes, and I am proving to him that my story holds water. The other agents understand this, and the tension has dropped considerably.

"The bags. What have you got in there? Do you have any weapons?" and the checking of each bag begins. "What's this?" "A power bank." "This?" pointing at the green bottle below the frame down tube. "Fuel." "What? Are you carrying fuel for what? A bomb?" "Sir, I need it for cooking." "Bullshit." "Let me show you, Sir."

I am forced to put together the stove and pretend to boil some water. "Do you make your own food? Why don't you eat at a restaurant?" and so on.

It must have been three or four hours since they escorted me to the station. Finally, the captain is convinced, and he releases me. "Okay, you can go."

"Oh, thank you."

As I rearrange my luggage on the bike, I turn to the captain, who is now staring at me distractedly, lost in thought, with a cigarette in his hand. "Captain, may I ask why you had me arrested?"

While he ponders this, he clears his lungs of smoke. "We got a call from the village because they suspected you were a terrorist. You know, we are about to have elections, and it was our job to check."

"Ah... Captain, excuse me, but do terrorists go around on a bicycle?" I laugh. And he with me.

"Sir, could you warn your colleagues in the next cities that I don't intend to kill anyone?" and I return to the bicycle.

"Yes, but please wash these clothes and change that torn shirt. It helps you not standing out."

The two officers who had escorted me to the station approach me and ask for a selfie. *First they point their guns at me and now the smartphones?!* Say cheese! Let's have a picture with the terrorist on the bike.

Life has to be taken seriously. Better to laugh about it than get pissed off. But these constant interruptions are not beneficial. I decide to stay on the main road for the next few days. Less hassle, more traffic, therefore safer. Maybe. In a week, I could be in Cameroon.

This theory will hold for a couple of days.

At the hotel in Ibillo, where I have spent the night, the owner greets me and says: "Stop by the military outpost before you leave and get a phone number." My eyes widen at this statement. "There are police along the road, but it might not be entirely safe," he adds by way of explanation.

This Nigeria is annoying me. I've been constantly on my toes for ten days now, which take a lot of energy. I no longer pay attention to the act of pedalling; my legs move automatically, but I can't concentrate. I need to get out of the country as soon as possible.

I ask to speak to the commander of the outpost, and the captain is happy to help. "Yes, alright, I'll leave you my number. Anyway, it's all quiet around here now. There are patrols."

"What was the problem?"

"Abductions. A group of people we were never able to identify. But it's been quiet for two months now."

"Oh, okay. Thank you, commander. I'll text you when I get to Auchi."

And I get back in the saddle. My heart is beating fast. It's not fatigue; it's anxiety. As I leave the city, I slalom between burnt tyres and Jersey barriers chucked in the road.

At the first checkpoint, the policemen look at me and wave, smiling. Shortly after, a man in his forties joins me on his motorbike. He wears a grey hat with the *USA2019* logo and a good-natured smile, and he slows down to my pace to exchange a few words. But I am paranoid today; anyone could kidnap me and goodbye world. I try to maintain an offhand conversation with him, using a deliberately annoyed tone. He doesn't leave. I'm travelling at a good cruising speed, so I keep busy pedalling and don't have too much breath for conversation.

The man who is accompanying me is an engineer, he has studied in the United States, and since his return has started a modest production of fruit-peeling machines. Perhaps everything is normal, and he is not interested in kidnapping me. Yet I feel an intense unease, he and I on this apparently dangerous road. *He's keeping an eye on me and will alert his team when we approach the "extraction" point*, I guess.

Second patrol. "Are you travelling together?" My travelling companion gets in first: "Yes, I'm accompanying him as far as Igarra, where I live." The answer seems to convince the policeman. *Maybe I'm just feeling paranoid.* The landscape all around does nothing to allay my fears: medium-low, indistinct scrubland, the perfect place to make someone disappear.

USA2019 is returning from the city, where he went the previous day to buy a spare part for a machine. Third patrol a few kilometres later. My supposed kidnapper tells me: "We won't stop for these guys; they are not real soldiers, and they will ask for money."

I am now at the mercy of events. I don't even want to know who these four or five people really are, standing by the side of the road next to a pickup truck, wearing ramshackle military clothes and carrying weapons. The good Lord will know what to do with me.

Fourth and the fifth patrol. Then nothing. *Goodbye, now he's going to pull out a gun and order me to stop.*

A few kilometres further on, a road sign indicates that we are entering his town, Igarra. A motorbike parked a short distance away starts to move and follows us a hundred metres behind. *USA2019* greets everyone in the village, some verbally, others with a wave of the hand.

"Here I am, this is home. I say goodbye to you here." He stops at the side of the road, pointing to a house not far away. The man who was following us stops beside us. He greets my bodyguard, then me. *I swear I don't understand anything anymore! Are you going to kidnap me or not?*

"All right, thanks for the company." And I try to leave. I was a bit grumpy, maybe.

"Don't you want to see the factory where I make the machines? I'll introduce you to my wife too."

"No, no. Sorry, I'm very late to get to... where I have to be today," I gibber.

My guardian angel does not understand this attitude but nevertheless asks me to take a photo of him and his workshop. He smiles. I try, too. CLICK. "Goodbye, and thanks again."

Off I go, fast as the wind. The guy who had been following us since we entered the village follows me until the last houses, and he stops. *Fuck him!*

At the mercy of events and the environment, I can't think anymore. *What will happen now?*

Ivan! I need to speak with Ivan. I'll talk to him a little while I'm pedalling. It will do me good and calm me down. I send him a vocal WhatsApp, to which he luckily replies at once. "My friend, keep breathing. And send me your position. I'll follow you from there."

I have two hours of pedalling ahead of me to get to Auchi and from there rejoin the main road. *No more roads with little traffic, never again.*

When I arrive in the city, my nerves have eased enough to realise that I am starving and parched. It's one o'clock, and I've been pedalling non-stop since this morning. People greet me like in any other village: "*Oyibo!!!*"[5] a boy across the road calls loudly. "*Oyibo!*" the market lady wants my attention. "*Oyibo! Oyibo!* where are you going?" and so on. One thing is sure in Nigeria, you don't forget the colour of your skin.

I study the map while sipping an ice-cold coke. There is only one climb to Uromi, where I would like to be this evening. Not bad.

I start off again, and, as I am leaving the town, another bike flanks me. No *USA2019* this time. One guy driving, the other two with guns resting on their legs. *I can't believe it. I'm in a video game.* "Stop." "No fucking way."

---

[5] *White man*, in the Igbo language.

"Stop!" And they stand in front of me, forcing me to brake hard. Is it normal that three young men stop a tourist with guns in broad daylight on a busy city street? *Evidently, it is.*

"Follow us."

What would you have done? I follow. We leave the asphalt, taking dirt side streets. All I remember is a lot of rubbish, scattered puddles and squawking chickens. I have no way out. And anyway, with the bike, they would catch me in a flash. I keep following them, trying to meet someone's eyes, trying to understand, to guess, *what the fuck is going on.*

We arrive in a courtyard. A fat guy is sitting on a root, and all around, some young people are messing around in the shade of a tree. One of the escort guys orders me to lean my bike against the trunk and go to him. He must be the leader of this gang.

The big man gets up, looks me in the eye and... starts laughing! *What the hell are you laughing about?*

My nerves are in tatters, and this smug guy is laughing at me. He turns to his friends: "Can't you see he's a tourist!" Clearly, they hadn't considered the remote likelihood that I might be a tourist. How silly of them. *Dickheads.*

"Listen to me, sorry. My name is John, and I'm in charge of these youngsters." Pause. I wouldn't know what to say, so I keep my trap shut. "It's a commando of young volunteers to maintain security in the city. You may have met some in other villages as well."

"Aaaaaaaaaaaaaaaaaaaaaah" that explains a lot. Mr. USA this morning, his colleague on the motorbike, these bad boys now.

"Yeah, well, let's say they scared me."

"Sorry about that, really. They saw you and thought you might be a threat. Usually, the white people we see all travel by car. You with this bike and luggage made them suspicious."

"Yeah, listen, I understand. I'm getting used to it by now." *Bullshit.*

An hour later, I'm on the main road, on a one-way uphill lane due to construction work. In front of me is an endless queue of cars and trucks. I'm sweating. The hot tarmac and the exhaust fumes are wearing me out. Check the map. A detour a few meters away. Good.

I have only covered a few hundred metres on this new road when three young men on foot stand in front of me, blocking my passage. They look somewhat worse for wear. I wouldn't be surprised if they tested positive in an impromptu breathalyser test.

"You can't go this way."

"Why?"

"The road is the other way; this way doesn't lead anywhere."

I've come to the end of energy, physical and mental. "You live here, and you don't know? You get to Uromi this way, and that's exactly where I have to go."

The eldest of the three pulls a cutlass out of his belt and smiles mockingly. "You have to pay to get through."

"How much?"

"One thousand naira." Two euros fifty. I don't bat an eyelid. I want this day to be over; I want to lock myself in a room and fall asleep. I put my hands in my pocket and take out a few coins to pay the fee.

"I have eight hundred."

"All right."

Bugger them.

Uromi is a tiny town but with an interesting market. The atmosphere *seems* to be more relaxed, the children giggle in the courtyards, and Nigerian dance music blares out from the bars. I grab some take-away food on the fly, I don't even notice what I have ordered, I find a clean hotel with 24/7 security, and I barricade myself inside.

I slept like a log for eleven hours, but when I wake up in the morning, one single nagging thought fills my mind and does not leave me. *Today I have to cross the Delta State, a red zone on the maps*[6]. *It's really*

---

[6] Please refer to the security sections of the French and English Ministry of Foreign Affairs websites.

dangerous there. More than yesterday? I can't pedal today; I don't WANT to pedal.

An hour later, I am at the bus station. One hundred and ten kilometres in Delta State separate me from the Niger river.

I arrive at the station late, and many of the parking spaces are empty. What remains is the usual chaos of people going about their business at the bus station and one minibus that is now overloaded.

"*Last seat,*" shouts the boy in front of the bus. That's lucky! I hurriedly approach him and haggle over the price, unconvinced. His colleague grumbles not a little when he sees the bike to be loaded onto the already overflowing roof of the vehicle. A large net holds all the merchandise: sacks of vegetables, aluminium rods, two little goats complaining about their accommodation—only their heads are sticking out of a jute sack—and a lot of other junk.

It takes us a long time to lift and tie down the bike. In the meantime, two burly ladies get off the bus and start complaining to the driver. Everyone is shouting at the same time, and although they use the local language, I can sense that they don't want to travel on this bus anymore.

The driver, obviously annoyed at having lost two customers, gets on board and starts the engine. The conductor and I jump in as the vehicle is already slaloming through the car park; I climb over bags and legs to get to my seat at the back of the bus.

We quickly emerge from the city's chaos, and finally, vegetation flashes past the window at great speed. A man in the front row gets up and starts singing a gospel hymn, and all the passengers immediately join in. A good alternative to the car radio, these songs accompany us for a full quarter of an hour. "... and God protect this journey. Amen."

"Amen," echoes through the bus.

As soon as the quiet returns, the conductor starts collecting the ticket money; when he approaches me, I ask him:

"How come those two ladies got off the bus at the last minute?"

He thinks about it for a while before explaining: "Travelling with a white man scared them. If anyone in Delta State knew you were on board, they might get strange ideas in their heads and attack the bus. But don't worry, that's a thing of the past."

The journey goes smoothly, and an hour later, the immense Niger River appears in front of us. As the reticular structure of the bridge fragments the view like individual frames of a film, the tension accumulated over the past few days melts away.

In Anambra State, and throughout the South-east of the country, lives the *Igbo* ethnic group. Here too, everyone keeps calling out to me, reminding me that I am white. But the language changes. *Oyibo* then becomes *Onye ocha*, and attitudes change too. People seem calmer, and everywhere I am welcomed in a more friendly manner. They don't exactly let off fireworks, but at least they don't pull out knives and guns, and when I stop, I don't get those suspicious looks that, unfortunately, I was beginning to get used to. The journey is back on track.

I arrive in the town of Enugu, exhausted. I need a break after the past few days. For the first time in Africa, I find a Couchsurfing host: Jackson, a twenty-seven-year-old computer science student. These three words give me confidence: Couchsurfing, twenty-seven, student. They smack of normality, after all I've been through.

Jackson lives in a former hotel, now converted to rooms for students and people passing through. The owner has built a church in the basement and, having appointed himself pastor, holds noisy masses a couple of times a day. Normality.

Normality? The whole of Nigeria is covered with churches, Anglican, Charismatic and Protestant. Looking to supplement your salary? Do you have the gift of the gab and can capture everyone's attention? Open your own church. Attract a flock of believers, and that's it. There are hundreds of these churches, and they are constantly growing in number. The best known are *Redeemed Christian Church* and *Living Faith Church*, which can be found everywhere and often welcome tens of thousands of members in monumental structures. In addition, there are other smaller churches—*Deeper Life Bible, Four Square Church*—or with funny names like *Laboratory Church of God, Run For Your Life Ministry, Jesus Election Ministry*. There is something for everyone, but especially for every budget.

Okay, explaining it like that may sound like I'm being overly cynical. I apologise to readers of the Methodist and Pentecostal faith. Yet the feeling I got on discovering this is that it is a real business, built on people's faith and wallets. I attended a Sunday service in the district of Asata. I felt like I was in a musical where the pastor directs the tempo, the choir follows and the crowd dances. In this engaging atmosphere, bodies move, hands wave, cries go up: that's what makes a church successful.

Jackson invites me for a beer in an outdoor club, joined by four of his friends. There's no better way to relax and takes one's mind off things: the right amount of alcohol, carefree talk, good music and dancing girls. City life here in Nigeria is so different from the countryside. There is a lot of money to be made, and if you want, you can treat yourself to all kinds of luxuries.

Leaving his flat, I owe a deep debt of gratitude to my new friend for providing me with distraction. I had been in dire need of disconnecting my brain from the journey before resuming it. I am just over two hundred kilometres from the border and should be out of the country in three days.

The border with Cameroon is considered a hot spot. I have been following the evolution of the situation for several months. In a nutshell, the two English-speaking provinces in the North-west have been demanding independence from the rest of the country for many years. Starting with a strike in October 2016 accusing the government of discrimination against the two provinces, the situation, backed by secessionist movements, has degenerated into a civil war. At the beginning of 2019, the war is at its height. Not the best time to cross.

I know someone who works at the border. From him, I learn that it has been closed again, officers won't let me through – it's too dangerous at the moment. The borders are closed to foreigners, but in the last year, tens of thousands of refugees have been crossing them to seek refuge in neighbouring Cross River State, Nigeria. They are brothers, part of similar tribes or ethnicities, and this has made reception much more effortless. Often, Cross River people have been hospitable to their neighbours and allowed them to live in their homes as brothers and sisters.

The only solution for me is a freighter that connects the coastal town of Calabar with Douala, Cameroon's economic capital.

Calabar is an atypical Nigerian town. On the banks of the river of the same name, and not far from the sea, it welcomes the traveller with its tranquillity and cleanliness. The boulevards are wide, and the relaxed traffic flows without any particular interruption. Many neighbourhoods are residential, with pretty pastel-coloured terraced houses. Calabar is famous for its Carnival, reputed to be the most remarkable on the continent. It's a pity I didn't get here the following month, but considering the previous weeks, I'm just glad I got here at all.

First mission: I go to the port. There is no certainty about the date of the boat's departure, but I'll grab a ticket in the meantime. I spend my days going around the city by bike or on foot. There is a serene air everywhere, and the threats bedevilling most of Nigeria seem so remote.

At the market, a woman beckons and pulls out a small jar containing broad beans from under the stall. She introduces me to *eseré*, a seed which has played an important part in the history of the region.

Since the dawn of time, Africans have sought justice by asking the gods to identify the guilty and the innocent during ceremonies. In an ordeal, a defendant was required to ingest a certain number of seeds. While the accused chewed, he would walk in a circle without stopping. If vomiting came before death, it was a sign of innocence; otherwise, he would get his natural punishment.

I look at her, definitely struck by the story, but at the same time intrigued by why she wanted to sell me this seed of judgement. The bottles on the counter contain extracts of this plant. Nowadays, it is used as a homoeopathic remedy for various diseases. "Madam, thank you, but I will continue to take paracetamol."

The cargo ship has been anchored for days without anyone knowing when it would leave. One morning I get a call from the captain. "We raise anchor at midday today."

With the bags already packed on the bike, I jump on the saddle, and a few minutes later, I arrive at the port, where I carry out the immigration formalities and load the bike. It sounds easy said like that. A long negotiation on the economic value of loading the bike actually preceded the operations.

I hand the bike over to Elvis, the guy in charge of the freighter's loading operations. He shouts out to a porter and entrusts him with the bicycle. Under his (my) supervision, the bike gets lifted on top of the mountain of goods lying on the ship's deck. Elvis climbs up to check that no damage has been done, and I follow him. We sit next to each other, our legs dangling over a mountain of baby nappies at the stern.

Stocky and with measured movements, Elvis is a 25-year-old who instantly inspires confidence at work. He tells me about his dreams, working hard to pay for his studies. "To become a captain," he tells me, "in addition to the right connections here at the port, you also need to study." He keeps an eye on his men as he tells me this. In the few hours we spent together, he demonstrated his diligence and precision, two qualities that will surely serve him well in the future.

I spend the afternoon on the nappy mountain. When he has free time during the day, Elvis climbs up for a chat.

Now six mighty men at the foot of the mountain are carrying a massive sack on their shoulders, singing in rhythm as they walk to give themselves a boost.

"It looks so heavy Elvis, what's in it?"

"Wigs for women." I look at him, surprised.

The wig business has been exploding for about ten years now, and it is not slowing down. For reasons of hygiene or just fashion, African women love wigs. Whether they are synthetic, worth a few nairas and made in China, or made of real hair, perhaps from a rural village in the hills of South-east Asia, every woman has her own.

I pop down to buy a couple of beers, and with Elvis, we enjoy our sundowners from the top of the (nappy) mountain.

I'm still on the summit of Pampers mountain, waiting for the ship to set sail. Another day is over on the *Brenda Collett*, the name of the boat. In front of me, the porters, who have been working hard since dawn, are now lying on the cargo enjoying the cool of the dusk. They listen to some music and tease each other as usually happens between comrades.

The next morning, I am still waiting up there while the ship fills up with more nappies, wigs, tanks, engines, cars, yams, wood, beer and other packages with unknown contents. Twenty-six hours after my arrival at the port, the siren sounds, the sailors weigh anchor, and off we go. The other passengers on board are happy—who wouldn't be, after a week sat on the port floor? However, onboard there is a tacit tension because the bay we are going to cross is one of the continent's two major piracy areas, along with the Horn of Africa.

"Don't worry, if they attack, it's for the goods, not us," a man in his forties standing next to me on the deck (unsuccessfully) reassures us.

According to the GPS, the ship is caressing its way through the water at a remarkable speed of ten kilometres per hour. At this speed, any pirates on a rowboat could easily assault us.

The hours pass, and to starboard, the horizon is swallowing the scorching tropical sun. The light gradually becomes dimmer, and some flames flare up in the distance, gradually becoming sharper and more intense. Initially, they are two, then three. A few minutes later, we see a dozen. Onboard, we can't explain what it is. Only time will help us solve the mystery of this twilight mirage.

As we get closer, the silhouette of an oil rig becomes clearer and clearer—a fire-breathing dragon lying on a placid sea. The roar of the beast closest to the ship is mighty. Dozens of dragons together create a unique and impressive spectacle, unforgettable in its singularity.

The flock of dragons has finally disappeared into the distance, and I return to the high deck where some passengers are singing religious songs. A young man leads the prayer, someone claps in time, and other passengers dance as if entranced. This spiritual fire warms me up, and I feel emotionally connected to the energies released by the chanting. I sit and gaze at the full moon reflected in the water; the ship runs freely on the open sea. It is only when the canopy begins to obstruct the view of the moon and the sacred chants fade that I lie down on the damp planks of the deck, lulled by the waves and the magic that still hovers in the air.

Tomorrow I will be in Cameroon, in a new world. And I have one word in mind: *hospitality*.

What does a person need when he arrives in an unfamiliar place, from a tiring situation, perhaps with a long journey behind him? He is probably hungry, needs to rest, or is cold. Above all, he needs someone to warm his heart, perhaps to talk to him and give him a smile.

I do not in any way want to compare my experience with the journey that thousands of souls undertake towards a new world and a new hope on derelict trucks and dilapidated boats. Yet, put in an uncomfortable position even for only a few days, I felt for the first time in my fortunate life what it means to feel excluded. I became the other, for no apparent reason except for the colour of the skin. I sought the dialogue; I sent smiles. *White*. I was turned away and shouted at. *Black*.

And I felt cold in my heart. The only way I can continue my journey is through being welcomed, looked after, and never abandoned. *Humanity*.

It has always been like that in my African days, where we are all human, all equal. This magic was interrupted for a few days, but it is already working again. A few days were enough to show me the necessity of welcome, being all human and feeling all *Together* in this world.

CAMEROON

If darkness exists, darkness is good.
When the Forest dies, we will die.

TRADITIONAL PYGMY HYMN

February

When we wake up, the ship is anchored in the middle of a river. During the night, we left the sea and sailed a few kilometres inland. I slept on deck because the passenger cabin was packed and the air unbreathable.

All around is green; it's the jungle. The equatorial forest I've been dreaming of for so long.

There is silence, and dawn is still far away. Only with the first light does the forest awaken. Prolonged chirping of sparrows, the irregular cawing of other birds, an orchestra of frogs croaking in the mangroves. A hidden monkey shakes the branches as it passes. The daily enchantment of the awakening of the world.

Even the last passengers with whom I shared the wooden planks of the deck are waking up. No one dares to speak; there is no need. A girl kisses her man on the cheek and leans against him, his warm embrace on her belly, her head on his chest. I am not the only one enjoying this moment.

A croaking voice on the radio in the cabin announces that the harbour is now open, and the captain can carry out the final manoeuvres. *But where is this port?* The sun peeps beyond the forest branches as the ship travels the last few metres and passes a bend. In the bow, at the junction of two branches of the river, a small pier comes into view, partly occupied by wrecks from another era—our destination.

From a distance, everything seems motionless, yet as we get closer, I see dozens of people on the pier. Some are busy with ropes, the team of porters is singing at the top of their lungs, reminiscent of rugby players before a match, the drivers are patiently waiting for the cargo of the ship. I enjoy my last moments on board, fantasising about what kind of not-so-legal trafficking might have passed through here.

When the poetic moment is over, I feel hungry, very. But the customs officer seems intent on postponing my meal. When I inform him that I am a tourist passing through and have nothing to declare, he phones his boss. "You have to wait an hour; the commander is coming from Douala." I try to dodge the invitation, but the officer is no longer listening to me.

It's time to fill my stomach. It's Sunday morning, and everything is closed. Everything except a little cafe that also seems to feature some culinary activity. The owner, who had been dozing in front of the TV just a few moments before, looks surprised at the strange customer that morning. The fan hanging from the sheet metal lazily stirs the air.

In the back of the cafe, onions are sizzling in the hot oil. I look for distractions while waiting: miracles are being broadcast on the TV.

The fictitious pastor of an equally unbelievable church has laid his hands on the knees of a lady who has a pained expression on her face. He shouts a prayer to the good Lord, and the patient begins to moan. The pastor abruptly removes his hand and orders her: "Get up!" and the miracle happened. The lady gets up and starts jumping for joy. "I can walk! I can walk! Thank you, Reverend, thank you, God!" The crowd that witnessed the scene is jubilant. I switch off: omelette and beans take precedence now.

The entrance curtain is pushed aside. A girl enters, wearing jeans and a red tank top. Twenty years old, maybe. And two fabulous eyes. And a pretty good figure. She sits down at the counter and orders a beer. "A Castel, please."

With one eye on the omelette and the other on her, I am going cross-eyed. The lady notices and does me a favour. She picks up her beer and comes to sit astride the bench in front of me, on the other side of the table. *Fan, spin faster, it's gettin' hot here.*

Tania is brilliant. She skilfully juggles with my stories; she knows many of the places I've been to, and every now and then, above all, she laughs, a merry laugh that warms the room even more. I am amazed to have met such a fine girl in this small forest village. Her father was ill, an incurable illness it seems, and she interrupted her studies to be near him. An intense empathy is born. There is a moment of silence and I don't feel the urge to say *anything*, as I smile at her.

The curtain of the restaurant moves again, and the customs officer blows in. "The captain has arrived. Come."

"Comin'." By now, besotted with her, I wish this omelette would last for another hour at least.

The procedures with the captain are hurried. "I have nothing to declare; I'm a tourist." He nods. "Yes, I understand. Just give me ten thousand CFA for my trip here." "Captain, I'm not the one who sent for you on Sunday morning for nothing. Ask your subordinate for the money." He smiles. I smile. Have a lovely Sunday.

I run back to the cafe, she's not there anymore. "Where has that girl gone?" I ask the bartender. He shrugs and goes back to watching miracles on TV.

I won't have any Cameroonian children, it seems.

Enrico and Biyen welcome me into their home as if I were a childhood friend. I have just arrived in Yaoundé, the capital of Cameroon. Similar to many other African capitals, but in the mountains. My mission here: to get a visa for Congo Brazzaville and wait for a package from Germany with essential spare parts for my bike.

Enrico, a grizzled fifty-year-old from Florence, is an Africanist political scientist, which means someone who knows a lot about Africa, its troubled history, traditions and cultures. He has worked for the European Union delegation for many years and lived in several countries before moving to Cameroon. Enrico tells me about Africa, and I read love in his words. He arrived in Mali at the time of his university thesis and has never left it.

As I see a brotherly feeling when he talks about Biyen. This depth of feeling is not even too hidden since he refers to him as *mon frère Burkinabe*. For more than ten years, Biyen has been helping him with household chores and has always followed Enrico wherever he has gone. I can confidently state he prepared the best meals I tasted on the trip. He is an artist, not just a chef. You admire his creations first, then you taste them.

To see them together, Biyen and Enrico, you would not think there was a working relationship between the two, but rather that of two inseparable friends. And in Africa, to express a bond of deep friendship, they use the word *frères*. Not blood brothers, but brothers of the soul. The respect and intimacy between them are the same as it would be in a blood relationship, and perhaps even more intense.

I have the feeling that I could have stayed at Enrico's house for as long as a month without getting bored, and I hope without boring him. We had exciting discussions about Africa and its politics. But we also visited the studio of a local artist, saw a musical dedicated to women's emancipation, and listened to lots of good music—a new, innovative Africa that values its talents and arts. Another Africa that I like very much. Much of what I have written about it in this book I learned from him during those days while talking on the bright patio between a glass of *jus de gingembre* (ginger juice), pungent to the point of spicy, and courses of fresh fruit beautifully carved by Biyen.

We have often gone to the market with Biyen. Everyone knows him, and he greets everyone, smiling like a good Burkinabe.

Two weeks flew by. I got my visa for Congo, but, unfortunately, the shipment from Germany was lost. I go to the customs almost every day, with the only result of becoming friends with the customs officers, but there is not even a shadow of the package. Contrasting emotions assail me: I have bitterness in my mouth because of the disappearance of the parcel and sadness in my heart because I have to say goodbye to two great friends. Expected difficulties on my journey over the next few weeks and the sluggish ease found in this house gang together to make me hesitate. In this emotional whirlwind, I set off towards the east.

As I move further away from the capital, settlements and cultivated fields become increasingly rare, interspersed with corners of virgin forest. On the fourth day of the journey, I stop in the middle of the morning. Today, I have not yet come across any villages, no palm or banana plantations and few vehicles on the road.

I am finally there! The beating heart of Africa: the equatorial forest. I have just arrived, yet I can already sense the magnificence and power of Nature in one of its highest expressions. I experienced a similar sensation when I was at the foot of Aiguille Noire de Peuterey in Northern Italy. We are tiny; we are guests. Entering the forest requires *respect*, and we ask Nature: "Excuse me, may I?"

It seems that this time permission is granted. One foot on the pedal, I move with the slightest noise, my head tilted upwards to admire this majestic vault, while at my sides runs the wonder of the mighty wooden columns.

In this Cathedral of Nature, even the track I am cycling on seems too much. It's an excessive intrusion into the intimacy of the place. Beyond this bastion, is the impenetrable darkness of dense vegetation. Occasionally, a ray of sunlight penetrates between the leaves and finds a corridor to illuminate the undergrowth. It's just like when the rays penetrate the stained-glass windows of the cathedral and exalt the floor with their mosaic hues.

Several times I stop in ecstasy and listen. A concert of rustling leaves and gentle shaking of branches in the wind, solo birds sing the praises of the great Mother, and I can do nothing but remain silent.

For a few days, I advance in this world far from the rest of the world. Only clearings and villages interrupt an otherwise continuous corridor of trees and shrubs: red earth and green forest. Green and red, in infinite variations, surround me.

One late afternoon, I am pushing my bike up a hill following a rough track. A boy on a motorbike is travelling in the opposite direction and stops beside me. Few motorbikes roam this region and, I assume with a good deal of certainty, even fewer cycle tourists.

"Where are you going, my friend?"

I look up, misted with sweat dripping incessantly on my eyes. "Yokadouma, maybe I'll get there tomorrow."

"EEEH!" the biker exclaims in amazement. "Listen, when you pass Agiep, there are no more villages for quite a while, and the track is not in good condition. If you listen to me, tonight you stop at the village and ask for my father. You can sleep there. I'll be back in a couple of hours."

The map seems to agree with him. But then again, online maps in these regions are so limited and lacking in detail that I often navigate by sight and with local directions.

I arrive in time for sunset and dinner. A bath in the nearby river washes away the sweat and the fatigue of the day. Later in the evening, I am sitting in the company of other young people chatting peacefully while the women are finishing preparing dinner. The conversation is enlivened by the palm wine, which quickly numbs my thoughts and camouflages the tiredness of the day. Every now and then, the guys exchange phrases in the local dialect; I think I recognise the Fang language, but I'm not sure—with over two hundred and fifty languages spoken in the country—and I take the opportunity to look around while the sweet wine slips down my throat.

A few huts are lined up on either side of the track, so similar to each other and those of the previous villages. With a square shape, the structure is built of branches woven together with mud plugging the gaps. It has a thatched roof, which, I hope for them, is watertight. Near the house, a few poles driven into the ground support a lattice made of entwined sprigs about one metre high. Pots, plates and a few other crockery items are left to dry protected from the relentless ants. In front of each hut is an iron tripod; under each tripod is a burning flame; hanging from each tripod is a pot with boiling water.

I have learned not to ask what animal I am eating in a continent where anything that runs or crawls can end up in the pot if and when it is caught. However, that evening I made that mistake: This time, there's a monkey in the pot, and they are the carriers of disease par excellence in the forest. *Let's hope it's well cooked*. But then again, in such remote places, you don't choose what you eat. If an antelope is caught, it's antelope for dinner. And if the monkey is caught...

I go to sleep with an itch on many parts of my body. In the last week, I have become acquainted with tiny black insects called *forou* that appear at dusk. They sting the most sensitive parts of the body, causing an irresistible urge to scratch. Because of the scratching, these spots have now started to bleed.

The terrified cries of an animal wake me up early in the morning. Not far from the tent, on the path entering the forest, a boy is killing a beast, probably caught in one of the many traps set by the people around the village.

I hope it's a rooster, perhaps the one whose crow has woken me up several times before dawn. As I get closer, I recognise a pangolin instead. The pangolin is a highly endangered mammal whose misfortune is the quality of its meat: delicious. Here, in the middle of the forest, where people live off what they hunt, no one cares whether the meat is tender, tough or inedible. Here, the pangolin is food like any other.

I don't want to see the animal's throat cut, so I go back to my bike to prepare breakfast. The goats! During the night, they have eaten all my bread, and now only the torn bag is left on the ground. While looking at them defiantly, I swallow jam by the spoonful; the slothful beasts pretend to doze off, warmed by the first rays of the sun.

Despite this slight hiccup, morale is high these days, and I enjoy everything going on around me. If only it could always be like this, carefree.

Of course, I would enjoy a single track like the one that leaves the village of Agiep, even with my morale down at the bottom of my boots. Little more than a path for the *villageois*, it winds for fifteen kilometres through the dense forest without interruption.

And I, feeling like a child as I return in these situations, enjoy it as rarely before. In addition to the slalom to keep me on track, I also have to watch out for the bushes that overrun the path at chest and face height. After being hit a first and then a second time, I decide that it's not so bad to be flicked by fragile twigs and damp leaves, even if from time to time, it's quite violent, and I don't pay attention to them anymore. In Agiep, they must have heard screams in the forest and wondered what it was all about. *Perhaps a gorilla has captured the stranger?* But mine are screams of joy.

There aren't many moments of pure cycling beauty; it is unusual for all the stars to be aligned, as in this case. But every now and then, it happens unexpectedly. In those cases, all you have to do is let the wheels roll, get a few twigs in your face and simply enjoy. It all made me feel Alive!

I will keep today in mind to remind myself that Happiness is everywhere and nowhere. Happiness is within us, in our choices, hiding in the most unexpected places.

And I can only give thanks. I have an immense feeling of gratitude to express. Who should I thank?

I don't know. God? Or myself for having made the fateful choice to leave? Or perhaps I thank the Journey.

By travelling, I have begun to learn who I am again, to know my inner self. I have learned that there is no single answer. I have understood that I am the experiences I live through, the decisions I make, I am always evolving. The journey is a school.

The Journey is that state of mind where there is an appetite for developing feelings, for expanding emotions. Journey makes me more sensitive. But this is not the result of weakness; those who travel are strong. Instead, it is a sensitivity full of openness to the world. I learn more and appreciate every little gift that nature gives me or that people give me. A drop of water resting on a blade of grass, the smile of a tired person. Life in its entirety is wonderful because it is composed of infinitesimal nuggets of wonder.

And it is as if I am being born again, this time with a slow, conscious birth, and I enter another life. I will learn things that will change me, not necessarily for the better. There is no better or worse, for I will see joy and humanity, but also misery and deception. My face and expressions will change, my ideas will change. I will learn things that I will probably not need in life. Or, perhaps I will, and in that case, I will finally be able to pass them on to others.

I live every moment of this life, intense and pure. People like to hear that. They crave it. And in the encounter with these people, the traveller is the impulse, the spark. Ivan, my brother, once said: "We travellers are the ambassadors of a world that smiles and welcomes us." Maybe the traveller doesn't know it, but indirectly, he spreads knowledge, instils stimuli and confidence in human beings. And vice versa, I have had many encounters that have helped me, sometimes materially, but above all, ones that have helped me to grow as a person. Travel is an exchange.

This is the journey. You strip yourself of everything, of thoughts, of suffocating defence mechanisms, of prejudices. You let them go, and so, naked before the world, you are like a sponge, ready to absorb everything, and there are so many worthy things in this world.

Yokadouma, a dusty town at the eastern end of the country. It seems like an oasis, in reverse. In an endless expanse of green, here is a dusty island where I meet life. I find it fascinating. Swarms of taxi drivers at the roundabouts on their 125cc motorbikes look around for customers, perhaps a lady leaving the market laden with provisions.

At the tables of the bar, some friends with beers in their hands watch the umpteenth *grumier*—the logging trucks—pass by. In vain, they wonder when the government will remember them, their town, and pave that damn road. Every object in the vicinity of that damn road is now tinged with red ochre, the red dust these giants raise as they drive through the town.

Yes, because the main road in Yokadouma is only paved for half a kilometre in one direction. The other carriageway is still a dirt track. The rest of the road is red earth, for two hundred kilometres before and three hundred after. One of the many African paradoxes: they have brought in the machines needed for the work. And then? *Then the money must have run out.* It will have gone into the pockets of a local governor.

In the meantime, the *grumiers* continue to travel on this track towards the capital Yaoundé and to the big port of Douala. It's quite a journey, thirty-six hours if you're lucky. An alternative route took me eleven days on the tracks and trails. Locals can only get to the outside world by asking these grumiers for a lift. Or the broken-down '73 Renault buses that daily cross the forest to the first town on the asphalt, on real journeys of hope.

I have to stop in Yokadouma for a few days. It seems that the parcel I was waiting for, after being lost in the online tracking systems, has now been delivered to the customs in Yaoundé. Enrico, too kind as usual, offers to pick it up and send it to me here.

He calls me a few hours later, live from customs, for a three-way conversation. In addition to the customs clearance, a fee must be paid for the *facilitation* by the clerk. "But facilitation for what? It's you who don't want to clear the package through customs!" exclaims Enrico, with his diplomatic verve. *Eeh l'Afrique.*

This means I have to wait a few more days, but those spare parts, in particular a new chain and the front sprocket of the transmission, are needed right now.

They are happy to host me at the Catholic mission, and I can stay as long as necessary, Père Joseph tells me. The only pledge to pay is to accompany him to at least two masses a day. In the following days, someone in the street begins to recognise me and say: "*Bonjour, Père.*"

One day Father Joseph and I go to the camp for Central African refugees, a few kilometres north of the city. This has happened countless times: at one point in history, a desperate crowd had to flee their country to save themselves in the neighbouring region—another tragic African reality. On the way, he tells me that for several years (since 2013), instability in the Central African Republic has led to deep repression of Muslims by Christian-majority militias, the Anti-balaka. More than a hundred thousand Muslims have had to flee to neighbouring Cameroon and have been welcomed in border towns, including Yokadouma.

We drive into the camp in the parish pickup. Father Joseph winds up the windows and makes no move to get out. "It could be dangerous for you."

I think about saying something but then drop the subject. I know for a fact that I wouldn't have convinced him. And I know with equal certainty that there would be no threat waiting for me among the wooden and tin shacks of the refugee camp.

With the engine running and the air conditioning fighting the heat, I look around. Here and there, among the tin roofs, I spot a few

UNHCR[1] tents, which arrived in this remote corner of Cameroon at the time of the emergency. As I suppose all too often happens, the camp was built in great haste to be temporary. Camp hygiene was a priority, so taps, latrines, and showers were installed. Five years later, more than three thousand people live here, and they have made it their home.

All the activities usually found in a village have sprung up inside. Someone cuts hair, someone else has opened a small shop, where refugees can buy everyday products: rice, oil, tomato paste and tins of sardines. And life starts again, a few kilometres from their old house.

"People can afford to buy a few things because the international aid organisations send them funds by mobile phone transfer," Joseph explain to me.

I look at him, amazed. It is indeed a widespread technology throughout Africa.

"I think it gives them more dignity." Then, to justify this statement, he continues: "Not having to wait for supplies and crowding around a vehicle for some food."

Joseph puts the car in reverse, and we head for the exit.

I have no more words. I don't even have any thoughts; my head is running on empty. Although I have not had the chance to meet anyone, the few minutes in this place have deeply disturbed me. After reading figures and statistics for several months, putting a face to these numbers has given me a strong jolt to the pit of my stomach. *Wake up Filippo, people are really suffering.* It was meaningful for me to be here, to bridge the gap between me and the pain of the millions of refugees worldwide.

The road to the border plunges me back into a green sea. The villages are far from each other and lie on the boundary between the forest and the track. The road is sandy, and I often make progress with

---

[1] United Nations High Commissioner for Refugees.

difficulty but always in the saddle. This road is reminiscent of a rollercoaster: a relentless succession of hills, where the quadriceps push hard to counteract gravity on the steep climbs and rest during the breakneck descents.

Once again, I'm grateful for these mighty tyres as I speed towards the next climb to take a few metres off my fatigue. It would be easy to fall over on this route: the front wheel sinks into a small island of sand and *voilà*. But not with these three-inch-wide doughnuts that float on every surface. It's a recurring thought these days. I would never go back to standard cycle tyres. Safety first.

I'm making slow progress through a puddle of sand, and I feel like I'm being watched. I stop—or undoubtedly it would be more honest to admit that I would have stopped anyway because it was such hard-going to cycle on the sandy ground—and my heart starts beating wildly.

A pygmy! Or rather, a pygmy woman, with a baby wrapped in swaddling clothes on her chest. I had read so much about this ethnic group, I knew I was entering the region where they live, yet the encounter took me by surprise. In hindsight, mine was a naive, almost racist feeling. We are all the same. And yet, the meeting moved me greatly.

Having seen many photos when I was still preparing for the trip, meeting her leaves no doubt in my mind. Obviously, her small stature speaks for itself. Her skin is dark but not black, tending towards a yellowish-red. Her nose is platyrrhine, with wide, well-spaced nostrils. The woman is probably returning from the field, as she is carrying a basket overflowing with cassava on her shoulders. By the look of it, there could be thirty kilos on her back. To take some weight off, she uses a sash running from the basket to her forehead.

I greet her in French; she seems to have understood but answers me in her own language. She gives me the feeling that she doesn't know whether to be intimidated or intrigued or both. Only now do I notice that she has another child with her. Maybe three or four years old, she is hiding behind her mother's figure and peeks out with apprehension and astonishment.

Amazed, I try to reassure them in the universal language of a smile, and she smiles back. Then, they set off again. Holding her mum's hand firmly in hers and her body attached to hers, the little girl looks at me curiously as they walk away along the large dusty road.

As I watch them continue on their way, I notice that in the forest, they carry loads on their shoulders and not on their heads, as I had always seen them do before. That would be a considerable hindrance in the tangled undergrowth. As a result, the baby sits in front of the chest, not behind. Pleased with this trivial intuition, I set off again with satisfaction, passing shortly afterwards mother and children.

Accompanied by a ranger and an armed guard, I lived for three days in the silence of the Lobéké forest, intending to look for gorillas and observe their behaviour.

I would perch for hours on that observation tower, twenty metres high over a wide clearing. Hearing nothing but the buzzing of the flies and the deep breathing of the dozing guard, my hopeful gaze flicked around the edge of the impenetrable wall of vegetation, to the rhythm of: *they're coming, they come, there they are, no it was nothing. Oh, maybe over there, but where are they?*

Then a snout, and a torso, appear among the tall grass. He checks that there is no danger in the clearing and, though suspicious, marches out into the open. He is followed at a distance by his young, his mother, sister, cousins and uncles; a whole family of lowland gorillas is now walking in the *baï*[2]. They are relaxed, and they look around, play and eat as a family would at a picnic; they are fond of the rush stalks that grow in abundance here.

---

[2] The name used by the Babenzélé pygmies to describe clearings in the forest, especially if they are bordered by a watercourse. This name is currently used by the international community.

The resemblance we bear to these primates is striking. I shuddered when I saw some of their gestures, so human. Gorilla mum rubbing her eyes in annoyance at the sunlight, a baby gorilla chasing away an irritating fly.

In all of this, the silverback gorilla, the dominant male, remains aloof. His job is to protect the troop; he feeds, like the other group members, but always on the lookout now that his family is so exposed in the clearing. Even from over there, more than fifty metres away, he inspires fear and respect. Better to watch him from the observation tower than to meet him on the bike.

It is time to leave the clearing that has been our home for three days and get back on the saddle. On the way back, I feel weighed down in the tangle of undergrowth, and I have to be more careful than usual about where I put my feet. A jeep is waiting for us at the collection point. On the way back, I shiver constantly. *I am probably tired, and I have not drunk enough.* In the clearing, I was collecting water from a river, which the guide said was clean enough to drink, but it was better not to risk more than I had to.

At lunchtime, we are back at the WWF headquarters in Mambélé, but I don't feel like leaving today. I'll take the opportunity to rest. I sleep all day, and I wake up when it's already dark outside. I turn over, my skin sticking to the crumpled mattress: I'm drenched in my own sweat, smelly. Oh Lord, I don't feel well at all. Those ten steps to retrieve a paracetamol tablet last an eternity. I stagger in the void and have to lean against the wall to avoid falling on the bike. *Better to go back to sleep. I'm not even hungry.*

I open my eyes again when the sun peeps out of the window. Twelve decent hours of sleep, and I feel slightly better. I stand up, albeit with difficulty, but a disturbing fear does not leave me. *Is it malaria?* First African rule when you are feverish: check for malaria. I wander around the centre looking for a quick test: there are none, and what's more, the field doctor is absent. The rangers can't tell me anything more, so

I go back to rest on my mattress, which has been lying open on the floor in a secretary's office for the last two days.

And there it is. Now it's revealed itself. I memorised them before leaving; according to the internet, the symptoms are: high fever (periodic), profuse sweating, chills, headache, muscle pains, nausea. I don't need the test any more: it's malaria.

It's the third day of illness, and I'm well aware that I have to get some treatment. Here at the WWF office, it is not possible. I don't have any medication, and no one is interested in the case. Perhaps malaria is as unimportant to the locals as flu is to us.

The camp electrician accompanies me to the nearby village on his motorbike. From there, I will hitchhike to the hospital, thirty kilometres to the north. Three grumier are parked and waiting at the village. It has rained during the night, and the road, already in bad condition, is now covered with thick mud. The passage of these vehicles would further deteriorate the track, so the local rule is: wait until the road is dry. *What do local regulations say about emergency transport to the hospital?*

The hungry truckers have packed into the only roadside cafe, which I go in to shelter from the sun and wait. While chatting with the owner, a *Bamilike*[3] from the North-west of the country, he suggests a coke therapy, claiming it will give malaria a headache. I thank him for at least putting a smile on my face, but how hard it is to smile. My head is sore, and my temples are throbbing intensely.

It is almost lunchtime when a police officer lifts the barrier, allowing vehicles to pass. My capitalist friend has found a free ride for me to the hospital; all I have to do is climb into the cab of the truck and hang on for a couple of hours. With the road in disastrous condition, it will take

---

[3] The Bamileke are a Bantu ethnic group of Cameroon distributed in the north and west, along the Cross River basin. Their name literally means *those at the bottom* (in the geographical sense), derived from the statement *mbale-keo*.

us two hours to cover those thirty kilometres in the lorry loaded with timber.

I get off at the village of Salapoumbè, which houses a *hôpital Catholique,* the only medical centre in the area. I stagger across the courtyard and make my way to the reception desk. When the nurse sees me come in, she doesn't need many words: quick to the lab, test, positive, artemether and lumefantrine immediately.

There should be a doctor in the hospital, but the doctor in the hospital is not there. A couple of weeks earlier, he had travelled to the capital for a course, and there is still no news of his return. In the hospital, there are four nuns from a French congregation. I am met by Sister Geneviève, who has been working to develop and support the structure for thirty-seven years. In Cameroon's remotest region, far from anything that smacks of modern civilisation, she immediately heard about my presence here. The Sister asks me a couple of questions, now that I am lying on a bench, eyes swollen and teary, while a band playing heavy metal music made my head throb. Geneviève invites me to stay in their house a few metres away: I can still get all the care I need and, in the meantime, not breathe hospital air.

"What are you doing here?" a worried voice, a North-eastern Italy cadence.

I open my eyes, heavy gates, and see the tiny figure of a nun smiling at me. "Hello, Sister, but do you speak Italian?"

"I am Sister Elisa, and yes, I am Italian. But don't talk now; rest." She speaks in a soft voice, almost whispering. She and five other sisters belong to the congregation of the *Piccole Sorelle del Vangelo* and live a short distance from the hospital. When I feel better, she says, I can move in with them, but for now, I have to stay here for treatment.

I lie in bed for four days, in the darkened room. I spend most of my time sleeping; otherwise, I am in a state of wakefulness but never fully receptive: voices, lights, in my head, all stimuli are muffled. I only see Sister Elisa come in and the nurses changing the drip: a dose of quinine, paracetamol, antibiotics, and repeat. Every movement costs me enormous effort, the metal band keeps hammering incessantly in my head, and I've lost all urge to eat and drink.

On the fifth day, I try to get up. My legs are unsteady, but I can stand. *Very good.* It will be another four days before the tests confirm the complete eradication of the disease. I am back on my feet again, short walks to the refectory and, when I am in good shape, a walk around the hospital. Five minutes, ten in the morning when I am rested, and I go back to bed, exhausted.

On the tenth day, I move to Sister Elisa's dwelling. That night, with the window open as usual, a strange song awakens me. *A yodel in the Cameroon forest?* I hear it far away, but I can only catch its echo, perhaps. I have never heard it before, but I am sure it is a Baka[4] chant. It comes intermittently when the wind does not accompany it elsewhere. A drum dictates a regular rhythm, and women's voices emit sounds that are new to me, repetitive and hypnotic. It never seems to end—a small gift from the forest for the sick cyclist. I would like to listen to the whole dirge, but the sounds come from afar, and I soon fall asleep again, lulled by this ancestral melody.

One morning Sister Elisa enters the room and sits beside me on the bed. "How are you feeling?"

"Like I've been run over by a train, Sister."

"Normal, you need time to recover. And you had a pretty bad case of malaria."

"Is it really always like this?"

A slight smile, "The first time is hard, then the body builds up its defences. I get sick at least once a year."

---

[4] The Baka are nomadic people living in the equatorial rainforests of Cameroon, Gabon and Congo. They belong to the large group of pygmy peoples, due to their short stature.

I don't have an answer, so she continues, "We caught it by the skin of our teeth, you know? Three days without treatment is a long time. It's good that you're strong."

"Yes, Sister, I suspected."

"You know, we get a lot of patients here. They often have malaria. On the fourth day, it is challenging to save someone. Did you notice the large Baka community here around?"

"I haven't roamed much, but yes, I have seen someone. And I think I heard them singing last night." I'm still struggling to put the words together.

"The big problem is that, when they are sick before they come here to us, the Baka go and talk to the witch doctor. They want to understand who sent them the illness. *Next*, they use traditional medicine. Often families bring their children here when it is too late, and we can no longer treat them. Sometimes they accuse us of not having done anything to save them.

"It's tough here, eh, Sister?"

"We've gotten used to it. The problem is with the drugs and the doctors. We're the only ones within two hundred kilometres, and you've seen the roads to get here."

As the days go by, I feel my energy coming back. The walks are now a little longer; I get to the last houses at the end of the village and return along the same road, the only one, before collapsing in bed. By now, the villagers have got used to my wanderings.

A Baka family is sitting on the ground in front of their house. They had said hello to me just before, as I was leaving, and now that I'm coming back, they call me and wave for me to join them. The man approaches me and extends his arm while deepening into a big smile. His upper incisors, triangular in shape, stand out to the eye. During a puberty ceremony, the teeth are sawn and chiselled to achieve this shape, enhancing their beauty.

This family has two houses. Next to the traditional igloo-shaped hut is a house built according to Bantu[5] standards. The first is built with woven raffia branches held together by a network of lianas; palm leaves, held in place with thorns, protect it from the rain. On the other hand, the second house has a rectangular shape, the masonry of dried mud and sand, and a roof of palm branches. Later I will see similar structures but with walls made of tree bark.

Only the man speaks French, and he translates our conversations to the family. He tells me that one of his sons had seen me pass by the week before on my bicycle and had enthusiastically reported the news to the whole family. "Now that I see you here, I believe it. Where's your bike?"

I report the latest events, trying to build up my attack of malaria as if I had emerged victorious from a deadly duel at Thermopylae, but they are not at all interested. *As if I were back home boasting about my epic defeat of the common cold.* They are more interested in me. It's not often they get to sit by the fire with a white man and ask him questions. And the same for me. It's not often you get to sit by the fire with a pygmy and grill him with questions.

This journey is uncovering an inestimable treasure, and what adds additional value is the cultural exchange. It is not only the cyclist who arrives in a village with his thirst for knowledge but also the locals, as they confirm time and again, are keen to know something about me.

It is also interesting to note that some aspects they find exciting seem trivial to me. And they are probably thinking the same about me. The knowledge they have of the West comes mainly from missionaries, so it is religious and historical. They have no other occasion to converse with a white person. In this region, they pass quickly by in jeeps on their way to the national parks or to the carpentry shops scattered here and there in the forest.

---

[5] The Bantu are one of the large families into which African groups are traditionally divided, according to linguistic criteria. They are the dominant group in much of Africa, spread across the continent.

This time, however, I am invited to their home, and my curiosity is overflowing. I ask them many questions, sometimes not even listening to the answer as I am already preparing the next one. I ask him if I can visit the houses. The man is proud to accompany me. The igloo is approximately one and a half metres high, with an even lower opening. I have to bend down to look inside. "What do you call your house?"

"This hut is the *mongulu*. My wife can build one in a few hours." *Their version of a camp tent.* After all, if they are often on the move, they must be able to build a shelter in a short time with the material they find in the forest.

I smile. The nomadic spirit, the need to move around, is a *necessity* for them. In us westerners, this spirit is hibernating, but it has not disappeared. In fact, it takes very little to reawaken this ancestral state of mind. The pleasure of pitching a tent always in different places, but still in contact with nature, comes from here, from our origins. Unconsciously, I am replicating what my ancestors did thousands of years ago, and I have the good fortune to do it for *pleasure*, not for necessity. Perhaps rather than nomad, the term wanderer is more suited to our way of life as light-hearted, aimless travellers.

I come back to the present. In the *mongulu*, there is nothing but a small fire burning in the centre and some large leaves on the ground. I suppose these keep you off the damp floor when sleeping. There is a smell of burning resin.

"It makes a lot of smoke, but there's no flame," I say, just making conversation.

"The smoke is to keep the insects and mosquitoes away."

"Mmmh, right." I go out, my eyes beginning to water.

Similarly, inside the modern house, a light smoke rises from the hearth. Beside and above are shelves. On one of them are pots and glasses, high off the ground to prevent ants from getting onto them. The boards above the fire are used for smoking meat and drying fish so that they can be stored for a long time. I notice little else inside. Mats on the ground next to the remains of a fire and a woven basket of vegetable fibres, the kind they use in the forest. Leaning against the outside wall are two solar lamps under charge. There is a lot of rubbish on the ground, including many empty alcohol sachets. Gin, so it says on the label, for sale at ten cents each. After tasting it, I can confirm that it is pure alcohol, and of the lowest quality.

Back in the courtyard, the wife has prepared cassava pasta with peanut sauce, which is a great classic in these regions. She invites me to stay. Towards the end of the meal, the man asks me if I have some money to leave him. "So, I can buy some alcohol." *Hell, you didn't have to tell me; I would gladly have given you some.* I spare him the rhetoric on the evils of excessive alcohol. It won't have any effect. I finish eating the fufu while watching the half-naked children sitting on the ground playing with a car—a sardine can and four plastic caps instead of wheels.

I am now exhausted and need to rest. On the way back to the mission, I think about the structure of the *mongulu*. Will it withstand the violent downpours in these regions, and will it hold up well in the wind? A few evenings later, I would get the answer from Walter Bonatti, who wrote in 1973: "I felt anguish, so exposed to danger and without any defence: nevertheless, I only decided to leave the hammock when the wind penetrated into the lowest layers of vegetation, quickly tearing my protective cover. This coincided with the first downpour of rain, which was immediately followed by a flash of lightning. I stormed into the Pygmies' hut and huddled among them until the next dawn. Unbelievable: that fragile-looking shelter of leaves had withstood the fury of a hurricane remarkably well.[6]"

In her little spare time, Sister Elisa comes to visit me, and we talk a lot. I'm glad to speak my own language without having to struggle with French. This helps to save my energy, really low these days.

---

[6] Bonatti, Walter, *Giorno per giorno, l'avventura,* Contrasto, 2014

"Besides running the hospital, our priority is to evangelise. To spread Catholicism here. Missionaries have been coming to these regions for a hundred years, but they have not been able to share their faith with the pygmies. "The Baka are strongly attached to their traditions, to the land. Evangelisation is tricky, and they have no interest. They come to mass because there is something to eat afterwards."

"So, you go to the forest for your activities?"

"No. By now, all the Baka live in villages along the road. They were forced to move by the government to allow easy access to education and schooling, they said. Need to monitor the population, that is." Most of the villages I passed through in recent weeks in this remote corner of the country were villages inhabited by Baka pygmies.

"They have altered their way of being and living. As long as the forest fed them, they stayed in the same area, and then they moved on." Sister Elisa has lived with the Baka for more than ten years and has taken the matter to heart. "Now they are forced into a more sedentary life, often living close to the Bantu people. And there is abuse and violence."

I can imagine. The pygmies have lived here for hundreds of thousands of years, and they are the only humans who have been able to adapt to living in the forest, the real forest.

"Sometimes they accept jobs from the Bantu, who often take advantage and pay them a paltry sum or provide them with alcohol and cigarettes."

"The saddest thing is that up to now, they have never had any attachment to money, they have never needed it, living on what the forest gave them. Pygmies are hunters, but they know all the plants perfectly, and they are also excellent fishermen. You should see them when they climb the trees to fetch honey from the hives, forty metres above the ground!"

"I met a young lady a few months ago in Sierra Leone. It was September. She had worked with *Forest Peoples*[7] in the past and said something similar. She told me that the pygmies have had a lot of problems with WWF and WCS. These organisations have kicked them off their lands to make them protected reserves, right?"

"Keep in mind that the Baka have no property. The forest belongs to everyone. These organisations chased them out of many areas to establish parks and protect the ecosystem. They were no longer allowed to exploit the resources of specific areas. No wood, no hunting. Imagine if someone forbade you to feed yourself as you always did from one day to the next. And some Baka were killed when entering these reserves, which were their home, while many others have been arrested and beaten up."

What harsh words Elisa is saying to me. It is terrible. Paradoxically, these organisations want to preserve the environment by excluding those who, by their nature, have inhabited and defended it for millennia. "My friend told me *Forest Peoples* worked to defend their rights. They went on to take legal action in the courts, of which the Baka obviously have no understanding. Now they have regained some rights, such as seasonal hunting of a fixed number of animals..."

"Yeah, unfortunately, I think this is a *sop* to silence the international community. They should come here and see what their social situation is like, to realise what little has been done. I pray that everything will improve in the coming years, or there will be no future for them."

She lets these words float in the air, but they are heavy words, and they sink into my heart. The Baka are people with exceptional strength and abilities unknown to anyone else, but *within* the forest. Here in our civilisation, they are weak; they are succumbing.

For me, the pygmies were a mythical tribe. Arriving in these lands by bike, for me, is the arrival in the heart of Africa, the wildest, most

---

[7] Forest Peoples Program is a human rights organisation that works with forest peoples around the world to secure their rights to their land and livelihoods.

primordial Africa. And it's magic. Yet, now that I am here, I feel guilty for what has been inflicted on them, as if it had been me who did it.

During one of my first trips out of the hospital after my illness, I was followed by a ragged man, whose age I couldn't identify, who insisted on having some money "to take care of his sick mother." And every time he opened his mouth, the air between us was filled with the pungent smell of alcohol.

Two weeks have passed since the day I arrived at the hospital, with a high fever and a weakness throughout my whole body. In the south, two hundred kilometres of forest separate me from the border, and only one village.

Even today, I thank her. Sister Elisa insists that I get a lift to cross this region. "Malaria is notorious for its relapses. If something were to happen to you in the next three or four days, you would be in big trouble," she warns me as I climb into yet another grumier.

We make a quick stop at the WWF building to retrieve my bike before resuming the trail towards the border. From the window, the view goes by unbelievably fast; I was no longer used to travelling at such speed. Nevertheless, several hours pass and the view is always the same, with the red earth road cutting through the otherwise uninterrupted ocean of trees.

We pass a turnoff in the road, where there is a sign to a hunting reserve. Just next to the national park. So, it is the Baka who threaten the fauna? Hypocrisy for sale.

Shortly after halfway through the journey, our attention is caught by a procession of cows and some donkeys laden with luggage on the edge of the track. A few shepherds appear from time to time among the herd.

The driver slows down slightly, and for a couple of minutes, we share the road with the cattle. One hand is always on the horn. As soon as he spots a cow approaching the centre of the track, he sounds it violently. *Does he want to move the beasts with sound waves?* Two shepherds walk side by side, chatting. As the truck passes, they make a gesture, asking us to stop. The trucker continues undaunted. "They wanted us to stop for a moment, perhaps?"

"No, no. They were waving."

Puzzled by his answer, I ask: "Who are they?"

"They are Fulani shepherds from Chad. They go to the South of the Congo with their cows, where there are rich pastures." Eight hundred kilometres travelled, and many more to go, the driver tells me in a tone of banality, as if they were going shopping at the market.

We don't talk much during the journey. I offer him a banana and some bread; he glorifies the Congolese rumba playing on the radio. I could get used to this luxurious way of travelling. The track jolts us for seven hours before taking us to our destination: Socambò, a peaceful village on the banks of the Sangha, where life flows monotonously and slowly, like the river that caresses it.

Beyond, there is the Republic of the Congo.

CONGO

*It seems to me I am trying to tell you a dream,
making a vain attempt, because no relation of a dream
can convey the dream-sensation,
that commingling of absurdity, surprise, and bewilderment
in a tremor of struggling revolt,
that notion of being captured by the incredible
which is of the very essence of dreams.*

J. CONRAD, HEART OF DARKNESS

March

"What is your mission here?" questions the border official while looking at me suspiciously. "I am here for the entry stamp on my passport," I reply, aware of the meaning of his question but reducing it to the next five minutes, not the whole trip.

Background to the opening: I have just crossed the Sangha, the lush river that separates Cameroon and Congo. These customs, typical of remote border posts, are bathed in the stillness of the hot tropical sun. I approach the *Control Passeport* office. Empty. *Police*, no one. I return to the forecourt and look around. Despite the temperature, I feel shivers running through my body again. This damned malaria has grown fond of me. On the other side of the street, a man comes out of the bar and walks quickly towards me. "Come on, follow me," he says when he gets beside me.

We enter his office, and he makes me sit on a bench on the other side of the desk. The policeman, in all his arrogance, sits opposite me, wearing glasses and taking my passport. One look at the document, one at me, then back at the paper.

With a glance at the open register on the table, I realise that few foreigners pass through here. The last one entered five weeks earlier.

"Why are you in Congo? What is your mission here?" the official asks. His voice is low, a Pavarotti of the frontiers.

"I don't have a mission; I'm simply crossing the country to enter Angola."

"With that bike," a mixture of question and affirmation.

"Yes, with that bike." On these official occasions, I always try to speak as little as possible; I leave it to them. The official is silent for a few moments while he flicks through the passport. I look around absentmindedly. The leaves on the trees through the window are motionless; there is not a breath of wind. The corrugated metal roof radiates a fierce heat, and my shirt is now soaked with sweat.

"Is it your government that pays you to do this?" I smell a rat.

"If only, but no! I travel with little money. In Cameroon, a plate of Couscous costs *cinq cent franc* (five hundred CFA), you don't need much to eat. Indeed, how is the food at the restaurant across the street? I'm starving." As always, I try to deflect uncomfortable conversations. This official, however, is a tough nut to crack and won't give up.

"I don't believe it. Do you have the map? Show it to me."

"Look, I don't have a paper map, only the one on my mobile phone. You can't see the route I've travelled, but on my passport, you can find the stamps of all the countries. I'll show you: Morocco, Mauritania..." and so on until the stamp that still smells of fresh ink, the one from Cameroon. More shivers, I feel cold again.

"Mmmh. You have to pay twenty thousand francs for the stamp."

With a haughtiness unveiled by the patience that is evaporating, I tell him: "No, it's free."

"I'm the boss here. I know how it works." An irritated note emerges in his tone of voice.

"All right, I apologise. Let me call the Italian embassy and tell them that they gave me the wrong information." Saying this, I pull my mobile out of my pocket and dial a random number. I don't even have a local SIM card. In fact, I have activated aeroplane mode to not squander my calling credit.

A moment of feigned waiting. "Mmmh, they're probably at lunch. They're not answering."

"Are you Italian?"

"Yes, from Turin."

"Oh, Cristiano Ronaldo." Bingo!

"Yes, but, listen, at Juventus, we also have other great footballers. Dybala is a phenomenon."

"But Real Madrid is still stronger, even if you have Dybala and Ronaldo."

"Then we don't get along, as I prefer Barça!"

After a few minutes of frivolous bar talk, I try to get a result.

"You know, I'd like to keep talking with you, but my stomach is growling. I'm going to the little restaurant across the street. Would you like to join?"

"No thanks, I've already eaten. But try the fish; it's excellent." THUMP. The entry stamp adorns the passport.

These conversations are ordinary in African countries. I don't feel like I've taken the officer for a ride. Everyone tries to pull their own weight, always respecting the person in front of them. It is often enough to make him laugh, to win over an African. They are the most jovial people I know, and smiles open many doors, especially at these latitudes.

I am going out into the square and the dazzling midday light. *I will leave the fish for another day. Fever's coming back. Give me a bed instead.* Four eternal kilometres later, I arrive in town, after a month spent in the forest. I reach the parish office and briefly summarise the situation to the curate. They have an empty room; I can put my tent and mattress there.

I stroll through the town streets, enter a hairdresser's shop, and ask him to give me a "shave and a haircut, please." I sit on the stool, and for the first time in months, I see my double in the mirror. He is pale, mostly emaciated, with pale cheeks and sunken eyes. His body has suffered a lot from the disease, but his spirit has not; in fact, he smiles serenely at me, knowing he escaped by a hair but is now ready to resume the adventure.

I have an important appointment here in Ouesso. I'm going to meet Victor, a cyclist from Madrid who has embarked on a challenge similar to mine. He arrived in the city a couple of days before me via Gabon. I'm enjoying a delicious frozen yoghurt—who knows why, on this trip, it has become one of the foods I crave the most for—sitting on a box in the little shop of a Mauritanian vendor when I see Victor riding his bike in front of the shop.

"Viiiictooor."

"Felippo, my friend!" We join in a long-lasting hug. What a joy to see him after so many conversations and difficulties overcome. Mutual friendship is born immediately.

My body insists on having a few more days of rest: the after-effects of malaria have not yet disappeared. I have come out of this illness with several kilos less, and after twenty days of inactivity, my shape is struggling to recover. I ask Victor for at least two days' patience, and then we set off.

Two days pass, and we set off. My body responds well to the first few pedal strokes. All my energy is back, *finally on the bike again!* Yet after just forty kilometres, reaching the first village, Pokola, I ask my partner to wait for me again. I can't stand up; my head is splitting, and I'm still shivering. Another diocese welcomes us and, for the next two days, I only commit to rest and eat. I don't need anything else at the moment.

Victor is amazingly patient, and I am so grateful to him. He has also suffered from malaria, so he knows how long the recovery takes. We both agree that we are about to tackle one of the most challenging legs of the journey. A week to cross the equatorial forest, in its purest state, to the Ubangi River. In this environment, you can't fool around. We will need all the energy we can get, and in this condition, I can only be a burden.

Pokola is an unusual village, in these parts and in the whole of West Africa. In Northern Congo, the word *Seibè* is on everyone's lips. CIB, *Congolaise Industrielle des Bois*, is the largest timber company in the country, owned by a Singaporean multinational. The government has granted them a land concession of about two million hectares on which they operate. At least on paper, they respect internationally recognised standards for environmental conservation. They are based in Pokola, which has undergone a radical transformation in recent years. There is lighting in the streets and houses, air-conditioned brick houses, well-kept gardens, roads in more than fair condition and a hospital that meets Western standards. In a nutshell, when you first see this town lost on the riverbank in the equatorial forest, the impact is astounding. Almost all the inhabitants are employees of the company, on which they depend in every way. The impression I get is that I am dealing with a paternalistic company.

But on the other hand, this is a real opportunity for the local population to grow professionally and economically. It is rare to find these conditions in a rural setting, less so in a city. Since the years of colonialism, every element of development has always arrived on the coast, often in the capital, and stopped there, leaving the countryside unchanged.

The fact is that even the two cyclists who have just arrived here can benefit from the CIB. In the evening, people take advantage of the coolness by hanging out in open-air bars, picking at grilled chicken and guzzling beer, perhaps a Ngok—unlike most food, beer in most African countries is brewed locally. A DJ plays the most popular songs of the moment. The Congolese are proud of their music; if anything, they import hits from the other side of the Congo River, from their cousins in the DRC. The base rhythm is often a rumba, on which variations in tempo and melody are played. Papa Wemba, Ferre Gola—*emperator de la rumba congoliana* recites one of his lyrics—Koffi

Olomide, and Fally Ipupa are known to everybody. To the rhythm of their songs, the local girls sensually sway their sinuous and exuberant hips. You certainly don't get bored at night in Pokola.

After three weeks, I am officially back in the saddle. So is Victor, who waited for me the whole time. I wouldn't have put up with another day of rest. After more than a year on the bike, this is now what I call life. Fatigue and wonder are now part of me, and I was already missing the breeze brushing my face. Now, the duo is ready to conquer the Congo forest. Loaded with energy and supplies, we have high expectations for the next few days. Off we go.

Shortly after leaving Pokola, we enter Likouala region. It's the remotest, the poorest. The road, which is as red as blood, is wide and runs straight ahead of us. I imagine that from above, the forest resembles black meat in which a long wound has been cut, still open and bleeding. The vegetation at the side of the road seems intent on claiming it back. The first layer of ferns and undergrowth is the most intrusive. Above, shrubs intertwined with lianas hang from the tallest trees. As we look up, the trunks lengthen towards those majestic giants whose crowns define the forest canopy fifty metres above the ground, and beyond.

Further and further, we enter the forest, leaving civilisation behind us. Leaving time behind us. We are returning to prehistory when time as we know it did not exist. Life went on the same way, day after day, for millions of years. When man was still an animal like any other, and the circle of life still flowed without our interference. Or perhaps even earlier, when the man was not yet born.

In this timeless tunnel, everything repeats itself endlessly. A tongue of red earth, intricate columns of fine wood at the sides and a sky covered by leaves. The legs follow the natural movement of pedalling. A movement that is always the same. There are no particular snags or obstacles along the way. Legs turn and turn. Only two elements indicate the passage of time: the sounds of the forest and the temperature.

The first hours of the day, pervaded by the morning coolness, remind us that millions of living beings coexist in this apparently inert environment. The chirping of crickets permeates the air. Hundreds of birds sing their praises to the morning, some with a long, high-pitched concert, others with croaking, sparse calls. An occasional stop is a must in front of such beauty. All of a sudden, a rustling of leaves makes us look up. It takes time to spot them up there, fifty metres above the ground. Two or three monkeys are jumping and chasing each other among the highest branches with improbable leaps and swings on the vines.

With the sun at its peak, only the crickets sheltering in the undergrowth continue their dialogue. Everything else is silent. The heat suspends life. The monkeys are now dozing in their nests, perched on high boughs or hidden among the thick branches on the ground. Exhausted cycle travellers can only snooze in the shade of a tree, hoping that the highest leaves will flutter with a breath of wind, which is rarely felt in this green labyrinth.

And then, the afternoon arrives. The cycle traveller wakes up from a refreshing nap. The birds resume their songs; the monkeys revive. It's time for them to feed. Somewhere in the depths of the undergrowth, forest elephants are awakening. Concerned people had advised against moving during the last hours of the day and the early hours of the morning when it is common to encounter these pachyderms crossing the road. The same goes for gorillas. *Yet, I would like to spot gorillas.* We catch sight of gorillas twice as they cross the track. From a great distance, but that's enough for an adrenaline rush.

There is one factor that we could not have imagined and which nobody warned us about: bees. Hundreds of them. They rest on the skin, sucking up the salts from our sweat. They look dozy compared to our local bees. If I move slowly, they don't care and keep buzzing around me. All day long, I am immersed in a swarm. The continuous buzzing is annoying, often beyond what you can bear. Thanks to a fresh and rested mind in the early morning, I can observe them quite serenely; I still tolerate them at noon; I try in vain to push them away in the late afternoon. The only solution to this assault is to pedal. As long as I keep moving, the bees don't show themselves. As soon as I stop, one, two, ten and then a hundred bees start buzzing around me again. I *Let it bee*, while studying a bee closely as it stretches out its ligula and starts sucking the sweat. Another one enters under my trousers, gets trapped. It stings. Another bee slips in between the open shirt and the skin. It stings again. I kill it with a brusque movement, and the other bees fly away frightened, whirling around furiously before attacking again. I start pedalling – it's the only way to get rid of them. With the first daylight, I can already hear them buzzing around the tent. They enter my mouth while I'm eating. I find them in my bicycle gloves when I put them on, and they sting. They land by the dozens on the handlebars of the bike when I leave it unprotected. Will they drive me mad? Even now, I can hear them, although night has fallen, and they have gone back to rest. That interminable buzz is now in my head; I can't get rid of it anymore.

And the *forou*? Tiny gnats that bite every exposed shred of skin. The itching is overpowering, and I scratch away until the stings become bloody, and then yes, I stop scratching; what a relief.

And the termites. They advance in orderly and compact platoons, like a large army, and it's better not to interrupt their march. One night, I killed some mosquitoes in the tent. In the morning, I found termites inside. They had eaten the fabric of the tent to get in and retrieve the corpses.

Please understand: I am not complaining. It is more an awareness of the hostility of the environment.

And man in all this? Here, man is a guest. He moves cautiously, often in groups, so as not to be overwhelmed. We pass military outposts, which are far apart: there, the rangers assigned to patrol the area live. Poaching is still a major problem in these parts. From a distance, the roadside huts blend in with the red earth and lush vegetation. Then, we come across the barrier that cuts across the road. A few strange looks emerge from the building. A little chat with them. Sure, you can pass.

Other humans are guests here in the forest. They are pygmies. Here, even more than in the South of Cameroon, they live according to their ancestral traditions.

One afternoon we are called loudly by a man who has appeared on the edge of the track. He runs towards us, seeming eager to exchange a few words with us. He speaks rustic French, which he proudly shows off.

"We own a lot of banana plants up ahead; Let me give you some fruit." The farmer runs towards the hut and comes out with a dozen bananas. Victor and I thank him, but we don't want to take all of them. One of his companions arrives, carrying a whole bunch with him. *Have they not understood? Maybe they thought that ten bananas are not enough?*

"Alright, we'll take some, but we want to pay. How much can we give you?"

The two look at each other, as they would like to give them to us for free, they say. We insist. The whole bunch for two thousand CFA. *Three euros for a whole bunch of bananas?* We give them the amount due, but we just walk away with only twenty bananas.

As slowly as we went in, we reach the end of the jungle. As we continue eastwards, the colossal trees become sparser; the forest crouches and retreats from the road. On the fourth day after leaving Pokola, we hear playful laughter. Shortly after, we reach a bridge over a wide river, in which children are sloshing around. Laughter, dives, racket. This playful and joyful environment is in stark contrast to the dark, austere forest we were going through.

Some girls on the bank, washing clothes and pots and pans, watch the little kids with amusement. One of them looks up at the bridge.

Two *mundeles*[1] are standing astride their bicycles. *What are they doing here?* The two cyclists have exchanged a knowing look and are now going down to the river. They have placed their bikes against a tree and are stripping off their clothes soaked in dirt and sweat. They are now alongside the girls: "*Mboté*[2]!!!" a joyful cry before running into the water and diving under the surface. The children exchange astonished glances. They have never seen a *mundele*, and now two of them are here, somewhere in the river. A bearded face breaks the surface of the water. "*Viens ici!*" He climbs onto the overturned pirogue from which the kids were diving just a few moments earlier. Some of them run away in fright; others giggle at the lumbering of the stranger, who grabs the closest kid and jumps, throwing him into the water. His companions are laughing their heads off. These funny *mundeles* don't look like the ones in the stories.

We left Pokola eight days ago, and the arrival in town is a relief, especially for the tired old Victor. The harshness of the environment has worn both of us out, but his bicycle's thin wheels have made the crossing more exhausting for him.

The road ends in Impfondo. Only the boats on the Ubangi River continue and keep this town in contact with the outside world.

"Victor, parish?"

"Let's try, come on!"

The map suggests there is a church nearby but, *hey! Where's Victor?* There he is, speeding after a pickup truck with a pretty girl sitting in the back. *That fellow certainly doesn't waste any time.*

The boys are back in town.

This is Mary, she is from Canada. She and her American colleagues are returning from the hospital where they work—an American hospital in this remote area of the Congo. Mary, Jesse, Sarah, Drs

---

[1] In the Lingala language, it means *White Man*.
[2] Greeting in the Lingala language. It could be translated as *hello*, or *good morning*. In this case, it is clearly *hello*.

Joseph and Rebecca Harvey live in what used to be an Anglican mission. Five or six villas of fine workmanship, scattered over a beautifully manicured lawn. Across the street, the river.

Jesse is a nice guy from Calgary, and, like his friends, he is immediately fascinated by our adventure. We will be his guests for a few days until the boat to the capital leaves.

The next morning Victor and I check the boat timetable for the capital Brazzaville—one every three weeks, we can't go wrong. Then, we go for a walk in the centre.

Impfondo is a typical frontier town. A Congolese Far West. The Far East, in this case. The main street is the hub of local activity. Two parallel rows of sloppy two-storey buildings or shacks house the local shops. From these, spill all sorts: from powdered milk to medicines, from hardware stores to fabrics. There are a few butchers, a fishmonger, even a betting centre that includes a hairdresser. It's all here, in this unkempt yet charming main street. Moving away from the centre, we discover a few clubs where people spend their evenings. But the skyline is dominated by a couple of banks and a desolate succession of shabby administrative buildings. They are either derelict or never completed.

The market is small compared to other towns of similar size. You can find everything. At first glance, it may seem confusing and disorganised, but every commodity has its place: clothing here, the food there, hygiene products here, frying pans there. You need experience to find your way around, but in the markets, the layout is often similar. This one is bursting at the seams. Merchants flood the streets, mingling with the bustle of people producing a great sense of chaos. I always enjoy looking for what I need among the stalls, often following the calls of the merchants in this lively and exuberant racket. Even more, I enjoy wandering aimlessly among the crowd, taking care not to trample on goods lying on the ground in the narrowest passages. Walking through this Babel, amidst the hubbub of the merchants bargaining and enticing customers, I am entranced by the market. I am overpowered by the smells: smoked fish, soaps, or pieces of meat stretched out on cardboard on the ground; fragrances that mix and disorientate the senses. Plump ladies advertise the tastiness of their *mikate*[3], which has sustained my calorie intake for the past few months. An old woman fries small fish; further on, piles of fabrics are stacked up in a kaleidoscopic jumble, and a cobbler also sells vegetables from his land.

From a particularly convincing lady, it must have been her not-entirely-negligible figure, or she simply shouted louder than the others, I buy three *mikate* just fished from the pan. She hands me a banana leaf, with the three balls still oozing oil inside. Nice and warm and fragrant, I think, as we approach a young shoemaker.

The reason for our foray into the market is to find a craftsman who can repair the bike bags worn out by a year of travelling. They now have several rips, so they're no longer water-resistant. Trying to pocket a little more money from the naive *mundeles*, the cobbler makes a bold request for *deux mille sefà* (three euros). "But no, *mon ami*. For this job, I won't give you more than five hundred!"

The prices of goods are not displayed on labels. The price is the fruit of the mood of the shopkeeper and the manners of the person in front of him. Bargaining is obligatory; it is part of market life. A good market trader is histrionic, but with an expansive, warm and accommodating manner, likeable and charming. Even though he may be slippery and shrewd, he's never ruthless as he has a vested interest in getting a sale.

On both sides, we pretend to be hard bargainers, but we already know what amount we will agree on. "One thousand five hundred then."

"No, no. We'll go to your friend over there; he'll surely give us a better price."

---

[3] In the Lingala language. *Beignet* in French. A dough of flour, sugar and yeast strictly fried in palm oil. With peanut butter spread on top, it is even more delicious (*mikate na mwamba*).

"Him? He'll ask for a lot more."

Stroke of genius. Victor approaches the shoemaker, hugs him, and with one swift movement, lifts him onto his shoulders and runs here and there among the stalls. Everyone is watching my Madrilenian friend's bizarre haggling strategy; the plump ladies have stopped their propaganda, and the whole market is giggling about it. Even the canny cobbler on his back is laughing. "*Mille deux cents?*" asks Victor. "*Mille deux cents, Mille deux cents!*" sings out his passenger joining in the fun. They have great bargaining techniques in Madrid.

The next day, to kill time waiting for the boat, I give my faithful companion a bath. Looking at my bike over these last weeks, I often thought it needed a thorough washing.

Have you ever had something apparently unpredictable happen to you, and yet when it does, you think: *I knew it?* That morning, it occurred to me. I flip the bike over, wheels up, and start cleaning—first the frame, then the drivetrain, the brake pads and finally the disc. With a sponge soaked in soap, I place my hand over the rear disc. Idea! If I spin the wheel, I'll finish faster. One hand on the pedal, the other on the disc, the wheel starts spinning.

I hear a loud shout in the distance. *Are they calling me?* I turn to see, and my fingers remain stuck between the disc and the frame. Zaaaaaac!

A stabbing pain explodes from the fingers. My first instinct is to remove my hand and hold it with the other, but the damage is already done. The adrenaline in my body is running wild, and my heart is beating like crazy. Taking a close look, I try to examine my wounded left hand. The tips of my ring and middle fingers are both mangled. Shreds of flesh dangle motionless, and blood flows copiously from the wound.

I run towards Rebecca Harvey's house, screaming. She appears in the doorway and lets me in, visibly frightened. Lying on the couch, I'm sweating profusely, my head is spinning, and I feel on the brink of fainting at any moment.

"Right away to the hospital, let's not waste time!" says Rebecca. Drawn by the shouting, Victor also rushed over and remained speechless. He tries to make a joke to lower the tension. Oddly, I remember my laugh from that moment, but not his joke.

With the pickup, Rebecca drives me to the hospital, where we go straight into the surgical ward. The doctor is not there, but there is a nurse, called Mary Rose, who lays me down on the operating table and demonstrates her skills in no time.

"Let's see what's happened."

I gingerly let go of my injured hand and hold it out towards her. Automatically, my head turns the other way.

"Uh, not bad. How did that happen?" I explain the facts briefly while she thoroughly disinfects the wound.

"Do you have the other piece of the finger with you?" It's one of those questions that you don't hear very often but, you know, might leave you unsettled. I look at Mary Rose, terrified. Then I glance at Rebecca, looking for an encouraging smile, but instead find she is staring at me with a worried expression.

"Um... no. How much is missing?"

"A tiny bit." *A millimetre, a phalanx?*

"Rebecca, please call Victor, who should still be home."

She looks up the contact in the phonebook and hands me the phone. Two rings. "Victor, hello?"

"My friend, how are you? What have they told you?"

"Listen, please go to the garden and see if you can find a piece of finger!"

Silence. The situation is surreal, and Victor can't help laughing. Me neither. My body is finally relaxing, and the tension vanishes.

"I'm going. "

A minute passes, my mobile phone rings.

"No, Fil, nothing."

"Shit. Thank you, Victor. See you later."

Later on, I asked myself several times: *what did Mary Rose want to do with that piece of finger? Sew it back on? Who knows.*

During this macabre scene, the surgeon arrived and started injecting lidocaine into various parts of my hand. I lose sensitivity within a few minutes. *More. Please, more.* The pain is gone.

A few stitches and I am back in the car with Rebecca on our way home. I think about the doctor's recommendations: change bandages every day and take great care not to get the wound dirty. An infection with the bone exposed would mean gangrene. And with that, bye-bye to the fingers.

In the hours before the boat's departure, the pier is buzzing with activity. Some market traders have moved here for the occasion; beggars wander about with their backs bent and one hand opened with the palm up. A toothless old man approaches me and asks me to pay for his ticket. There is a constant bustle of porters carrying all sorts of goods on the boat. Passengers get on board, but they soon return to the bank as the wait may be long. They set off in the only boat available for the next few weeks, and Victor will join them. At this latitude, the rainy season will begin shortly, but for now, the river is almost dry; numerous sandbars border the few navigable areas, and only *baleinières* can travel in these conditions. One week to get there, some days tied up, another week to return. That's twenty days of waiting. What am I going to do?

It was a bitter farewell, I think, while, with a plate of rice and *saka saka*[4] on my lap, I watch the small pier slowly emptying. I have dreamt about travelling on these boats on the Congo River for a long time. Now that the opportunity has arisen, I am stuck with a bandaged hand that must not get infected in any way. I let the reader imagine the hygienic conditions on board these wooden boats, overloaded with people, goods and goats. Victor seems to understand the situation, but

---

[4] A typical Congolese dish made with fish, cassava leaves and palm oil.

I am sad to see him go like this. Yet another cycling companionship interrupted too soon. *Adios Victor, maybe we'll meet again!*

At the hospital, I am now a family member. I go there every two days for the dressings and, while she cleans the wounds, the caring Mary Rose distracts me, so I don't mind the pain.

Mary Rose is of Rwandan origin but has lived in Impfondo for some 20 years. How did she come to the Congo?

In 1994, one of the bloodiest genocides in African history took place. The Hutus, the majority ethnic group in the country, killed almost a million Tutsis and moderate Hutus[5]. Despite this, the new government was led by Tutsis. Fearing reprisal attacks, two million Hutu refugees from Rwanda were welcomed by President Mobutu in DRC[6]. In the wake of this tribal hatred, Rwanda, Burundi, and Uganda invaded DRC in 1996 and marched onwards to conquer Kinshasa. Their intent was to defend the minority of Congolese Tutsis and free the country from Mobutu's pro-Hutu dictatorship. During this march, the enormous Hutu refugee camps were attacked, and the Hutus were abused, raped and murdered: estimates of the number of Hutu refugees killed vary from two to three hundred thousand[7]. Like many of her brothers and sisters, Mary Rose was in one of these camps at the time and was forced to flee westwards into the heart of the forest. In miserable conditions, they crossed the immense country then known as Zaire and covered more than two thousand kilometres on foot. I met quite a lot of Rwandans in Central Africa, and I imagine a good number of them found refuge here in the same period.

---

[5] There is endless literature on the genocide in Rwanda. To delve deeper into the subject, let me suggest *The Rwanda Crisis*, by Gerard Prunier. *Sometimes in April* and *Hotel Rwanda* are two films set during that period.

[6] Democratic Republic of Congo. Not to be confused with the Republic of Congo, Congo Brazzaville.

[7] Prunier, Gerard. *Africa's World War: Congo, the Rwandan Genocide, and the Making of a Continental Catastrophe.* Oxford: Oxford Un., 2009.

"It took us six months, or maybe more. The first months it rained all the time, we walked and slept in the mud. We often couldn't find food. My husband and many of my brothers died on the way while others stayed in DRC."

"And how did you come here?"

"Ouch!" I let out a groan in pain.

"I'm sorry, am I hurting you?"

"No, no. I saw you were about to touch my finger, and I felt pain just at the idea."

"Tell me if I'm hurting you. So, when we crossed the river for the umpteenth time, I was exhausted, tired from the journey and the hunger. We arrived at the banks of the Ubangi with my brothers; there were more than ten thousand of us. We had had enough and decided to stop. Only eight hundred of us received refugee status, and we were allowed to stay here without any problems." Despite the memory of those atrocious moments, Mary Rose continues to recount the facts with extreme calm with her warm voice.

"I got married here, and now I have two children.

I smile at her, not missing the peaceful expression in her eyes. "Were you a nurse, also in Rwanda?"

"No. I was a seamstress. You see, I do have some fabrics over there. I make ends meet." She says this as if to apologise for her side activity.

"And now you sew people up."

"Yeah."

We burst into a roaring laugh.

After the last change of bandage, I walk back from the hospital, crossing the whole town. Life is running its normal course, but I look at it through different eyes. Perhaps already clouded by a veil of nostalgia. The butcher, who we have taught how to cut meat into a real steak, sees me passing in front of his shop and greets me with his hand holding the knife. In the shade of a tree on the riverbank, a barber is cutting a customer's hair while chatting relaxedly with those waiting.

Despite the hot time of the day, some guys are still piling up sand by the side of the road, to be sold later. They usually go to the river to dig in the early morning, when the sun is still snoozing, and possibly the freshness of the river cools them down as they work.

I am experiencing mixed feelings. With its life as slow and idle as the river that runs through it, Impfondo has won me over. This oasis of calm that welcomed us after the darkness of the forest wants me to be here. Yet, I need to get back on the saddle and pedal. I've spent more than a month recovering both from malaria and the injury to my hand. I miss that routine in the saddle that I had made my own.

It's time for me to get going again. Since there are no other boats in the coming days to reach the capital, I should go back the same way I came through the forest for a thousand kilometres. However, I don't feel like it, not alone, especially not with this slow healing wound. *AirCongo* offers me a quick but controversial solution. I'd rather not take a plane. It's like cheating at a game whose rules I wrote. Hypocrite.

A shiny Xian MA60 twin-propeller—an aeroplane designed by the Chinese aviation consortium—is waiting on the runway. I board the plane with a mixture of remorse for the *shortcut* and sorrow for leaving my friends, who have helped me so much over the past two weeks.

After take-off, the small town, now so familiar, flows past the window. The plane flies over the river for a few minutes before turning southwest; the forest seen from up here is just as impressive. Gradually, the vegetation becomes thinner and thinner. We are flying over a green savannah when a sudden loss of air causes the aircraft to lose several metres. Some worried passengers let out a scream. "Beeeeeeh," complain two goats in the cabin. Their bleating elicits a nervous laugh from the passengers, and the flight continues without further incidents.

In Brazzaville, humid, oppressive air hits me. Although the rainy season has not yet begun in the North of the country, here in the South, it is coming to an end. Nevertheless, frequent and rapid downpours underline that it is not yet over. I am leaving the airport with some regret, but happy to be back in the saddle in a few days. The noise of traffic, horns and confused voices remind me that I have spent the last two months in the forest, and all that is suddenly over.

Brazzaville lies on the northern bank of the Congo River. Kinshasa, the capital of the other Congo (Democratic Republic, DRC), shines across the water on the opposite bank. You don't find any single bridge across the river on the 600km-stretch that separates the two *Congos*. Not even between the two capitals, which are thus connected only by boat.

I'm going to the port for information on the timetable and tickets. Despite the official price, the cashier asks me for more money and an unreasonable extra charge for the bicycle. I don't intend to give up. But although I approach the question politely, the person in front of me raises his voice, quickly getting on to French colonisers and the arrogance of *us whites*. At that point, I shrug and walk away. I will find another solution.

While I am thinking of other possible solutions, I go to the embassies of the next countries: Angola and DRC. At the Angolan embassy, I complete my application in just a few minutes. However, I know from several experiences reported online that foreigners can't obtain a DRC visa here. My experience has taught me that it is worth a try.

"Good morning. I would like to apply for a tourist visa," addressing the secretary.

"Are you a resident here?" Her experience must have taught her how to cut a conversation short. "Yes, I have a residence visa for one year." Silence on the other side of the counter. "*Ca va,* follow me," the first hurdle cleared. She ushers me into the office of a diplomat who greets me in a friendly manner; I interrupted him while he was mopping up his plate with a little piece of *kwánga*[8], but with a quick lick of his

---

[8] A laborious way of preparing cassava, with the fermentation of the cassava. Depending on the region, it is given the form of a stick or a loaf.

fingers, he's back in business. After a brief account of my journey, he explains the visa requirements. "Fifty thousand CFA," *not bad, elsewhere it costs much more,* "passport photos and an invitation letter."

Ouch, I already knew that. All week, I've been looking for a reliable contact in Kinshasa, but I haven't come up with anything.

"Sir, I don't need an invitation. I'm in transit on my bike, and I'm not visiting anyone."

He looks at me and gives me a smile that means everything and nothing. "Without a letter, I can't issue you a visa." He is adamant on this point.

"Fine. Listen, I'll look for someone willing to host me, and I'll be back." I get up to leave. But as I'm heading to the exit, he says: "Wait... come, sit down." I return to my seat. The official puts his hand on my arm and moves closer to reduce the physical distance between us. In a confidential tone of voice, he reveals to me: "If you want, I have a friend who does these things. You know, the letters have to be made official at the foreign ministry. It's not easy." He wants $175 for this *favour.*

Here comes the point. The Congo has an unfortunate reputation as one of the most corrupt countries in the world. You don't hear about it here, but it permeates society at every level. It's the norm. I have read that it is widespread in many African countries, but personally, I have never been confronted with such explicit situations before arriving in Congo. Okay, except for the time when *I* tried to bribe a civil servant in Burkina.

Let's start from the top of the social ladder. Denis Sassou-Nguesso, seventy-seven years old, president of the Republic of the Congo for thirty-seven years. He has some thirty children with several wives—I am told by some Congolese, these are costly to maintain—and he recently bought a $7 million flat for one of his daughters, paid for in cash. In recent years, he has been investigated in France for corruption, where he laundered a lot of money from public finances and oil royalties. With influential supporters in Europe and America, he controls the market, primarily in oil and timber. To secure a third term in office, he even changed the constitution before the last elections. I would entitle his biography "A good man."

Going down the hierarchy, most politicians and high-ranking military officials are in their jobs thanks to their connections and relatives. Corruption is widespread in every government sector, especially in the management of earnings from the oil industry, which accounts for 90 per cent of the country's exports.

At the local level, the police and the army are also involved in corruption. A driver, be it a truck or a public bus, always has a wad of money at hand, ready to hand out at the first checkpoint. Similarly, a shopkeeper must be ready to pay, even more so if he belongs to a minority ethnic group that might not be appreciated in a big city. What about the population?

The population is the victim in all of this. Oil is the country's main source of livelihood. In 2014, there was a sharp drop in crude oil price, and the country fell into recession. Today, the government can no longer pay all the salaries of civil servants. Doctors and teachers are often forced to work without pay. Corruption, albeit with a different form at this level, is not so much a sign of moral weakness among people. It becomes the only means of survival, so you do not go hungry and at least manage to feed your family. Inspired by the hierarchy above, everyone feels entitled in their own way to ask for something.

Recently, I asked myself: "Why does nothing change in these countries? Everything has been the same for thirty years.[9]"

The prevailing opinion is "*Whatever Works*", to quote (improperly) Woody Allen. These mechanisms, which have become so well-oiled over time, enable everyone to get something to survive on with dignity

---

[9] The question does not refer exclusively to Congo Brazzaville, but to most of the Central African states. In Cameroon, Paul Biya has been in power since 1982, with seven mandates, in Gabon Ali Bongo succeeded his father after 40 years in power, Teodoro Obiang is also celebrating 40 years in power in Equatorial Guinea.

in one way or another. The fear is that a change in government will break the system, always to the detriment of the poorest segment of the population. But the problem is that nothing really works, or maybe just a bit. The bureaucratic apparatus is often a money-eating machine, with no positive outcomes for the country's development. It's like that in The Congo, and it's like that in many other African countries. How many times have I heard the sad condemnation: "The State has forgotten about us"?

The underlying problem is aptly summed up in a sentence I well underlined in the book *Half of a Yellow Sun* and which I quote here: "The real tragedy of the postcolonial world is that the majority of people had no say in whether or not they wanted this new world; rather, it is that the majority have not been given the tools to negotiate this new world[10]." None of the major African parties that would lead to independence existed before the Second World War. With independence, colonial governments left the newborn nations without any handover and often manipulated elections to ensure that their allies emerged victoriously. Africans found themselves with a democratic political structure that they were unable to manage, the previous social structure being, in many cases, tribal. Some of the colonial period's repressive laws nevertheless remained. Governments could censor the media, ban public meetings, and detain political opponents. New leaders inherited states without adequate infrastructure and public services, or it just took a few months for the system to collapse, as in DRC. African presidents found a way out of those impasses by centralising more and more power around them, leading to the birth of forty-year dictatorships. Over time, this process gave rise to the logic that those who attained a certain public office were entitled to personal benefits for themselves and their families.

---

[10] Adichie, Chimamanda Ngozi. *Half of A Yellow Sun*. 4Th Estate, 2019.

Even the occasional cycle traveller finds himself sucked into this conspiratorial vortex. As far as I'm concerned, except for one time when I was forced to pay a *toll* at gunpoint—but that wasn't a real *corruption*—I have never given in to those demands, nor did I intend to do so this time at the embassy. Rather, I preferred not to visit DRC. With an internal flight connecting Cabinda and Soyo in Angola, I am offered a simple and reasonably cheap, but at least legal, way to cross the Congo River. Second flight in a week. So be it.

"I'll think about it, thank you and goodbye." I turn around and walk out through the door.

ANGOLA

> *I come from one of the richest countries on the planet.*
> *Yet the people of my country are among the poorest of the world.*
> *The troubling reality is that*
> *the abundance of our natural resources*
> *[…] is the root cause of war,*
> *extreme violence and abject poverty.*
>
> DR. D. MUKWEGE,
> NOBEL PEACE PRICE LECTURE 2018

April

If a friend asks you why you fell in love with that girl or man, you probably blush, don't know what to say and stammer something about her beauty, her smile.

Many have asked me what my favourite country was of all those I have crossed. My immediate answer is Angola. Never before have I had such an emotional reaction from the instant I entered a country. Why? It's beautiful; the people have beautiful smiles…

Angola hit me in the stomach, like a fist that leaves you breathless. Then, slowly but relentlessly, it took over my heart and has never left it. It is in me. Here is an expert voice to help me, the writer Pedro Rosa Mendes, who wrote about Angola: "From a place like this you come back empty. Even the soul becomes thinner.[1]" A part of me remained there, not like in Congo, where a piece of my finger lies, but a part of my soul remained trapped. I like this vision. Unlike Rosas Mendes, however, I walked away saturated. Angola has replaced that fragment

---

[1] Mendes, Pedro Rosa. *Bay of Tigers*. Jonathan Ball, 2003.

of my soul with its smiles, its rhythm and the warmth of its people, but also with its complexities, sacrifices and uncertainties. Maybe that's why I'm glad I left it at the *right* time. It is like, after a hearty lunch, you feel the need to get up from the table for a walk. You're glad you have eaten well, but you wouldn't be able to eat more unless you forced yourself.

Let me start with a premise. Angola has gone through twenty-seven years of civil war. *Twenty-seven!* And it was not the longest war in Africa. More than five hundred thousand deaths, an economy in collapse, roads and bridges destroyed. It's the country with the highest infant mortality rate.

Why? Angola could be one of the wealthiest countries in the world. Yet Angolans are among the poorest people in the world. Each region possesses incalculable riches: oil on the coast and in the territorial waters, massive diamond deposits in the province of Lunda Sur in the North-east of the country. Water flows in all four directions from the plateau in the centre of the country. Not to mention gold, and iron, and copper, platinum, uranium, rare-earth metals, lead and zinc, tin. My list is not exhaustive.

Already by the end of the 1960s, there were the first outbreaks of military conflict. It began as a war of independence from the Portuguese colonial regime. The scale of the conflict grew rapidly. South Africa invaded Angola from the South at the behest of the USA. Russia and Cuba sided with the MPLA (Movement for the Liberation of Angola), led by the charismatic figure of Agostinho Neto. On the other side were the FNLA (National Front for the Liberation of Angola) led by Holden Roberto and Jonas Savimbi's UNITA (National Union for the Total Independence of Angola). It seemed that whichever side had control of Luanda on independence day would secure power. It was Agostinho Neto who declared independence on November 11, 1975. Yet, the war did not end that day. The Angolans found themselves embroiled in a fratricidal war without knowing the real reasons behind it. It was a war of the poor: at times, they carried fake wooden rifles to make it appear as if they were armed. They had no uniforms, so there was no way to tell until the last minute whether one was friend or foe.

In the mid-1980s, Angola became the African country where the Cold War was at its fiercest. Then, with the end of the Soviet Union, the great nations lost interest, leaving the Angolans to fight among themselves. Two attempts at peace in 1989 and 1994 came to nothing. Until the end of his life, Savimbi carried on his insane campaign, largely financed by the sale of diamonds from mines in the province of Lunda Norte. When he died in 2002, the ruined UNITA party signed the peace agreement.

Angola and the Angolans will need many years of peace to recover. Most of the population still live on less than two dollars a day. Healthcare is inefficient, and infant mortality reaches record levels.

A fifteen-minute flight took me over the river—and the country—Congo. As the plane approaches the mouth, I watch the ocean's deep blue become stained with yellow and ochre. At peak flow at this time of year, the Congo River carries fragments of silt and clay, sucked up over the 4,700 kilometres of its course, into the Atlantic Ocean. The water is muddy for tens of kilometres. It catches my attention from the low altitude at which the turboprop flies, but the effect is evident from the satellite images.

Leaving Soyo airport to the south, I pedal through a flat, sandy environment. A recently built multi-lane road interrupts the monotony of the landscape. Here the road signs are bilingual: Portuguese and Chinese.

In these vast spaces, there is something that does not make sense to me. I don't notice it at first, but it becomes more and more jarring in my perception as the morning progresses. *But what is it?*

The sun, that's what! It's behind me, even though I'm heading south. As long as I was near the equator, in the forest and under gloomy weather, I didn't notice it. But yes, I am in the Southern Hemisphere, and my biological compass has started to freak out. My senses were calibrated to the sun's position. I could now tell instinctively if I was going in the wrong direction. I think back to the crossing of the Sahara, when, at noon, blades of light would strike the white sand and asphalt in front of me and explode, blinding me. But today, my shadow is there in front of me.

Treebeard, an Ent in Lord of the Rings, said: "I always like going south, somehow it feels like going downhill.[2]" I really like him for that. I've always enjoyed going south too. But will it still be like that from now on?

This is how my thoughts wander as I cycle along this endless, monotonous, paved road. How boring! A quick study of the map reveals a track that leaves the main road, reaches a small town called Ambriz and continues along the coast.

I take a rough path that climbs up sheer red sandstone hills, giving me enchanting views of the sea. The clouds travel fast across the sky, and I can't compete with their shadows on my bike. They slow down as the day progresses and begin to gather: vague omens of rain.

I'm climbing the steep slope, my gaze wandering in search of a passage between stones, until a black patch a palm away from the wheel catches my eye. I pass it and turn around; one metre away, a black cobra is staring at me, head raised, and hood expanded. A rush of adrenaline pours into my bloodstream. Should I run; should I stop? I stop. *When will I ever meet a black cobra again?* In the blink of an eye, the snake has already disappeared among the shrubs. I remain petrified for a long time, and my hands continue to tremble. Did I dream, or did I really pass by him? But now, let's get back on the saddle! There is still a long way to go.

Ambriz is a surprise. It stands on the end of a peninsula that separates the open sea from a lagoon dotted with salt pans. Entering

---

[2] Tolkien, J. R. R. *The Lord of The Rings*. Mariner Books, 2012.

the main square, I have the impression of having travelled ten thousand kilometres in a few moments to the square of any village in the Portuguese countryside. Now home to the navy, a Dutch-built fortress from the end of the 18th century dominates the square. The garden has probably seen better times but retains a certain elegance with its geometry. All around, the houses are unquestionably colonial in style, low and painted in pastel shades, the brightness of which now belongs to bygone days.

There are many signs of the war. Among them is the old town hall on the main street. Only the façade and the clock tower are still standing in its memory. I look at it, wondering if the plant climbing on the back is keeping the tower up, or vice versa.

In short, a Portuguese village in Angola. Not too surprising, you might say, since Angola is a former Portuguese colony. But I have never come across a *French-style* town in the former French colonies I have travelled through. This is indicative of the different style of colonisation adopted by the two countries.

France adopted a centralising strategy, aiming to *civilise* the locals and thus destroy any traditional power base. Economically, France was interested in exploiting the abundant resources, especially mining, that the land offered. These colonies produced what they did not consume, and consumed what they did not produce. All of colonial life took place in the capital. Colonists ventured inland only for business.

Portugal, on the other hand, intended to stay. Its influences are much more pervasive, architecturally, culturally and culinary. The colonists built numerous *fazendas*, the farms. Their idea was that a higher level of moral and economic progress would make the colonies, seen as an integral part of the mother country, more profitable. In this process of cultural integration, missionaries played a fundamental role.

Here I am in Luanda. I enjoy a few days of rest, in the excellent company of Sergio, my contact here in the city, and other Italian friends. I share good food and splendid days at the beach with them and recharge my batteries.

Luanda was a key outpost of the Portuguese colonies. It was initially built to house thirty to fifty thousand people, but by the end of the war, one million refugees had crammed into the urban area, which had been a haven since the beginning of the war. The South African army, deployed in support of UNITA, arrived within a few hundred kilometres of the capital, but the guerrillas never got in.

Today the population exceeds five million. The majority lost everything during the war—family, home, business. They flocked to the big city. "Because there's money there; there's work," a young man I met in a remote village in the highlands told me.

Studying the physiognomy of the city, there are some imposing skyscrapers on the seafront called the *Marginal*. These have been built in recent years by the Chinese. These buildings overlook the villas of the colonial period, where wealthy Angolan business people and a large number of expats now live. The middle-class lives in the City and the surrounding residential neighbourhoods, juxtaposed in a dissonant manner with a sea of decrepit buildings and wooden and tin shacks.

It's really challenging for the government to scale up the infrastructure so it can cater for such huge numbers. On paper, it would like everyone to have a decent home to live in. Along the main roads out of the city, you see ugly, monotonous blocks of flats. But if you take a rickety side street, you can lose yourself in a maze of shacks and dilapidated shops, with traffic going crazy everywhere.

Moving further away from the city centre, you come across an immense industrial zone on the outskirts. You might think that all of Angola's industrial production comes from here. There are also several Chinese companies along the road. If there is any business to be done in Angola, the government deals with the Chinese. Finally, the countryside. More and more empty, more and more desolate, the further one goes. The signs of war are still there; no one has bothered to remove the rubble from these abandoned lands.

You still hear a lot about it in the city. Today there is the port, banks and houses, but until 2011, on the seafront not too far from the city centre, there was the largest black market in Africa, and perhaps in the world. More than three hundred thousand people came daily to *Roque Santeiro*, named after a famous Brazilian soap opera, to buy all kinds of goods. Legal and otherwise. It provided an essential service, especially during the war, as it was one of the few places where you could find both food and weapons.

I leave Luanda behind and, at lunchtime, I arrive in the town of Catete. A commemorative plaque in front of a recently constructed building reminds me that it is the birthplace of the first Angolan president, Agostinho Neto. The building is a cultural centre dedicated to him. A young man is walking along the pavement, and soon he catches me up. I ask him if events are sometimes held here, but he shakes his head: "*Não.*" Answering my next question, he suggests a nice little restaurant where I can get something to eat.

The spacious interior of the place is clean enough and tidy. There are no other customers, just a lovely waitress sitting cross-legged watching TV. As soon as she notices me, she smiles brightly. *Is she smiling at me because I am the only customer or a charming globetrotter?* She seats me at the table closest to the buffet: an abundant buffet, all for me.

"Take whatever you want, my treat." With the plate in hand, I turn around and see a sturdy Angolan approaching.

"*Bom dia.*"

"*Bom dia. Eu sou o General Manuel De Carvalho, mas todo mundo me chama Pakas.*[3]"

"Pleased to meet you, General. And thank you for the offer, but don't bother. Everything looks delicious, and I'll pay with pleasure."

"No, no. I insist; this restaurant is mine."

I return to the table. The general asks if he can sit with me.

---

[3] *Good morning. I am General Manuel De Carvalho, but everyone calls me Pakas.*

"What do you drink, beer?"

"A coke will be fine, thanks."

"*Manuela! Traz duas Coca-Cola aqui*,[4]" he orders, addressing the waitress.

I'm ravenous, and without even waiting for the drinks, I plunge the knife into the steak.

"Do you like it?"

Hmmm.

"Where are you from, boy?"

"Today from Luanda, General."

He nods.

"General, I saw an elegant building at the entrance to the city, the cultural centre. It's admirable that the state is supporting culture, even outside the capital." I must have hit a nerve. The general emits a grunt that I interpret as, "Maybe, but is money wasted."

"They spent loads of money on that building, and no one uses it. It's been there, unused, since the day it opened."

"I see."

"Here we are in the province closest to the capital, yet we are mile away from the prosperity you saw there. Here, there is poverty everywhere. And the government spends money on useless projects instead of helping the population."

"I'm sorry that things…"

The general doesn't give me time to finish my sentence. His empty coke bottle is passing from one hand to another, and without looking up, he continues: "This government talks and talks, but the population is getting poorer and poorer. In Luanda, they are busy with the Chinese, with foreign companies, and nobody cares about these people, who have nothing to eat. I'm lucky, as you can see, I have a pension and a restaurant to run. But did you pay attention, on your way here, how much poverty there is?"

---

[4] "Manuela, bring two Cokes here"

I lower my eyes to follow the bottle that keeps rotating in his hands: "And the government is doing nothing?"

"The young people! The government must focus on the younger generation to lift this country out of misery. We can't go on for the next twenty years asking for aid from China. Nothing will ever change. We will have a generation that has not studied, that will never be ready. Angola cannot improve without them."

The last statement leaves no room for a reply. A moment of silence falls over the table. I need to assimilate what the general has just told me while he watches the TV. Reflecting on the meeting, I can only feel grateful. Pakas is a cultured man and seems to have held a prominent position in the army. So much so that he can afford to talk about sensitive topics without fear of repercussions. His privileged view of reality helped me to understand a little more about this country.

"General, did you fight for the MPLA during the war of independence?"

His gaze focuses on an unspecified point behind me. "Yes," he sighs, "a long time ago."

He lets me know he doesn't want to talk about it. It is not hard to understand. Today, Angolans don't want to hear about the war anymore. They have suffered too much, too many unspeakable things. Today, Angolans are trying to move forward with their best assets: industriousness and a smile. And music. A music video by a local artist is playing on the TV while Manuela cleans the counter with sensual dance moves.

The wide-open space on the plateau in the province of Cuanza Sul reaches towards the infinite horizon. I have the impression that the earth extends so far because it has stolen some space from the sky. And a few moments later, I think that perhaps it is the immense sky that is appropriating a piece of land.

The distances seem endless. I pass some *fazendas* as I cycle along never-ending fences, with one eye on the bumpy road and another on the sky. Ah, what amazing skies Angola has given me. Especially the midday sky. Against an exceptionally bright and uniform background, in the mid-morning, sparse cotton balls appear, and over time grow to fill the vastness of that otherwise monochrome blue.

As I pedal along, I can't help but admire the sky, enchanted, my mind busy trying to recognise shapes in the clouds before the wind shuffles the cards and creates new ones. But this pastime is not suited to the uneven roads of the highlands. There is nothing to it but to stop, put down the bike and contemplate in silence. The lush grass sews the wounds in the rocks on either side of the track and sways when a breeze caresses it. I am often and easily distracted. The road continues relentlessly until I reach the gate of a *fazenda*. My calls drag the guard out of the lodge. He doesn't hide a wide yawn, and the annoyance at my wakening him. I won't be allowed to continue along that path. The GPS, which is very accurate in other countries, in Angola has already shown its shortcomings. Now it has led me to a dead end. I ask it for directions along another road that will not disturb the guard's rest. The response is a journey of one hundred and forty kilometres, to cover about twenty as the crow flies.

I argue my case with the guard, who has regained his good spirits. He refuses to let me through again but suggests another solution to the impasse. "If you continue along the fence," he points to his right, "you will come to a village and, from there, a path goes round the hill. No one uses it anymore though, so it might be in bad condition. I think it's going to be hard to get through on a bike."

On the GPS map, I have an empty area in front of me; nothing is marked. About twenty kilometres to the east, a thin white line is lost in the grey sea of the map. *Are the two roads connected?*

I proceed like a submarine in a sea of grass. Grass underneath, grass in front, and sometimes clumps of grass taller than myself, blocking my view of the sky. But I am advancing almost blindly: I have no way of looking at the sky. Keeping my head out of harm's way, I do my best to dodge the branches that still hit the rest of my body. At the same time, I try to make out the vague hint of a path in front of me. The brushwood clings to the handlebars, and several times I run the risk of tumbling over. As time goes by, this sea of green shows no sign of diminishing, but the grass gets lower, and finally, I can see ahead of me. I only detect more green. Then, suddenly, the undergrowth stops, and the path reappears under the wheels. I follow it with my eyes as it goes into a delightful grove.

I take advantage of this for a break. Thorns have caused several cuts, and trickles of blood are flowing from my bare arms and legs. My glasses now have a few more scratches, and numerous tufts of grass have been caught here and there between the bike bags. I'm sitting on a moss-covered boulder and munching a packet of cookies. Crunch... crunch... crunch... the packet is now empty, and silence returns to the grove. The rays of the afternoon sun are penetrating the sparse undergrowth and painting shimmering tricks of light. There is silence all around—only the music of a gentle wind playing the leaves on the trees can be heard. I close my eyes for a moment and inhale deeply, several times. My heart slows down. The breeze caresses my hands, and I let my mind fly away.

Finally, I open my eyes. I feel totally regenerated when I jump on the pedals and take to the trail again. Elegant, exciting, it unwinds in a docile descent through the plants of this ancient forest. I press on, exhilarated by this amazing place so isolated from the rest of the world. No thoughts, no worries, just me, the bike and the wind. I let it carry me, as if on a stream, through this primitive world.

In Calucinga, a good meal of rice accompanied by potato leaves and a chicken wing, followed by a quiet night, recharges my spent energy. Leaving the village, I should follow another dirt track that will take me to Bailundo in two days. But the track is not there. Or rather, there used to be one. The Chinese are paving Angola at a pace that not even Google and its satellites can keep up with.

Not too bad. Favourable wind and smooth asphalt make it almost effortless. Gentle green hills accompany the ride under the usual immense blue sky—I could call it Angolan Blue. There are not many villages along the road, so I ride fast. I could reach Bailundo in a day at this pace, but I arrive right on time for lunch in a lively little village not marked on the map.

The central square, dominated by a majestic tree with a canopy that seems to obscure the whole world, is invaded by a garish market. Typical scenes of crowding and confusion that I am well used to but which never bore me. I slowly push my bike among the stalls and vendors displaying their goods on the ground. Many greet me cheerfully as I pass. A man offers me a packet of *ginguba*, peanuts, while another jokingly asks me how much I want for my bike horn—*not for sale, sorry!* In the area where fruit and vegetable sellers have set up, I ask where I can buy a juicy pineapple.

They point to a woman sitting on a low stool nearby. By Jove! She is African womanhood personified, not a pineapple seller. She sits there with her legs spread out, peeling pineapples, and she watches me while I stand rooted to the ground, speechless. She is in her forties. Her straight black hair is gathered into a slight bun. Framed by her ebony skin and delicate face, her lips look even more voluptuous. She wears a red top that is tight enough to leave little to the imagination, and a floral fabric is wrapped around her waist. The skirt doesn't do its full duty and hangs over her thigh, held only by her knee, revealing a slender, athletic leg.

"Want to taste?" Her voice brings me back to the real world, where she is handing me a wedge of pineapple. As she reaches towards me, her skirt slips off her leg, leaving it entirely uncovered. I can't hold back a look full of desire. This is how I want to remember her, the most attractive pineapple seller I have ever met and probably will ever meet. She has noticed that I'm undressing her more and more with my eyes, but, more cheeky than innocent, she doesn't bother closing her skirt.

She is undoubtedly used to being stared at in a certain way due to her disquieting beauty—disquieting for her admirers, not for her.

In any case, reader, if you are by any chance rooting for me, know that I didn't get anywhere, but at least I got two juicy pineapples.

I am still stunned by this blow to the heart as I leave the market on the main street. Under the big tree, as always, life is teeming. Taxi drivers are huddled around their motorbikes, waiting for customers. A trader has rolled out a carpet on which he has neatly arranged belts, and a group of older adults are sitting around discussing the weather and the legs of the pineapple seller. I ask for directions to a place to eat, but I also stop to chat with them. In a bat of an eye, a large crowd has gathered around us. I look around and meet only smiling faces that inspire friendliness. They ask me for photographs together, and one guy even wants my autograph. Unbelievable! A policeman makes his way through the crowd. "What's going on here? Step away from the gentleman at once."

"But no, officer. We were just talking. They were not disturbing me."

"No, no. I don't want them bothering you. Where are you going?"

"Just across the street. Some guys told me there's a Malian dude who prepares grilled chicken."

"Yes. That's right. Come on. I'll take you." And he escorts me across the street, my bodyguard.

Sitting at the table, I dust off my *françafricain* with the cook, Idriss, while the policeman stands at the entrance, with his arms crossed. *Heaven forbid all these fans should disturb my lunch.*

I finish the chicken, a little bit charred, to be honest, and on the way out of the restaurant, the policeman invites me to the station. "The captain would like to see you."

Formal diplomatic handshakes between the parties, complete with photographs. "We are pleased to have you here in our community."

"Captain, I thank you; you have welcomed me like a star."

"Not many people come through here, and even fewer tourists. The police must leave you with good memories of this country."

Once again, Angola, despite its difficulties and contradictions, amazes me with the goodness and genuineness of the people who live there. They deserve so much more than what they have now, with everything they have had to suffer.

"Felipe?"

"Yes, Captain?"

"An officer will escort you as far as Bailundo to make sure you arrive without any problems."

A smile escapes me, inevitably, "Captain, I have a feeling that nobody in this country would ever let anything happen to me." No argument. And there will be an escort.

The officer follows me on a motorbike taxi. We ride side by side to have a chat, but sometimes he lags far behind. That's a funny situation! I also *take advantage* of him as a cameraman and ask him to shoot a video.

Just outside the village, we come alongside a cultivated field. An old woman is bent over picking vegetables. She interrupts her work, slowly straightens her back and greets me with a wide movement of her arm and an even wider smile, that's tired but at the same time full of energy.

I return the greeting, and at that moment Claudio Lolli comes to mind, with that song of his "that resounds more in the chest than in the sun.[5]"

> We are the ones who make the earth rich
> we who bear
> sleeping sickness and malaria
> we harvest cotton, rice and wheat
> we plant corn
> all over the plateau.

---

[5] D'Elia, Gianni. *Riascoltando gli Zingari Felici*.

We penetrate forests
we cultivate savannas
our arms reach
farther every day.
From us come the treasures taken from the earth
with which all others
remain favoured.[6]

I am officially in love, with the pineapple lady and with Angola.

The city of Huambo welcomes me with its energy and liveliness. Once a UNITA stronghold, it has now risen from its ashes with the best of intentions. I came to the city to extend my Angolan visa, but I stayed on a few more days. The rhythm and vibrations that run through this city have won me over, and what's more, it is attractive to the tourist's eye. In particular, I am fascinated by the statue of Agostinho Neto that dominates the view on 11th November Square. The poet president. He is sitting on the ground, his rifle lying behind him, with a pen in his hand, perhaps composing one of his poems.

After waiting for a week, I am told that my visa cannot be renewed. I will have to exit Angola, get it validated for another thirty days, and then return. Seventeen hours by bus take me to the border crossing of Santa Clara. In Namibia, I eat a sandwich at Burger King, a leap into the modern era, before repeating the same gruelling journey to be reunited with my bicycle.

Mission accomplished. Now I can retrace my steps, travelling with no hurry to the border. Studying the map, I identify a river flowing south in an ideal direction for me. The Rio Cunene, one of the longest rivers in Angola, has its source not far from Huambo on the Biè plateau. The river then flows until the border with Namibia, forming a

---

[6] Lolli, Claudio. *Ho Visto Anche Degli Zingari Felici (Conclusione)*.

natural boundary for almost four hundred kilometres. I decide to follow it as closely as possible, as far as the roads allow.

The route I pick is quiet at the beginning. The roads are in poor condition with little traffic. I cross the river for the first time at Matala. The Cunene is different from other African rivers. It is a proud river with an aggressive character. It's full of energy from the mountains and sweeps away every obstacle in its path. It digs inexorably into the rocks, creating bends or waterfalls at will, and no plant is allowed to desecrate its banks. It has nothing in common with those immense rivers of West and Central Africa, which flow peacefully, so much so that at times they seem motionless, and welcome boats and animals on their waters. Sometimes plants and mangroves grow in such abundance on the banks that you cannot even get close to them. And the bank itself is not clearly defined as the waters overflow into stagnant flood plains. Not so the Rio Cunene. It is either water, or nothing. It is turbulent, or still.

The track heads south from the village of Mulondo and follows the river for two hundred kilometres before rejoining the asphalt road to Namibia. Much of it runs through Bicuar National Park, once the home of large animals, including elephants, buffalo, and various species of antelope. During the civil war, almost all the beasts were killed and sold to buy weapons and supplies.

I travel along a sandy track, quite hard in some places and loose in others. There is no hint of human or animal activity. With little variation, the route runs through a colourful but monotonous woodland. In particular, one widespread plant attracts my attention: the *mopane* tree. It doesn't stand out because of its size, just over ten metres, but because of its unusual butterfly-shaped leaves. Once again, I fantasise about what it would have been like to cycle through these forests two hundred years ago. Maybe I would have had to stop and wait for a herd of elephants to cross the road, or I would have chased an antelope for a few metres. In 2019, there is none of that. It's a day of sand and *mopane*.

At another time, it might have gone unnoticed, fragile and bare as it was. But that tree, with its pale green leaves now becoming yellow, touched me. I had to stop and admire it. That tree had a fundamental meaning for me. It meant the seasons were starting to roll again. After more than a year in the forest, where the weather was always the same and the vegetation always green, I had almost forgotten the beauty of the seasons. This tree reminded me of that beauty. Today, the spell was broken, and the seasons were free to move. This tree would probably not have the same meaning for an inhabitant of the equatorial forest, where the value of changing between the rainy season and the dry season determines the rhythms of work in the fields and fishing. Nor would it have the same meaning for an inhabitant of the desert, for whom the more rapid change from day to night, from heat to coolness, is significant.

But it was meaningful to me. I then sat at the base of the trunk, listening to the first dead leaves crunching on the ground, and wrote him a letter.

Dear tree,
I sit here at your feet and write you this message because, seeing you from afar, I was stirred.
Your leaves are beginning to take on shades of yellow. There's nothing strange about that. Autumn is coming. There, you have reminded me of the beauty of the seasons, which mark the rhythm of Nature at our latitudes. […]
You know, your colleagues near the equator, comforted by abundant rains and the sun at its zenith, have hair that is always vigorously and luxuriantly green.
But as I move away from the equator, you are the first tree I have met that is willing to refresh its colours from year to year. […]
And for once, I like to think that I went to find Autumn and didn't have to wait for its arrival.

*Thank you,
An admirer of yours.*

Twelve hours have passed since I left Mulondo, and finally, after one hundred and thirty kilometres, the village of Mucope comes into sight, illuminated by the last rays of the sun. For the second time, my route crosses the Rio Cunene. The air was boiling until late afternoon, and the sand, plentiful along most of the way, has considerably slowed down my progress. Only in the last few hours has the temperature cooled a little, bringing some relief to my tired body.

A few words with a villager and a policeman are enough to direct me towards the shelter for the night. At the town hall, the mayor interrupts what seemed to be a critical meeting and welcomes me with great pleasure. The mayor invites me to join the other guests at the table, where they have just finished a plentiful buffet washed down with wine and beer. There are still a few delicacies left over, and, taking advantage of their concentration on the meeting, I clear the trays, indeed polish them as if they had never been used. I sit in a corner with the eyes on my plate and my ears tuned to the conversation.

The problem is serious. Here in the Huambo region, the rains have been generous this season. All around, the vegetation is green and luxuriant. On the other hand, there has been no significant rainfall in the South of Angola for the last six years. Indeed, the total absence of rain during the previous wet season has brought the population to the point of desperation. Not only have they been unable to farm, but their livestock are also beginning to die from the drought, and drinking water for the population is becoming increasingly scarce. The herders have had to abandon their homes and migrate to the central provinces of the country, where we are now.

In this meeting, the administrators of all the municipalities in the region are trying to agree on possible solutions that would allow the many affected animals to come. A big part of the area is, in fact, uninhabited, and there is not enough land near the wells for all the incoming cattle. The only ready solution is to open new water wells in the nearby Bicuar National Park so that herdsmen and cattle can exploit these lands. This requires permission from the provincial authorities.

Sitting at the table and listening to these words, these issues seem far removed as I am coming from the North, where water abounds. Yet, from the next day, I will find myself living in contact with this new reality.

I set off early in the morning and immediately find myself sinking into a thick layer of sand. The passage of the herds of cows has ruined the surface, forming several banks of sand. The few bikers who are tackling the track are also having difficulty. Yet they are able to use the gas throttle, and with the right balance on the rear wheel, they manage to move forward slowly.

I push on. I try pedalling on the side of the road, where the trees are not too dense, but quickly give up on that idea as my tyres get punctured by loads of thorns. The gentle mopane had now made way for more aggressive vegetation of shrubs and thorny plants. I continue to get punctures, and the sealing fluid squirts out of the tyres, working its miracle several times over. I send my thanks to the inventor of tubeless tyres, and return to my sandy beach of a track, well over a thousand kilometres from the coast. Today counts among the top three of the most demanding days of the entire trip.

The morning is well underway when thankfully my luck changes. A truck is travelling in the opposite direction, carrying goods northwards. The sand has become harder under the weight, and I can faithfully follow the track, with some difficulty, but still remaining in the saddle. I double my cruising speed, covering perhaps ten kilometres in the next hour. It feels like flying.

Throughout the day, I meet herds of cows going up the road in the opposite direction. Puffs of dusty clouds, first silky and then thick as fog, announce the approach of the cattle. Barefoot, dressed in a few rags and only carrying a water bottle, the cattle drovers advance. They are children; they are young; they are old. They are exhausted. No one talks, no one laughs. One step after the other, their stick preceding them as they cross that arid land.

And here, at last, is the asphalt. After three days on (or rather, in) the sand, I touch the tarmac near Chiulo, a collection of metal sheets and burning shacks. From here, with the wind at my back, I follow the road to Cahama.

This land exudes abandonment and misery. I try to imagine what this region might have been like before millions of slaves were deported and the advent of the civil war. Perhaps it was a populous area, dotted with villages. Now it is deserted, as if a tornado had swept through—hundreds of kilometres of emptiness. On his way to the Southern front during the war, Kapuściński passed through here in 1975 and wrote: "Time passed, but it was like standing still on the spot. Always the same smooth strip of asphalt in the middle of the red crumbly earth. On either side, always the same faded and parched curtains of scrub, the same sky of blinding whiteness, the same emptiness of an abandoned world whose presence was betrayed by not a movement, not a voice. In this motionless, dead and essential scenario, our truck moved forward [...][7]," and my bike moves forward, pushed by the east wind. I look around. I would say that still today, everything matches his description.

Here in the province of Cunene, the drought has hit hardest. Most of the cattle I have come across in recent days may have come from these lands. Sometimes I pass large tanks beside the road; they are clearly empty. Next to each of them, there are lots of brightly coloured plastic buckets and basins. Women and children are waiting in the shade of the trees. Waiting for what? For the tanker that will bring the water. I don't see any villages nearby; just sparse settlements and the wells of these small households are dry.

---

[7] Kapuściński, Ryszard. *Another Day of Life*. Vintage Books, 2001.

I pass three children on the other side of the road. Three water containers. Big, small, small. Like the three bearers. They walk fast in a line, silent. *Where do they come from? How far do they still have to go?* Hell, why so much injustice? When I was their age, I was splashing around in an inflatable pool in the garden. Instead, these three souls travel miles under the scorching sun to drink a sip of water. My heart tightens. I would like to smile and greet them cheerily as I love to do with everyone I meet, but I can't. Who knows what kind of face I'm pulling? They watch me go by, say nothing. I am helpless. I have no way to help them except by leaving them the half-full bottle of water I still have. A smile. Thank you, kids. You make me feel a little better. I move off, but their souls remain close to me.

The Catholic mission in Cahama seems deserted. I push my bike into the sand of the football field, and I approach the goal. Three men are sitting under a tree deep in conversation. They greet me warmly as soon as they notice my arrival.

"*El Padre chega em uma hora,*" the oldest one reassures me. I sit with them, sheltered from the fiery rays of the sun. After the usual questions, due more to politeness than to heartfelt interest, the conversation dies down. Two hens chase each other a short distance away, and their calls are the only sounds to be heard. I have always felt at home in Angola. Even now, sitting silently with three Angolans under a tree, I don't feel uncomfortable or embarrassed. I feel at home with them: they are welcoming me without showing it openly.

Crossing the football field, a stocky man comes up to me with his arms outstretched and an even wider smile. "Here's the father," one of the men anticipates my question.

"*Bem-vindo, filho.*"

"*Bom dia, padre.*"

He exudes joy and fulfilment from every pore. His smile is contagious. I don't even need to ask him for a room – I'm already his guest "since the Lord decided that you would stop here." Fr. Alijandro is Mexican and has been running this mission for five years, together with another missionary.

He gives me time to put my stuff down in the room and proposes a village tour. He has to make some visits and would be happy to show me the area. I accepted with enthusiasm. Everywhere we go, the community greet him with affection, like a lifelong friend, and this first impression is confirmed by all the people we pass.

The son of the mission warden is to be married the next day. Fr. Alijandro passes by his house to visit them. "Are you ready? Do you need anything?" His every action is imbued with altruism. He lives to serve, as good Catholic doctrine teaches. Obviously, they invite us to attend the wedding, at least for the celebrations held at the groom's house.

On the way back, I share my thoughts with him. "Father, you are well received by the community. I can see that you are a key man in this town."

He breaks into a broad smile. "We are here to serve. I have seen that it is only by setting a good example that people understand Christian doctrine. Here they are not scholars: catechism is useful, but only to the few who attend."

"Well, I was lucky to meet you then."

"Do you know that if you passed by yesterday, you would have met a fellow cyclist?" The statement leaves me stunned. There are so few of us cycling this coast that the chances of accidentally meeting another cyclist are close to zero. It turns out to be Blanca, a Spanish lady well known in the milieu. At the age of sixty-one, she is cycling alone through the whole of Africa, East and West; she rides fifty or sixty kilometres a day. Nothing stops her. Blanca is exceptional, not only for making the journey at that age but for doing it alone. Many women worry about the idea of travelling alone. In some respects, it's easier, but in others...

Shortly after sunset, the party begins. In the courtyard of the groom's family house, there are several people, all gathered around the newlyweds. They have just returned from her family, where they participated in the first half of the party.

"Tonight, there are only relatives from the groom's side. And a few uninvited drunkards. Those two you see over there are the girl's parents. They are the only ones attending tonight." Fr. Alijandro points to a smiling couple conversing with some ladies.

The guests of honour wear a suit made of the same fabric, a *pagne* with geometric patterns in different green shades. From the very first moment, the groom gives the impression of being proud of his bride. She is a beautiful girl with delicate and elegant features, as confirmed by the many admiring looks she receives from guests during the evening. On the contrary, the bride doesn't look radiantly happy. It's as if this wedding is not to her liking.

I meet many guys, and the evening proceeds nicely. Alijandro and I are the guests of honour, and the groom's father invites us to serve ourselves first at the buffet, followed by spouses' parents and then the rest of the family. I am ill at ease, a feeling that increases dramatically when the last guests arrive at the table just to find all the food has been eaten.

After dinner, the music, which until then had been muted, takes centre stage, and I take the opportunity to learn a few dance steps. There are some brilliant loose-limbed dancers on the floor in front of me, and soon I resign myself to my usual clumsy style of dancing before leaving the dance floor, maybe to find some girl to talk to. On reflection, the situation is bizarre. Almost all girls aged twenty to twenty-five, especially here in the rural environment, are already married. I should turn my attention to the fifteen-year-olds, but it feels strange just thinking about it.

The bride has been sitting all evening with a cryptic expression, maybe even one of annoyance. She doesn't seem to be enjoying the party. She is invited to stand up and accompanied to the banquet only when they came to the cutting of the cake. Fr. Alijandro is at my side. "Father, the bride doesn't seem very happy about this wedding, huh?"

"I think it's due to some tradition related to obedience. The girl can't get up from the table and has to maintain this detached attitude."

"Ah..."

Dozens of ritual photos, and no one is cutting that tempting cake, covered in cream. I haven't eaten many sweets in the last year, and I wait with a greedy desire to plunge my fork into that sponge cake. Yet I am convinced that every other person invited does not see many desserts in their lifetime. Maybe that is why no one seems eager to taste it.

Fr. Alijandro has a toy Chupa Chups dispenser with him, and a few minutes later, every kid at the party is wandering around contentedly with a stick in his mouth. The music starts up again at high volume; now, everyone is dancing. I am fascinated by the dexterity with which they all move. Unable to dance, I could only match them in fun and enjoyment of the evening, so I work hard at it until late at night.

The next day is Sunday. I take part in Mass with pleasure, in a church full of people. The church has been carefully designed, and I am pleased to observe some of the details. A sloping roof at a great height above the ground conveys the warm air through large gaps to the outside; large fans rotate in the ceiling by natural convection. This keeps the room cool, and attending Mass does not involve as much hardship, as I have often experienced elsewhere. Behind the white stone altar, a massive full-wall window offers a view of the trees behind. With the breeze blowing today, they form a lovely decorative effect.

The celebration continues for the next three hours. Songs and dances, organised by the adolescents of the parish, follow one another with brief interludes. The congregation contributes by clapping, dancing or improvising choirs, and the women express their joy with high-pitched shouts that enthuse the arena. The vibrant clothes of the faithful mirror the acoustics of these songs and fill the hall with a special mix of colour and sound.

At the end of the Mass, many people surround Alijandro, eager to talk to him. After waiting in vain, I sneak into the crowd, say a quick goodbye, and get back on my bike. After half an hour, I hear a car honking behind me. I turn around and find the Father smiling at me and waving from the car window. On his way to another service, he has had a puncture and lost time changing the tyre, and it's getting late. No, not in Africa. "Mass starts when the priest arrives." To tell the truth, I'm happy to have met him again, and this second time I greet him with the great respect he deserves. While leaving Cahama, I weigh up the value of this encounter. I'm sure it will remain among my fondest memories. I stand up on the pedals as his car passes me, and Alijandro shouts: *"Felipeeee! ¡Conserva tu sonrisa siempre!"*

At your orders Father, I will. And I smile at him while his big face is still watching me from the rear mirror.

A few months ago, a cycle traveller sent me a photo showing his bicycle with the impressive waterfalls of Ruacana in the background. I've been looking forward to visiting the falls throughout the trip, and now I can finally go there. I looked up the falls on Wikipedia. With a width of seven hundred metres, they are among the most impressive in Africa, after the Victoria Falls.

Leaving Cahama, there are about two hundred kilometres of track to reach these waterfalls on the Cunene river, at the border with Namibia. The map shows only a couple of villages on the route. I opt to divide the itinerary into two stages, hoping that on the third day, I will reach the frontier and the waterfalls.

There is no hint of life as I pedal through the acacia and mopane forests. The further southwards I travel, the more the whole province seems depopulated. The few abandoned settlements make the environment look even worse by adding a melancholic note. It's easy to understand why. I pass so many empty farmyards. All the cattle that did not die on the way, are now grazing further North in the province of Huambo, where there has been no shortage of rain this year. And all the herdsmen migrated with them, too.

In the distance, barren mounds become visible, and I soon reach them. Here, sparse plants alternate with high stacks of boulders. I have no way of knowing where they come from.

The savannah I cycle across looks sad and barren. That's why I'm so surprised when I reach a village at midday, not marked on the map. And I am even more amazed when I spot the inhabitants. The town itself looks just the same as all the previous ones—dusty streets between earthen walls and metal roofs. But if I look at the inhabitants, I might guess that it's Carnival: they are all in costume.

Looking out of a window, two busty ochre-skinned ladies take a good look at me as I pass by. Buxom ladies with bare breasts. A few moments before, they were talking with a girl from another ethnic group, as I could make out from the clothes she is wearing. Now all three are staring at me inquisitively.

Their way of dressing looks extraordinary. I have already seen several pictures in photo books. The Himba are one of the few semi-nomadic populations still existing, and they proudly wear their traditional clothes. They speak a Herero dialect, which indicates they came originally from Namibia. The women are especially eye-catching, with their unique hair and skin decorations. They usually smear their bodies with a paste of fat mixed with ochre obtained from soft stones that are laboriously crushed with harder stones. This practice gives effective protection against the sun's rays, and especially against insect bites. I have much to learn from them.

The same ochre stone is mixed with mud and used to decorate the hair. The hairstyle changes as you get older. Little girls have two large braids that fall in front. When they reach child-bearing age, they divide their hair into many smaller braids. The two women I have just met also have an animal skin decoration on top of their hair, similar to a crest. They are married.

And the men? They, too, use their hair to signal their readiness or otherwise to procreate. Their hair is shaved, except for a single central tuft combed into a braid. When a hat covers this tuft, they are married men.

In a nutshell, the arrival in this village leaves me stunned. I have landed in a new world… yet another one. And, surprise, in this world, there is a power line, which means only one thing: a bottle of ice-cold coke, to which I've become addicted and helps combat my profuse sweating.

I turn to the girls and try to make myself understood. "I'm looking for a *loja*." Evidently, they don't speak Portuguese, but they get the meaning and point me towards a plain-looking hut. However, a pile of textiles on the outside suggests that it could be the place I'm looking for. Inside I find the shop assistant, a boy in his early twenties, I would say, leaning on his elbows at the counter and intent on having a conversation with three colourful maidens. The *Mwila* girls love to dress in bright patterns, a bra, a skirt and a headscarf. Lots of pearl necklaces decorate their bare necks.

They are sizing me up. Is this unexpected encounter more surreal for me, or my entering the shop for them? As a matter of fact, the three of them exchange an apparently amusing joke and leave, smiling at me. The shop assistant, on the other hand, does not smile. *He was probably making good progress in flirting with the girls.*

I look around the dimly lit place. The shelves are almost empty: I notice sardine cans, tomato paste… in short, the usual things. I ask what drinks he has, and as he lifts the refrigerator door, a big man enters, and with a stentorian voice and a big laugh, he offers to buy me a fizzy drink. He is the owner of the shop. And he is also one of the few people I have met in the village who speaks Portuguese.

In front of the shop, a crowd of onlookers has gathered. I am certainly more interesting to them. The owner's expansive nature lends itself well to the role of interpreter for my story, which is interrupted from time to time by a comment in dialect and subsequent laughter. A hilarious moment is the *Mwila*—or *Mundhimba*? —class. As always, when I meet new ethnic groups, I want to take home a handful of words useful for brief conversations.

"How do you say hello?" "*Mbapiti.*" I try to repeat to memorise: "*Mbapiti.*" The audience nods in satisfaction. "And thank you?" "Thank you is *mbapandula.*" I repeat: "*bapandula.*" "No, no. Mba, *mbapandula.*" And so on.

I finish my drink, and my lesson, and set off, well behind schedule for the day. At the village, they warned me that this is a lion hunting area, and a night in the tent could be quite *eventful*. Better to aim for Chitado, the next village along the track.

If this remote village thrilled me, leading to my leaving with lots of positive energy, Chitado arouses the opposite sensation in me. A sad-looking agglomeration of houses on the banks of the Rio Cunene, neglected, soon to be uninhabited. Sand has invaded some buildings that now look abandoned; wrecked cars lie by the roadside or in the courtyards. I try to get some information from two passers-by about a place to camp, but they are both drunk and mumble something in the local dialect, pointing to the town hall. I will spend the night here, but with a feeling that I want to leave soon. If nothing else, I'll keep the lions away tonight.

Forty kilometres of rocks, sand and corrugations separate me from Ruacana. The dam on the reservoir attracts numerous herds of goats and cows, with whom I have to share the road to the bridge. *I don't hear the sound of rushing water. How strange.*

After the customs formalities, to compensate for all the efforts I made in the previous days, I set off towards the well-known panoramic point from which I can admire the waterfalls in all their magnificence.

A few steps from the car park towards the escarpment, and I can only see a bare rock wall in front of me. It's little more than damp. For seven hundred metres. The attendant accompanying me explains the dam is closed during this period of extreme drought, so water is rationed. A large part of Northern Namibia is supplied from this reservoir.

NAMIBIA

Nothing is yours except the essentials
- the air, sleep, dreams, the sea, the sky -
all things tend towards eternity
or what we can imagine of it.

CESARE PAVESE

June

Namib means land of nothing in the Nama language. *Opuwo* means *the end*. My question is: why not go to the end of a land where there is nothing? What will be there beyond the end?

In the first few days in this empty land, I come across a few settlements, connected by a long, straight strip of asphalt. Poor villages, indeed. But here it is another kind of poverty, not the misery I have encountered daily in other countries. It is a less blatant poverty, poor people in a more affluent country.

At regular intervals, a lay-by at the side of the road gives motorists a moment of shade to rest from the fatigue of travelling through these infinite spaces. I have landed in another world.

I am crossing a wide expanse interrupted on the horizon by a chain of low mountains. In the midday heat, many dust devils graze on the plain, chasing each other like horses at play. Some are moving towards the road. I sprint on my pedals to reach the centre of a whirlwind, but it doesn't let itself be caught. Beyond these pastures and a barely visible pass between the mountains, Opuwo comes into sight. On the outskirts, there are car wrecks and tin shacks swept by the dusty desert wind. As I approach, my first impression is that I have reached a village in the American Far West.

But Opuwo turns out to be a charming town, albeit not very large, and not too populous. And with a particular appeal. Paradoxically, I find there are many people in the street, considering it's the end of the world. Perhaps it is because I am returning from the other side of the line that divides the civilised world from the wild, ancestral one. Perhaps Opuwo, the end of the civilised world, is the beginning for me. Depends on your point of view.

Here humanity is noisy, colourful, and has different forms. This is a crossroads of theatrical characters. It is mainly women who contribute to the lively folklore. Many Himba, even in the city, maintain their nonchalance with traditional costumes and bare breasts. There are the Herero, whose women wear lavish Victorian-style dresses and large triangular-shaped headdresses. The story goes that the Herero women, traditionally clad in animal skins, in the same manner as the Himba, were encouraged by German missionaries to wear clothes in the European fashion of the time. The fashion was appreciated, and to this day, they wear this outfit with pride. With their slow gait and dignified attitude, they look like grand ladies of the court out for a stroll.

In addition to the Himba and Herero, there are also other ethnic groups here in town, and they almost always wear traditional clothes. Moreover, there is no shortage of men and women in western dress. Jeans and a shirt for him, a short, low-cut dress for her, both with earphones in their ears and smartphones in their hands.

Finally, there is one last type of person. The tribe of tourists, so difficult to meet in other countries. Here they wander around seemingly at ease wearing khaki shorts with large pockets, possibly a white shirt and mountain boots. A female specimen is lowering the rear window of a car to take pictures of the local people with a safari lens. The car drives off as the window closes again. A pack of tourists is crowded into a bus with huge wheels to tackle the Namibian dirt roads and large windows so that the natives can watch them. One daring tourist gets off the bus and is immediately attacked by some street vendors trying to put a tribal bracelet on his wrist. Feeling uncomfortable now, he has to retreat into the pack.

The supermarket is the place where the modern and the traditional blend together most notably. It is impossible to hold back a smile as you watch a Himba woman, goatskin skirt and bare breasts, select some imported products and pile them into the trolley.

That is where the charm of Opuwo lies: in this coexistence of tradition and modernity.

In Opuwo I have another appointment with Fred, my best friend and travelling companion. Luckily for him, I'm in an excellent mood this time. He won't have to put up with hours of complaints, as he did in Liberia, but only stimulating anecdotes about my current great love, Angola.

Together we leave the city, cross the pastures on the plateau where the tornadoes roam, and plunge back into the great void. The Namibian roads allow our thoughts to flow and free our imaginations to wander without limits. We are inspired by these apparently limitless lands and a horizon that disappears into the distance in every direction.

But this serenity is short-lived. In fact, the track is soon covered by endless corrugations, the infamous *washboards*, and piles of gravel on the sides. This is not good for the rear wheel, which in recent weeks has again been damaged on the rim at the nipple joint, for the second time on this trip. To avoid the front wheel getting stuck in the gravel and, even worse, the constant annoying vibrations, I have to limit my attention to one metre in front of me and no further.

This is how we proceed, slowly, in this *namib* for a few days. Tiny, distant villages remind us that where there is water, there is life. On paper, the town of Palmwag is the right place to stop and rest for a day while we prepare the itinerary for the next stages. There are hardly any distractions along the road, so we push hard on the pedals to get there in three days. We have to overcome endless descents and ascents on gravel tracks where the bike sinks in, and we make slow progress.

The track gradually rises until it flattens out on a barren plateau. We have reached *Damaraland*, the land of the Damara people[1]. It is precisely this bareness that makes the environment magnificent. Up here, the view is impressive: we are on another planet, perhaps Mars. Everything is on an extended scale so that the distances are multiplied and the valleys are endless. The horizon is only interrupted by tabular reliefs, which remind me so much of the *mesas* in Arizona, and conical mountains—both phenomena have been shaped by weathering due to the unremitting force of the local winds. I feel like a Lilliputian in these immense lands. The monotonous landscape amplifies this sensation even further: a few shrubs, some dry trees and stones scattered as far as the eye can see.

Not even the plants belong to this planet. As we move southwards across the plateau, so dry after six years without rain, the vegetation thins out. The only plant still alive is the *Euphorbia damarana*, *melkbos* in Afrikaans: a pertinacious wonder of nature. It is a shrub a couple of metres tall and without leaves. Its structure is composed of a tangle of small, tubular, and smooth branches. They contain a milky sap that is, apparently, poisonous. I fell in love with this monument to resilience.

A sturdy branch is moving in the distance. As we approach, we recognise the elegant silhouette of a giraffe's neck sticking out beyond the sparse tree canopy. It's my first encounter with a wild animal in a long time. I join Fred as he stops to observe the giraffe plucking leaves from the acacia tree. Looking at it, I can hear the wind instruments from the Jurassic Park tune. It is impossible for me not to recall, if only for a moment, the great saurians of the Jurassic era. Looking more closely, we also catch a glimpse of its calf, stretching its neck to reach

---

[1] A population of Namibia. During Apartheid, the South African government, which controlled the country at the time, ordered that all Damara be transferred (deported) to Damaraland.

the lower twigs. Their movements are slow, measured, and we copy them to get a little closer. The mother gives us a hard look before turning away, with the baby following her. Finally, a short gallop brings them back to a safe distance.

We resume cycling, and in a short time, we make other encounters: an ostrich notices us from afar and escapes, running away wildly; flocks of springbok graze quietly in search of food on the arid soil. As we pass, they stop all activities to keep an eye on us. *Predators or harmless?* At the first sign of flight from one of the herd, they all follow in leaps and bounds. Not by chance, the early Dutch settlers, on seeing these animals, had called them jumping goats, *springen bok*.

If it weren't for the constant passing of white pickup trucks rented to tourists, it would seem as if we were still in that prehistoric world, where man had not yet begun to have his impact on fascinating nature.

Here we are, after another exhausting day, in Palmwag. What is there in Palmwag? Not much, at least not what we expected. The track is closed off by a gate. Here we run into a police checkpoint and a veterinary checkpoint for the control of meat in transit. We managed to conceal our secret supplies: a kilo of mortadella, a gift from Fred. Some lazy Himba are sitting in the shade of a small grocery shop, waiting for tourists. A petrol pump and a dozen or so cottages—I imagine for workers, as I don't think there are commuters over these prohibitive distances—complete the depressing village. A few kilometres further on, there are a few shacks and a campsite. Nothing else.

As we pass by, a man gets up from his chair on the porch and extends his arm to call out to us, "Hey! Hey!" He is the only one who shows any interest in our presence: the campsite manager. After minor negotiations, he offers us an excellent tent site at the bottom of the valley, not far from the bed of a dried-up river. Only a few puddles remain, and, in a blazing sunset, several flocks of birds come to drink, making a great noise. As darkness falls, so does the silence. If it weren't for the baths and the barbecue grill, it would be just like camping out in the wild this evening too, surrounded by nature.

The same caws of the previous evening wake me up early while Fred manages to keep dozing. After breakfast with a view of nature, we devote the day off to two activities. The highest priority is fixing the damage to the rear wheel. Because of cracks in the rim, some nipples have shaken loose—scotch tape. Then at least I can no longer hear them rattling in their seat, and can forget about them—panacea.

Furthermore, Fred would like to visit a real Himba village, far from the tourist circuits with their living museums. Not least, we have a chance to rest and recover our strength. Okay, there are three things to do.

The unbearable heat and its incessant hold over the vast stony ground prohibit us from walking during the hottest hours, so we head for the village in the late afternoon. The manager gives us a few simple directions: "Walk towards that mountain for half an hour; the village is at its foot."

More than an hour has passed since we left the camp, and we are still wandering among the stones, following this barely visible path over the hard, uneven ground. After the umpteenth hill, the village is still out of sight. The sun is setting.

"What do we do, Fil?"

"Shall we go back? It's almost dusk."

Night still falls too fast at the twentieth parallel. Only a faint crescent of the waning moon illuminates the ochre ground, which tends to absorb light rather than reflect it. For fun, we decide not to use our mobile phones to illuminate the path but advance slowly, barely spotting it, until we reach the campsite.

In the morning, when we have packed our stuff, we look for the campsite manager. Simultaneously, an angry shepherd arrives in his pickup truck and slams the vehicle's door, cursing: "Bloody lions!". He speaks to the manager, who we discover is also a ranger at the wildlife conservation area where we are.

"Last night, three beasts have killed two more cows. They are a huge problem. We must kill them."

The heated discussion continues in the local dialect for a few minutes. Finally, the shepherd resigns himself and turns to go back to the pickup. Before he goes, Fred asks him: "Excuse me, but is your farm nearby?"

The shepherd points south with a gesture of his head: "Over there, a couple of kilometres away."

Our gaze points to the area where the two white cyclists were walking in the dark the night before.

I've been through a lot with Fred. In the snow, on the rock and on the bike. He's a person I trust blindly, and after several years we know each other perfectly. I know what he needs, he knows what I need, and often we don't need to talk. A glance is enough to ensure we are on the same page.

This explains why on a windy afternoon, with the sun approaching the horizon, we take a track not marked on the map. This track should then join another one, which should eventually lead somewhere. We have about two hours of daylight to get somewhere; we cannot stop before, because we are crossing an area inhabited by elephants.

We travel across a stony monochrome heath. Ochre tending to brown, burnt by millennia of sun. It has been beating down all day, and now, in the late afternoon, the ground releases more heat than the sun does.

From a crossroads, two tracks diverge, equally uneven. The first one turns to the left and descends towards the valley; there *should be* a river, the map says, but with the current drought, I wouldn't be surprised if all we find is sand and stones. The second track continues slightly uphill towards the mountains to the west. If there are animals, they might be at the river at the end of the day and during the night, rather than in the mountains. We thus continue westwards.

The track we want to reach, which will finally take us somewhere, is over the mountain. We struggle along on the gravel of this dilapidated surface, hoping to find a pass that will take us to the other side of the mountain range. For two hours, we ride over a lifeless land, and I would bet my bike that there is not a soul for many kilometres around. Here and there, pale earthy bushes stain the desert, but they don't look very lush.

Beyond a hillock, the road dips down a few metres and finally climbs up the mountainside before disappearing over a saddle. The worry that had crept in during the previous hours disappears in a flash, and once again, we feel full of energy. We both quickly climb the few hundred metres that still block the view of the next horizon, and at the summit, we stop, panting. It's one of those moments in which it is inevitable to ask: "Jeez, where on earth have we ended up?"

Behind us, the view is lost over the plain, monotonous in appearance and colour. Ahead, the last rays of the sun illuminate some sections of the track as it winds its way through these Martian mountains, towards a valley in the distance. Looking closer to hand, where the shadows have already fallen, I catch a glimpse of faint lights coming from behind a small hill. As we get closer to the lights, we come across a luxury resort. Welcome to Namibia.

As the sun has now set, it will offer its benefits only for a few more minutes, so we camp near the hotel bungalows, out of sight.

With its landscapes, Namibia fascinates the visitor during the day, but in my opinion, it gives its best with its night sky before the moon rises. The stark, dehydrated clarity of the sky in these regions allows the observer to travel back in time, to millions of years before his birth. And without maps or knowledge, the traveller just scans the Southern skies, finding unknown constellations. For fun, he can identify some of them and guess their shape. The only certainty in his poetic ignorance is the Southern Cross, which catches his eye as soon as he raises his head.

At the first light of day, we take advantage of the resort to stock up on water and enjoy a cappuccino with cocoa by the pool (courtesy of the management, thank you). Chatting with the waitress, we learn that we are in a protected area used for safaris. Obviously, the staff dismiss any chance of our finding our way out of that maze of tracks, which run dangerously between lions and elephants. Just as obviously, we decline the invitation to retrace our steps and go the longer way round.

The quality of the track is the same as the previous day - horrible. Yet, with the whole day at our disposal and a breathtaking view in front of us, we cycle on without any worries. At the moment, there is only one track descending lazily towards the valley floor, so there is no risk of getting lost. Suddenly, a smooth, flowing roadbed takes the place of the scree. Thus, we can enjoy a run off the track, tracing new paths on the compact, virgin gravel.

We continue until we reach the valley floor and the bank of the Aba Huab River. Given the size of his bed, it must have been quite an abundant river in days gone by. Several tracks split off in different directions here, but one, the one most trodden, crosses the river bed and runs parallel to it on the other side. It seems likely that this area still receives water from the mountains from time to time, as imposing, well-spaced trees dominate the entire panorama of the valley. Sturdy branches and twisted trunks, a canopy of green needles is evidence that there is still some water underground.

Obviously, in this environment, one would expect to encounter many animals. On the ground, I recognise footprints of various ungulates, hares, giraffes, lions, and the unmistakable print of the elephants. The child in me, and in Fred, is excited by this vision, longing to meet an elephant. What is more, these regions are home to a rare population of pachyderms adapted to desert life. These animals can go for several days without drinking and can march more than sixty kilometres every night in search of water. In dry riverbeds, they dig holes to reach deep water. For these reasons, it is complicated to find them.

We move forward in this motionless, primordial world for a long time, but we do not find any beasts. Finally, the trail leaves the riverside, and Damaraland, to climb up a small valley that will lead us back to civilisation in a few hours.

"Oh, you'll see the sea when you're still sixty kilometres from the coast." This is what an old man tells us as he remembers the road we will take shortly. We have just reached Uis, a settlement built near a tin mine, one of the world's largest open-pits. As we fill our bottles in a restaurant, the owner's father tells us of yesteryears with nostalgia, when the price of tin still justified the mine's existence. In 1991 the mine was abandoned, and this outpost risked the same fate as interests moved elsewhere. Namibia, so arid and apparently devoid of riches on the surface, hides a priceless treasure in its depths: diamonds, gold, uranium, lead, and copper. Nowadays, Uis is trying to revive its fortune with a few tourist attractions nearby—in Namibia, nearby can mean more than a hundred kilometres away—but in the near future, with new mining technologies, the mine should be active and profitable again.

From the settlement of Uis, the road descends gently towards the sea in a straight line of a hundred and ten kilometres. The afternoon wind hinders our pedalling, and we make slow progress, too slow, in a crescendo of nervousness and frustration.

Fred is in the slipstream behind me. We have been riding in silence for a couple of hours, occasionally swapping places. I hear his voice; he is shouting something, but the wind carries his words away. I turn around and signal for him to join me.

"Fil, when does the road start going downhill? This is too much of an ordeal."

I check the GPS: "Fred, we have already gone down six hundred metres." We hadn't noticed it. We were tricked by the rushing wind and the almost imperceivable slope of this monotonous landscape. We crouch out of the wind behind our bikes to munch on something other than sand. It is still mid-afternoon, but we decide to camp, hoping that the morning wind will be our friend. We can't even smell the sea promised by the old man from Uis.

It is not yet dawn. Shy shades of orange interrupt the otherwise deep blue of the night on the horizon. It's pretty cold, and the prankster wind is now pushing us into the arms of the ocean. On the coast, a thick fog obscures the view, and the humidity condenses on my glasses. We begin to smell the sea, before we see or hear it.

I cycle on almost blindly, following the markings on the road. A cold shiver runs up my spine. I haven't felt this sensation since the snow-capped mountains of Morocco, which I crossed a year ago. And the temperature seems even lower with the humid Atlantic breeze. Winter as I remembered it.

The mouth of the Swakop River, that's what Swakopmund means. It is a German town on the coast of Namibia. It is said jokingly, but maybe half seriously, that the Germans built this town here during the colonial period to remind them of the damp, cold climate of the northern coast. The city was founded at the end of the nineteenth century, and the architecture reflects the style of the time, with facades decorated with exposed wood, large windows and pointed roofs.

Coming from a desert environment, but especially from a year and a half of Africa, this already sharp architectural contrast looks even more out of place. We stroll through the streets of the centre, and it is bizarre to find German delicatessens, bakeries, and cake shops of excellent quality. Charming bistros and classy restaurants, where you can find game or freshly caught fish, complete the range on offer.

We have spent two more fulfilling weeks together, but it is the end of the holiday and time for Fred to go back to work. For me, however, it's time to head south into the desert.

Looking at some satellite photos, I was struck by an abrupt break in the desert, marked by the Kuiseb River. To the north, the environment is arid and rocky. According to Wikipedia, the prevailing winds in the region blow the dunes northwards, but their advance is blocked by the river. For me, this is another opportunity, perhaps one of the last, to venture into remote regions.

I leave the tarmac a few kilometres after Walvis Bay. A despotic wind is blowing from the east, trying to send me back to the coast, but I have other plans. About four hundred kilometres separate me from Sesriem, a tiny tourist resort, where I will find my next supplies. In between, there is nothing but a research centre and a petrol station.

I cycle on with difficulty through a bleached landscape—white, sun-hardened sand. The sun reflects off the ground, and a blinding light whitens the sky. All around me is emptiness, interrupted only by the shy mountains that I am leaving behind. The breeze slows me down a lot, and I struggle to keep my balance, buffeted by incessant cross-winds.

Along the way, I pass through a few settlements belonging to the Topnaar clan. The huts in these villages are scattered so far apart that they do not give the impression of real communities in the spirit that marks the rest of the continent. I am inclined to think that the huts are deliberately spread out so each one has access to water. I have brief exchanges with these people. They are completely disinterested in me, only advising me to cycle with care and make sure I take sufficient water supplies. I obey.

I pass the outpost of Rooibank, where water is drawn from wells on the river bed to supply Walvis Bay's town. On the banks of the dried-up river are a few huts, but I don't see anyone nearby.

I don't like planning, except for the bare minimum. I had anticipated that it would take three days to reach Sesriem, so I bought food for a possible fourth day. In this first stage, I covered far fewer kilometres than I had planned, so I was already mortgaging the buffer day.

Basking in the air conditioning in the supermarket, I had estimated that ten litres of water a day would be enough, and perhaps overdoing it. Yet, I've finished my quota in just half a day, and not having refilled the bottles at Rooibank, I'm almost out of water. A torrid wind continues to sweep relentlessly across the plain, raising swirls of dust and sand. Nothing else moves in this world. There's just me, pedalling.

The evening is coming, and my romantic travelling spirit pushes me to cross the riverbed and enter the desert for a while. Trees, shrubs, and weeds reveal the presence of water below the surface, but it only takes a few strokes on the pedal to return to a lifeless environment: the Namib Desert, the oldest in the world.

I reach a small transverse valley, bordered by high dunes that limit my visible universe to a uniform burnt orange colour. Over time, the oxidation of iron minerals darkens the sands more and more. The more intense the colour, the older the dune. The more intense the colour, the closer the sunset.

I check how much water is left - a little more than a litre. It's better to keep it for the next day. For dinner, I just chew on a bit of bread and a handful of biscuits, which gum up in my parched mouth and take away whatever appetite I have left.

I sit on the top of a small dune in the middle of the valley. As is often the case at this time of day, the wind has died down, and now a deep silence fills that emptiness. Awe and wonder. Nothing moves, only a dung beetle paws at the sand next to the bike, leaving a distinctive trail behind it. I lean back, my hands sinking into the sand that has already forgotten the heat of the day. I stay like this for a long time, contemplating the Evening Star and all the other stars lighting up one by one. Some of the shyer ones will only peep out later in the night, but even now, the Milky Way shines magnificently.

In her diaries, Etty Hillesum wrote: "The human being also searches outside for the landscape he carries within. [...] The inner world is as real as the outer world. One must be aware of it. It, too, has its landscapes, its contours, its possibilities, its boundless terrain. And the man himself is the small centre where the inner and outer worlds meet. The two worlds feed off each other.[2]"

She invites us to probe within ourselves, not to neglect either of the two worlds, but to be receptive to the signals coming from both. As he travels *physically* through space, man is also called on an inner journey, and to try to find a balance between these two worlds. There can be no harmony with the outside world if one does not thoroughly investigate one's self-awareness. As I wrote before, silence is a light for the soul. The desert is silence. Over to you to complete the syllogism.

And as I pedal through Namibia, this concept, which I like very much, comes true. Here I often wander in the silence of vast expanses, and in the solitude, I can listen to myself and learn something new about myself. In this emptiness, I love to leave my thoughts free to wander and get lost, and yet, if I remain in the present moment, I can expand my self-awareness.

My soul speaks to me, and I listen attentively. These days it communicates its serenity to me and needs nothing more than to continue through the desert.

With the body, the same happens. I can almost hear the noise as it works like a machine with its repetitive movements. In an analogy with the engine, if the mechanism is well oiled, everything works correctly; at the slightest sign of it being damaged or broken, I can hear it and fix it.

Now there is stillness within me; there is peace. The human being also searches outside for the landscape he carries inside, says Etty. Here, there is quiet outside. In that nursery of stars, I am a grain of sand confused with the billions on which I sit. I am in harmony with

---

[2] Hillesum, Etty et al. *An Interrupted Life*. Henry Holt, 1996.

my surroundings, I am One with the universe. I have established the balance; the circle has closed.

Now all is silent here, under a blanket of cold stars.

I have slept like a stone, the only one within miles. It is still dark when I come out of the tent. Only a faint glow tinges the eastern sky while I try to swallow some biscuits, accompanied by short sips of water. I am enchanted by my surroundings and linger a while longer in contemplation. In the forest, this hour would be filled with birdsongs, while a village square would be traversed by pawing goats, but the desert is still. All is silent.

But I must hurry! My goal to reach Gobabeb Research Institute before the wind starts blowing from the east again and slowly but steadily draining my energy.

I retrace my evening steps and go back to the other side of the river, the arid and stony one, where the track runs. The sun rises, that intense orange and all the other shades of sand come back to life around me. Sunrise is still rapid at these latitudes; just enough time to play in my mind the introduction to Thus Spoke Zarathustra. The melody lends itself well to the impetus with which the daylight suddenly envelops everything, and the sun becomes fully visible above the horizon.

The half an hour it takes to get back to the road and onto my saddle are enough for me to realise that I am not going to make my goal. A first sharp gust announces the return of the hot desert wind. My water bottles are soon empty, but I have covered a little more than twenty kilometres in two hours and as many more separate me from Gobabeb. For a moment, a thought pops into my head: perhaps I should cycle at night, with a calm wind. But then I think I would miss so much beauty… and a touch of splendour is worth the pain, perhaps.

On the river bank and close to green trees, a small settlement of a few well-spaced-out houses appears. I head in that direction. A dog senses my presence and starts barking nervously, runs towards me and stops a few metres away, gnashing its teeth. The racket has led a man to the door of his house. With a commanding shout, he calls the animal back to him and takes some short steps towards me. He is wearing blue overalls and greets me with rather fewer teeth than he should have.

A few pleasantries and I get straight to the point: "Do you have any water?" He doesn't understand English, so I pull out an empty bottle and shake it to show there's only air inside, while I point to it with my other hand. He nods and invites me to follow him into the house. He sinks a plastic jug into a barrel and fills a bottle with the precious liquid. While I guzzle down the fresh water, the man does the same with the other bottle.

Yuck! It's salty. He looks at me and smiles. "Yes, unfortunately, it's not very good, but that's all we have," his expression suggests.

What a life! I ponder as I walk away after multiple and appreciative gestures of greeting. *What do they live on around here?* They don't have any animals; they can't grow anything on this land, and it's a heck of a long way to the nearest shop, about eighty kilometres away. I don't have an answer for you, dear reader, so I get back on the bike and go on my way before it gets too hot.

The Gobabeb tank tower! It is the first building of the compound that I spot in the distance. A few kilometres from my destination, the road turns south and, blown by the winds, I fly to the water reserve.

I walk wearily into the research centre. A secretary inspects me while I shake the sand from my hair, and she immediately gets me a bottle of water. This time, it's not salty but pleasantly bland. A wild wind is still raging outside, but here in the shelter of four walls, I can calmly contemplate it as a spectator, for a few minutes at least.

Gobabeb is world-renowned for its research into desert environments. I am fascinated by this topic and would like to take the opportunity to look around. But the bad weather conditions exclude any outdoor activity, according to the secretary. All that's left to do is to hydrate, load up with water and plunge back into the wind.

My travelling companion is waiting for me, leaning against the fence, always ready. Tied to the frame, the Tibetan prayer flags, a gift from a great friend, are flapping wildly. *Come on, it's hard, but we don't give up;* the bike seems to infuse me with vigour as I lift my scarf up over my nose and adjust my cap. I greatly appreciate the symbolism of this ritual. It gets me going, and I often perform it with a smile as it reminds me of Sylvester Stallone in Over the Top. "It's like a switch that goes on," he recites before the final contest.

North of the compound lies an immense plateau of gravel and compacted sand. According to the GPS, for the next sixty-five kilometres, the track lazily but relentlessly climbs to an altitude of one thousand metres. The wind is unhindered on the barren plateau, and, as usual, is blowing straight into my face.

I don't know what the temperature is. Maybe it's not excessive, but with this scorching wind and without a hint of shade, I'm suffering a lot. After a couple of hours, I stop sweating and start shivering - they are the first signs of dehydration.

Five sips of water every five minutes is the new rule. No more. If I could quench my thirst with four, I'd be happy. At the fifth sip, I am never satisfied, and probably not even at the tenth. Water alone is no longer enough, I should replenish my salt and sugar levels, and I dream of a coke.

And yet, after drinking, for a few moments, my concentration shifts from my parched throat to the scenario in which I find myself. There is nothing in any direction, not a shrub, nor a boulder. It's a blank page between two chapters of the book that God has written. This emptiness exalts me, recharges me with energy and keeps me going as if I wanted to penetrate this inhospitable world more and more. I still fondly remember that afternoon when I managed to travel half my planned distance under an unrelenting sun and finished ten litres of water in four hours. Numbers and sensations.

In the late afternoon, a mountain comes into sight on the northern horizon. Maybe I would call it more a mound of rocks than a mountain, without wanting to offend it. Mirabib, the map says. I decide to call it a day and to cycle towards it. It will provide me shelter for the night and hopefully give me some protection from the wind. That same wind that has smoothed these hardened sandstones to its liking and given them such bizarre shapes.

With my energy running out, I finally arrive at the rock and walk around it, looking for a place to pitch my tent. At the end of that afternoon, browned by the sun and whipped by the wind, I saw a mirage, or so it seemed to me at first.

A massive truck, military green in colour and with thick tyres, stands out among the ochre of the rocks. A lady in a swimming costume is sunbathing on a deckchair, and two kids are playing video games in the shade of the vehicle. It is so surreal, so far from the context in which I was and still am. It's a German family travelling for a few months in southern Africa. The Germans love to travel in these huge, camper-like *things*.

My throat burns and begs for relief. I tell the lady in a nutshell about my trip and nonchalantly ask if she can leave me some water. The mother, a blonde in her forties, hands me a small bottle, *half a litre*. I empty it in the blink of an eye. *Maybe the boy is dehydrated. I'll give him another bottle.* I empty this one too while her husband arrives. He's a stocky guy whose biceps are bursting out of the short sleeves of his shirt—in some way he looks just like his truck. He has witnessed the scene from the door of the camper and is more down to earth. He scolds his wife with a smile and fills all my bottles. Then, I move away to the other side of the rock to give them some privacy. But I'm immensely grateful to them for their kindness and to destiny for letting me meet them. *What luck!*

In the morning, I reach the main road after a couple of hours' pedalling before the wind picks up. There are no obvious differences from the track I have just left, except for the stream of vehicles. In the last three days, I have not seen a single car. Now, every ten minutes, a tourist bus or a rental pickup passes by, decked out for desert expeditions, and with the camping tents folded up on the roof. Goodbye solitude.

The GPS announces that there are still two hundred kilometres to go to the petrol station. I was supposed to get there that morning according to my initial plans, but I'm in no hurry, and above all, I have other *almost* desolate lands to enjoy.

A big dust cloud is getting closer and closer. I raise one arm into the air. I don't even know whether it's to salute the return to civilisation or attract attention. A white bus, with the name of a travel company printed in large letters on the side, slows down and stops beside me. The cloud of dust that had been travelling behind the bus continues on its way and envelops me. Only then does the automatic window open.

"Hey there. Alone in these parts? Do you need anything?" the driver asks.

"Well, if you have a bottle of water to spare, I'd appreciate it." Without a second thought, he opens the fridge behind him and hands me two bottles.

"Here, cold. All for you."

That might be enough to be grateful to him forever, but some elderly ladies travelling on the bus, who had witnessed the scene, handed me a packet of biscuits, a coke, and a hot sandwich.

"Wow, thanks! But there's no need for all these delicacies."

"Eat, eat. It's a long way," replies a lady, definitely a grandmother by trade.

Alone in the middle of the road, I watch the bus drive away as I open the can. That unmistakable metallic sound followed by the effervescence of the coke. Better than gold, right now.

The continuous traffic of vehicles at high speed damages the quality of the track, so I have to cycle carefully. Every now and then, some tourist stops me; winds with his window down to see what I'm doing alone on that road and, possibly, to leave me some water.

I pass the fuel station in Solitaire, famous for its apple pie, and stop for a few days in Sesriem, which has the reputation of having the highest and most splendid dunes in the world. As you may have guessed, there is no shortage of interaction with tourists these days.

Beyond Sesriem, the uneven road surface, covered with gravel, becomes even more challenging and requires my attention for most of the day. Around me, there are no great distractions. Everything is always the same. The road runs long and straight between plantations of stones toasted by the sun. In the distance, I see a hint of a mountainous relief made of red sandstone. In front of me is a straight stretch of about thirty kilometres, and I'm not kidding. All slightly downhill, I can see the end, down there after a curve and behind the mountain. I spot yet another dust cloud coming in my direction. It's a pickup truck that will reach me in a quarter of an hour, at least. If the driver is a good soul, he will slow down and ask me if I need anything. If not, a cloud of dust and gravel will run me over at full speed.

It's the animals that make this region so enchanting. Ostriches, giraffes, and antelopes. Numerous, and of different species. My favourite by far is the oryx. It is a large beast with a grey-brown coat and elegant black streaks on its face, belly, and legs. With its elegant head with two long, strong ringed horns, it is easily recognisable from a distance.

They make no sign of fleeing when a pickup truck comes swiftly alongside them, but as soon as they see the cyclist, the whole pack runs away.

The rosy light of dusk is about to leave the valley when I come alongside yet another herd. The nearest specimens raise their heads and peer at me. One of them starts to run, and the oryx beside it chases after it. They are galloping along the side of the road, a few metres from me. I have to stand up on the pedals and speed up so as not to miss this marvel.

Despite their bulky size, the two oryx are running gracefully across the uneven plain. Their every step on the ground raises a puff of dust; the warm evening light makes their coats shine even more glossily. The leader lengthens his stride and leaps over the mound of gravel on the roadside before crossing right in front of me, while the other heads for the mountains. A moment later, I can no longer see them, hidden by the dust they have kicked up.

By good luck, I come across a knoll not far from the road. It would seem to be the ideal place behind which to pitch the tent. I head in that direction, and after pedalling a bit, I find myself following animal tracks. Judging by the number and shape, it could be a herd of antelopes. In the delicate eventide, I reach a suitable place to camp, devoid of stones and hidden from the road.

Night falls and, while washing the saucepan, I hear some animal calls that I do not recognise, like short howls. I use my headlamp to find out what's making the noise. I can't see anything. I shine a little closer, and the reflection of four eyes freezes my breath. My heart races; I am petrified. I don't know how much time I stay frozen, but then I unzip the tent and dive in, careful not to make any noise. In complete darkness, I don't know what to think or hope. I'm a mummy in my sleeping bag. In the next half hour, I hear the same noises twice more, then nothing.

I am restless. Here alone, hidden from view from the passers-by on the road, who knows when they will find me in case of an attack. I finally fall asleep, but it's an anxious sleep. At every noise, I wake up and listen with bated breath.

Deep in the night, I hear footsteps, ever closer. A hoof hits a stone. They are antelopes, thank goodness. I exhale. I think back to all the tracks I had unwittingly followed to reach my campsite. It must be a large herd. For a few minutes, the animals move back and forth a short distance from me and make short, low calls.

I'm too inquisitive. Even as *I'm shitting in my pants*, I open the zip trying to damp down any noise and, stretching an arm under the outer wall of the tent, I take some pictures. The dim light of the new moon isn't enough for the sensor, and the result is a completely dark photo. I open the outer zip, and, holding my breath, I peep outside. About ten metres away, there are five or six oryx, some lying down and others standing, unmistakable by their horns. They haven't noticed my movements, so I watch them entranced for a few minutes.

Before plunging back into my sleeping bag, I cast a last glance upwards to the sky: the dark background of the night is interrupted by a soothing profusion of distant stars indifferent to my presence.

I spend the next few hours in that limbo between thought and dream until a faint glow appears in the sky. With measured movements, I leave the tent; not a soul is in sight. The Namibian silence surrounds me. Could it all have been a dream?

The Richtersveld National Park, in a remote region in Northern South Africa, has long captured my interest when studying maps. The reason for this interest lies in its remoteness: a desert area of mountains and deep gorges. Yet, as I approached the border, I was increasingly hesitant about the idea of crossing the region. I had found that ten litres of water are barely enough for twenty-four hours at these temperatures. Moreover, Richtersveld seems entirely uninhabited, so I would need water for two days, but I have no way of loading more on the bike.

A cyclist friend I met the week before must have picked up on my negative thoughts, and one evening I read a WhatsApp message from him.

"*Salut, Philippe!* When you reach the border, take the road that follows the Oranje river upstream. You'll see how beautiful it is there."

Without hesitation, I reply, "Okay, thk! I'll let you know :)."

My arrival at the border with South Africa leaves me stunned: a thriving river welcomes me, surrounded by rich vegetation and with plenty of water. A sudden change, after more than a month spent in barren Namibia.

The road upriver is as enchanting as my friend had described it. The mountains plunge sheer down to the road. To my right, a dense tangle of trees and shrubs tinges the riverbank with green. Beyond lie the arid Richtersveld mountains and South Africa. During the morning, I meet numerous families of baboons that come down to the river for drinking. However, when I pass, they run to cling to the rocks at the side of the road, from where they can study my movements in complete safety. Another novelty in this region is the cold weather. The climate is humid and, used to the furnace of the highlands, I feel it even more so.

Some warning signs remind me that I am crossing an area of diamond mines. I am strongly advised not to leave the main track. Shortly afterwards, I see several trucks working on the other bank, and a plane lands at the mine, raising a lot of dust.

In the mid-afternoon, the gorge I'm travelling through suddenly opens up into a wide valley. The overhanging rocks make way for gentler hills, and the view extends for several kilometres. Vineyards as far as the eye can see. Welcome to Aussenkerh, says a sign. Soon I will cross the last frontier on this journey.

Camped on the Oranje banks for my last evening in Namibia, I reflect on this country. It is an inhospitable land for man. Wild nature is the master here, and it's almost impossible to tame. In Namibia, empty spaces are extreme environments for human life. It is equally difficult as in the forest, which is instead so dense. Only a few people have adapted their lifestyles to live here, and then only by bowing to natural laws and living as much as possible in harmony with their surroundings. The starry sky in its immensity, the most enchanting I can remember, is the reward for their tenacity.

SOUTH AFRICA

Every person [...] shall be classified [...]
as a white person, a coloured person or a native [...]
and every coloured person and every native [...]
shall be classified [...]
according to the ethnic or other group to which he belongs.

POPULATION REGISTRATION ACT, 1950

July

"Where are you from?" the border official asks me.

"Italy!" I exclaim excitedly. I am at the last border of this journey. Today marks the end of the frontier ritual.

"You are a strong guy. Give me a five, brother!"

I reach out with my arm, and after the pop, I jump on the pedal and push. Here I am, cycling into South Africa. I probably wouldn't have bet a cent on myself achieving this before the journey began. And yet, with calmness and determination, one can accomplish a lot. Day after day, this is the only way to go far.

I remember a morning in Southern Congo. I had just started the day, up a gentle asphalted climb in the lush greenery that follows the rainy season. Suddenly, I still don't know why and how, but I raised my head to the sky and smiled. At that moment, I thought of Cape Town and said to myself: *Yeah! Now I'm sure I'll get there.* For the first and only time. Another important lesson to me from the Journey: I don't have to think about it too much to create something unique and meaningful. I let myself be inspired, sure. I go with the flow and take care of the little things, the details—one brick at a time.

The weather in this region is acting up, especially as it is winter. Low temperatures, dropping below zero at night. Lots of wind and rain. However, I have to admit I was missing it a bit.

I could follow the main road and get to Cape Town in a few days. Obviously, I don't, and look for alternative routes. I pass from the north's arid environment to the verdant coastline, the barren highlands in the centre and the cold mountains before descending back to the coast and the iconic Table Mountain. Every evening kind farmers host me on their property. Much of South Africa's land lies beyond fences and barbed wire, so I turn up at the farm, hat in hand, asking for hospitality. I have never been refused; indeed, I have often received an exceptional welcome. A bottle of wine, a barbecue, grilled fish, a cake prepared at the last minute in my honour. Exquisite people, even here.

One evening I come to a farm—a sizeable one-storeyed house with a spacious garden. I call out loudly but get no answer. A passing farmer suggests that I go inside and wait, as the owners will be back soon. At ten o'clock in the evening, nobody has shown up yet, and I decide to pitch my tent in the garden, ready to face the charge of trespassing. The owners come back around midnight. The car moves forward down the lane, and the headlights light up the tent while someone is closing the gate. I look out, and a lady is approaching under the gentle rain. With the most pleading look I could muster, I briefly tell her what's going on. After a glance at her husband, the woman's reply was: "Oh my dear man, you don't have to worry. Sleep peacefully. Indeed, would you like to have a beer with us first?"

At dusk on July 20, five hundred and sixty-five days after leaving home on that freezing January 2, from a soaked campsite among the rows of vines laid down on a hillside, the elderly owner points to Table Mountain in the distance. The last rays of the sun make it stand out against the blurred background of sea and land. I am quite calm, not particularly excited. I share my emotions with a group of buddies who have gathered there for a barbecue, the *braai*, as they call it in South

Africa. They invite me to spend the evening with them, which, between a song, a glass of wine and a pork chop, continues joyfully until late.

On July 21, shortly after midday, I am at the port of Cape Town, queuing up with other tourists for the ritual photo from the famous yellow frame that encloses part of the pier and Table Mountain. I lift my bicycle onto the frame and dive into the picture, as some people applaud, and a man cheers me on: "Yeah, man!" I ask someone to take a picture of me, and shortly afterwards, I am sitting on a bench a few metres away. The bike is leaning against the backrest behind me. At that moment, perhaps for the first time since I left home, I feel alone. In the hustle and bustle of tourists at the pier, I had no one to share the moment with or, to be more precise, no one close to me or who could understand what that moment meant to me. I called mum, dad, my sister Martina, Fred. No one answered. I started laughing, *how sad*, I thought. A few moments later, the phone rang: Enrico, from Cameroon. *You're a great man, Enrico!*

I spend two weeks in the company of some interesting people. I climb Table Mountain, of course; I visit wine cellars, just as obviously. Cape Town is seductive. What's more, the spring sun and a pleasant breeze invite me to stroll through the colourful streets of the hill, along the wide waterfront and to the marina. Yet something bothers me. Everywhere, people talk about white, black, coloured. Skin colour determines your life.

In South Africa, I had the impression that racism is still widespread. It often lies under a thin layer of respectability in people's speech, and it is present in the segregated compounds of blacks and coloureds. A village is either white or black. If it is big, there are two well-separated neighbourhoods. The example of Springbok is glaring: the two areas of the city were built on different sides of a mountain. The whites stay with the whites, the blacks with the blacks and the coloureds with the coloureds. Yes, because, to be precise, some are not really black; they are of mixed ethnicity. These divisions were strictly classified under the Population Registration Act of 1950.

Categorising humanity according to colour is even more disturbing for me, after travelling through countries where, at least in my experience, racism is almost non-existent. Of course, everywhere I travelled, I have been called *white: Monsieur le Blanc, White Man, Toubabou, Mundele, Branco, Oyibo...* and a hundred other names that I don't even remember. However, the intention in calling me these names has never been, except in isolated cases, to put me in a different race with which to behave differently. It was just their way of identifying me. Don't you know my name? Am I the only one with white skin in miles? You call me white, and I turn around. In some areas of Angola, the white man is beginning to be associated with tourism, and then my name becomes *Tourist*. Near a dam being built in Guinea, all the whites were Chinese, and again my name changed: *Chinois*, Chinese. That's the intent of the nickname. In some countries, the white person is associated with giving money, so people ask me for money.

In South Africa, Apartheid ended twenty-five years ago. Nobody mentions it anymore. But high walls with video surveillance separate white houses from the rest of the city. And invisible walls exist, which are more challenging to cross or break down. People walk on the same sidewalk, they pass by each other at the supermarket, yet they are on two different planets.

In the elegant white villas of whites, the cleaning lady is black, the gardener is black. On a construction site, the worker is black, the supervisor, maybe, is white.

Early this century, the government (which is black) introduced the *Black Economic Empowerment* (BEE) programme, a criticised race-specific initiative—i.e., based on skin colour. The BEE was launched to reduce inequality between *Whites and Blacks*[1], by providing the latter

---

[1] Coloureds are excluded from this programme.

with opportunities not available to the former. Among many aspects, this translates into selection for a job based only on skin colour.

At this point, I ask myself, why doesn't the government focus on improving the quality of education for all instead of further fuelling racism within society? I have no direct experience, yet many of the people I talked to were critical about the education system. The only good schools, and I speak from direct experience here, are private ones (Obviously! To charge five thousand euros a year, they must provide an exceptional level of education). But clearly, the typical South African family, with an average monthly income of eighty euros, will never be able to afford it. These schools do, however, provide some scholarships for black students.

In the draft itinerary I have designed to reach the far South of the continent, I would like to circumnavigate the Cape Point peninsula. This would mean exiting Cape Town along the coast and from there continuing on to Cape Agulhas. Following this route, I would have to cross Khayelitsha for a few kilometres. Khayelitsha is a side effect of Apartheid. In those days, no blacks were allowed to live within the city limits, so they settled on the plains to the east of the city. After the end of Apartheid, large numbers of blacks came to the town searching for work and naturally settled here, in this neighbourhood. It is estimated that around one million people live here today.

While staying in Cape Town, something strange happened to me, or perhaps better, something that would have been highly unlikely only a few weeks before. Over the past few weeks, I was almost always in the company of whites. Being with them, made me develop fear and prejudice. This prejudice also applied to Khayelitsha and its inhabitants – just this name created distress and revulsion among whites. "You must not go through there; it is dangerous." "Watch out, they'll rob you, and if you don't get it, they'll kill you." And so on. Protected by high walls and barbed wire, 24/7 guards, even my mind started to barricade itself, to get defensive. I was becoming racist too.

I then passed through Kayelitscha on a day of torrential rain. From the top of a small hill on the outskirts, there is a good view of the area. Sheet metal shacks as far as the eye can see, or at least as far as I could see under the heavy rain. Officially they are called informal settlements. Khayelitsha still gives the impression of a village, but it is confusing, broken up by the impromptu arrival of thousands of people and the rapid construction of new houses. For the outsider, it seems chaotic, but there is a semblance of order at least for those who live there.

People watch me full of curiosity, as they have done for the past two years. Greetings, shouts of encouragement and smiles. *Fuck racism.*

The Southern coast of South Africa has something magical, as one would expect given how beautiful it is. Sheer mountains, rich and colourful vegetation[2]. In addition, an abundant fauna populates its seas. Along the coasts, I have spotted penguins, seals, and dolphins. In the right season, whales and sharks also live in these rich waters. Flamingos, cormorants, eagles, and many other birds fly over them. Every bend brings a new and surprising view. I come across small settlements with a few fishermen's houses followed by elegant holiday resorts. In both cases, you only need to travel a few kilometres away from the towns to be immersed in luxuriant nature once again. I arrive in Cape Agulhas enchanted with the wonder of the trip. This town is mainly devoted to tourism, and now that it is out of season, the second homes are empty. A shopkeeper invites me not to worry about the bicycle, "this is not the city; nothing happens if you leave it outside," as in the rest of the continent.

The Southernmost point of Africa can be reached by a wooden footbridge resting on the rocks. A large miniature model of Africa and a modest monument with an inscription celebrate the traveller's arrival.

---

[2] Characteristic vegetation, called *Flynbos*, meaning *fine bushes* in Afrikaans, due to the many needle-like plants in the region.

Another panel reminds us that the Atlantic and Indian Oceans embrace here.

Leaning against a low stone wall is another bicycle loaded with luggage. I smile, perhaps a little moved. On the last boulders not submerged by the waters, in search of the real Southernmost point, I meet Kim, a South Korean. He, too, started the journey at home but crossed Africa along the eastern coast.

I am happy to have met him here today. After taking some photos, we sit on the rocks to have lunch together. The frugal lunch of the cycle traveller: bread, cheese, and a big piece of chocolate to conclude. We exchange a few anecdotes, stories of encounters and events, but these are few words. In silence, we watch the waves crash on the coast, the Southern breeze carrying the drops of water that rise into the air after the impact. Some of them reach us.

What I have lived, he has also lived. In this silence, we are close, in intimate. Any other words would only be a distraction. This is not a celebration. We both know that it is not the goal that matters, but what we have created, how we have shaped ourselves and adapted to the world. We have joked, and we have cried, we have contemplated the wonder of Mother Earth, we have suffered, and we have shared. We have Lived every day. This is the most important celebration: the celebration, at every moment, of the Life that has been given to us.

Thank you, *Mama Africa*.
E Viva la Vita

"And in all of this, what did your mum say?"

MUM IS ALWAYS MUM

by Carla Villata

"Mum, I need to talk to you..." this is how my journey with Filippo, Fili, Papo began. These are the nicknames we call him in our family.

"I've decided to leave by bike. I don't know yet for how long and where to: towards France, Spain, then I'll see."

A multitude of questions filled my head. I ask him why he has made this decision. I share my doubts and fears with him, but Fili is ready, convinced, determined to go.

On a cold, sunny morning in early January, he set off with his bike, loaded with everything he might need for a real trip. I was not aware that I would not see him again for such a long time.

Kisses, hugs, last recommendations, high-five and... go! With dad Ezio, grandma Maria and the faithful dogs Barolo and Joy, we watch him go. I still have captured in my heart his first pedal strokes beyond the gate. He was looking straight ahead; if he had turned around, it would have been worse.

Hoping that he would return after a few months, I began to digest his choice. But as time passed, instead of turning around, he landed in Morocco.

This is where my first real worries began: the desert, the immense distances to be covered alone on my bike, under a suffocating sun, unlikely to meet anyone and with the risk of running out of water.

I often phoned Martina, my daughter. She was the only one who could give me courage: "Come on. Cheer up, Mum!"

My days became interminable: I concentrated on my work, trying to stay busy and not to think.

My mobile phone became a precious companion: I switched it on countless times, hoping to receive a GPS signal from his bike, or a message. Every time I didn't see any new notifications, I became more anxious. Maybe there was no signal where he was, or worse, he had had an accident. When I finally received the message, "Mum, so tired, but everything's fine", I felt really relieved and often cried with happiness.

The geographic atlas on the table was always open on the page of Africa to follow his progress. Ezio and I measured the distance with our fingers to understand how much time he still needed to reach the next destination, further south.

At that time, some young people had been kidnapped in Burkina Faso. I thought of them, of their families. They will be devasted. And I with them.

In the meantime, my heart and mind continued my journey with Fili. I stayed close to him, but the days always passed too slowly.

I felt so happy to hear him in the evening, tired but calm, joyful about the kilometres he had travelled and the encounters he had made along the way. He would tell me about the exuberant and inquisitive children who ran to see the stranger—white, tall and with a giant bicycle. *Toubabou*, they called him!

He sent me photos of them. The smiles on those kid's faces filled my heart with positive energy.

Listening to Fili, I realised how important those smiles were for him. They made him feel good, and he felt at *home*.

It was exciting to hear him talk about rice and chicken dishes. The same chicken and rice that the women of the villages cooked for him to celebrate and as a sign of their welcome.

Day after day, Fili was savouring Mother Africa embodied by her welcome, smiles, humility, and dignity.

He was learning that happiness is not only made up of material things but of a lot of sharing. He was having a once in a lifetime experience.

Later on, he met Ivan, a guy from Assisi, also on a bicycle. He was riding along the same road.

Finally, a few words in Italian and some company as he pedalled.

I was happy until the time came to cross Nigeria, a complicated country with a high kidnapping risk.

I had advised him to fly over it, even though I knew he would not have followed my advice.

During his few short phone calls, I could feel his anxiety and sense how worried he was. He would have preferred to cross it together with Ivan, but his friend had chosen another route, and they had separated.

As I write this, I do not know in detail what happened to him: I will find out myself by reading his book. One evening, after he came home, we were waiting for him at the table for dinner. He came into the kitchen and said: "Sorry I'm late, but I was writing my piece on Nigeria. I still get the shivers when I think about it."

I didn't say anything. I just felt a tremendous pang in my heart.

The worst, most endless days were when he contracted malaria in a forest in Cameroon. I was devastated with grief when I realised it was impossible to help him. Moreover, there was no telephone reception in that area.

My first thought was to get on a plane and go to Cameroon to bring him home.

But my Papo was too weak; he had a high fever. In that condition, it would have been dangerous to travel, and unwise.

There, he met Sister Elisa, an Italian nun, who became his guardian angel and, although I don't know her, I will always be grateful to her.

In the meantime, Martina, equally worried about her brother's condition, repeated to me: "Come on, Mum, he's going to be okay!"

Lying on the sofa, crying and praying, I begged my mum to help him from up there. And so, she did.

During *our* long journey together, I also remember the day the phone rang, and a firm, determined male voice asked: "Are you Carla Villata?"

My heart thudded. I felt on the brink of fainting and had to sit down on the stool. The two customers who were tasting wine in our cellar saw me sit down and realised that that phone call had scared me, a lot.

"Here is the commanding officer of the Carabinieri at the Italian embassy in Congo Brazzaville…"

And I immediately interrupted him: "Fili?"

He continued: "I have your son here in front of me, Filippo Graglia… congratulations Madam, you have a smart and very polite son".

Bam!!! The heartbeat of the previous seconds first made me fall silent, and then I finally uttered an exclamation: "Aaah!" Luckily, the officer handed the phone to Fili because I screamed a string of inappropriate words, shouted at the top of my lungs, which I hope the Carabiniere didn't hear.

These are the kind of phone calls a mother dreads receiving when she has a son away from home, even more so if he is in Africa, alone, on a bicycle.

"You know, mum, I met Victor, a Spaniard, also an engineer. We'll ride together for some time."

Good!

Then one afternoon, he phoned me and told me he had just come out of the hospital. While servicing his bike, he had accidentally amputated a piece of the ring finger of his left hand.

The doctors advised him not to start riding again immediately, as he needed to be treated to avoid gangrene risk. As a result, he rested for another twenty days or so.

These long and forced stops made him nervous and impatient. So much so that I barely managed to get a word in edgeways on the phone. Besides, he did not post any news on his social pages during this period, and I was often been asked in the village why he stayed silent. People talk and comment, sometimes inappropriately. All this hurt me!

Every mother wants her son to be happy. Fili, despite his mishaps, was happy, which was enough for me.

My happiness exploded when he arrived in Cape Town. "I'm proud of you, Papo!" were my first words.

Proud of what you were able to do on your own, with your bike and with so much willpower. You overcame difficult and challenging moments. You accepted everything and everyone with respect and humility, always with your wonderful smile. You have shown me that with determination and help from people, you can go far. You have enriched yourself inside and taught me that one should not be afraid of the unknown because, to grow, one must be open to the world. Thank you!

My only regret on our journey is that I didn't pedal with you!

You're great, Papo!

I felt the most intense happiness and joy when I went to the top of the hill in Albugnano to wait for you. Finally, I saw you again, surrounded by your friends also on their bicycles.

"My beautiful Papo."

"Mum, you're here too?"

I wanted to be there, to hug you first, and to ride the last few pedal strokes of our journey together.

Pedalling... five kilometres all downhill, but I can do that!

I felt so happy. It was like I could touch the sky with my finger.

Mum

P.S.: Thanks to all those who, in these long twenty months, have been close to me, even if only with a friendly word.

I would like to dedicate a page to thanking a few people. Each one of them has given his or her contribution, to help bring about this book.

Isabelle Patterson and Peter Greenwood, first of all, spent a whole month revising this book. I am infinitely grateful to you for this. Wine and Easter cakes will never be enough to repay you.

Sara Hancock made an enormous contribution as she patiently helped me correct my English grammar.

Many others have done their best to correct one or more chapters: François Loncke, Dave O'Grady, Fr Michael Smyth, Edward Nelson. Without them the book would probably not yet be published.

I would also like to thank Annabel Targett, Kristen Meiburger, Idil Kanpolat, Mary Gorobtchouk, and Rebecca Harvey because with their precious insights have helped perfect the book.

Finally, thanks to Mamma, for her contribution and for her patience during these two years of travel.

I have to say thanks to someone else.

And it is to you, who have bought the book and, if you have got as far as these words, perhaps even enjoyed it.

You may have noticed that the book has been self-published. No professional translators were involved. There were no graphic designers to do the layout, no professional editors, literary agents, publishers, or promoters. In short, I have rolled up my sleeves to make this book complete, and I hope enjoyable.

If you think I have succeeded in my aim, I would like to ask you a few minutes of your precious time to write a review on Amazon or on any another platform where you purchased the book. A few lines, a sincere comment.

Or, even faster, share a cover photo on your social networks. I am only asking you to make a small effort, but it will make a significant contribution. Word of mouth and feedback are the main channels for disseminating this work.

And if you have any questions or would like to write me a message, please contact me on: https://www.facebook.com/aroundabout2020.

Thanks again! And may the wind always be at your back in cycling and life.

Filippo
Castelnuovo Don Bosco, February 22, 2021

CONTENTS

A ROUNDABOUT 9

TIME 13

JANUARY 2 17

MOROCCO 21

WESTERN SAHARA 55

MAURITANIA 61

SENEGAL 83

GAMBIA 97

GUINEA BISSAU 107

GUINEA CONAKRY 117

SIERRA LEONE 139

LIBERIA 141

IVORY COAST 159

BURKINA FASO 177

NIGERIA 195

CAMEROON 217

CONGO 243

ANGOLA 267

NAMIBIA 297

SOUTH AFRICA 321

MUM IS ALWAYS MUM 331